THE BEAUTY BIAS

The Beauty Bias

...

THE INJUSTICE OF APPEARANCE
IN LIFE AND LAW

Deborah L. Rhode

UNIVERSITY PRESS

2010

OXFORD
UNIVERSITY PRESS

Oxford University Press, Inc., publishes works that further
Oxford University's objective of excellence
in research, scholarship, and education.

Oxford   New York
Auckland   Cape Town   Dar es Salaam   Hong Kong   Karachi
Kuala Lumpur   Madrid   Melbourne   Mexico City   Nairobi
New Delhi   Shanghai   Taipei   Toronto

With offices in
Argentina   Austria   Brazil   Chile   Czech Republic   France   Greece
Guatemala   Hungary   Italy   Japan   Poland   Portugal   Singapore
South Korea   Switzerland   Thailand   Turkey   Ukraine   Vietnam

Library of Congress Cataloging-in-Publication Data
Rhode, Deborah L.
The beauty bias : the injustice of appearance in life and law / Deborah Rhode.
p.   cm.
Includes bibliographical references and index.
ISBN 978-0-19-537287-8
1. Women—Legal status, laws, etc.—United States.   2. Beauty, Personal—
United States.   3. Women—Health and hygiene—United States—
Sociological aspects.   4. Sex discrimination against women—
Law and legislation—United States.   I. Title.
KF478.R48 2010
346.7301'34—dc22   2009033283

1 3 5 7 9 8 6 4 2
Printed in the United States of America
on acid-free paper

Contents

. . .

PREFACE ix

ACKNOWLEDGMENTS xvii

CHAPTER 1:   INTRODUCTION 1

The Personal Becomes Political: The Trouble with Shoes, 3
The Costs and Consequences of Appearance, 5
Surveying the Foundations: Social, Biological, Economic,
Technological, and Media Forces, 7
Feminist Challenges and Responses, 9
Appearance Discrimination: Social Wrongs and Legal Rights, 11
Legal Frameworks, 14
A Road Map for Reform, 19

CHAPTER 2:   THE IMPORTANCE OF APPEARANCE
AND THE COSTS OF CONFORMITY 23

Definitions of Attractiveness and Forms of Discrimination, 24
Interpersonal Relationships and Economic Opportunities, 26
Self-Esteem, Stigma, and Quality of Life, 28
Gender Differences, 30
The Price of Upkeep: Time and Money, 32
Health Risks, 35
Bias, 41

CONTENTS

CHAPTER 3: THE PURSUIT OF BEAUTY 45

Sociobiological Foundations, 45
Cultural Values, Status, and Identity, 48
Market Forces, 49
Technology, 53
The Media, 54
Advertising, 65
The Culture of Beauty, 68

CHAPTER 4: CRITICS AND THEIR CRITICS 69

Nineteenth- and Early-Twentieth-Century Critics, 71
The Contemporary Women's Movement, 73
Critiques, 74
Responses, 77
Personal Interests and Political Commitments, 80
Beyond the Impasse, 86

CHAPTER 5: THE INJUSTICE OF DISCRIMINATION 91

Ensuring Equal Opportunity: Challenging Stigma and Stereotypes, 93
Challenging Subordination Based on Class, Race, Ethnicity, Gender, Disability,
and Sexual Orientation, 95
Protecting Self-Expression: Personal Liberty and Cultural Identity, 99
The Rationale for Discrimination and Resistance to Prohibitions, 101
The Parallel of Sexual Harassment, 114
The Contributions of Law, 115

CHAPTER 6: LEGAL FRAMEWORKS 117

The Limitations of Prevailing Legal Frameworks, 118
Prohibitions on Appearance Discrimination, 125
A Comparative Approach: European Responses
to Appearance Discrimination, 137
The Contributions and Limitations of Legal Prohibitions
on Appearance Discrimination, 139
Consumer Protection: Prohibitions on False and Fraudulent
Marketing Practices, 141
Directions for Reform, 142

CONTENTS

CHAPTER 7:   STRATEGIES FOR CHANGE 145
Defining the Goal, 146
Individuals, 148
Business asnd the Media, 151
Law and Policy, 154

NOTES, 163

INDEX, 239

[vii]

Preface

...

I have always had issues with appearance, but seldom have I wanted to share them openly, let alone write a book about them. In this culture, some measure of anxiety is hard to avoid. Susan Brownmiller, one of feminism's founding mothers, identified part of the problem: "Who said 'clothes make a statement?'" she asked. "What an understatement that was. Clothes never shut up. They gabble on endlessly making their intentional and unintentional points." The same is true of weight, hairstyle, makeup, and related choices. That creates problems for those of us who have no statement. I've always wanted just to blend in, to remain aesthetically unmemorable. Unlike other women, who seem embarrassed or affronted if they turn up in the same outfit as someone else in the room, I have been greatly relieved. If some fashion faux pas has been committed, at least I'm not alone.

Imitation has always struck me as the safest strategy, but when I came to Stanford in 1979 as the second woman on a law faculty of thirty-six, my only female colleague had a style I clearly couldn't follow. She wore flamboyant prints and bold colors—statements everywhere. By contrast, the progressive male colleagues with whom I identified wore sweaters and corduroy pants. That seemed fine to me. After all, I was a feminist and an academic, pursuing the life of the mind. Why squander time and money on fashion?

I had outfits in three color rotations. Gray corduroys and black turtlenecks alternated with black corduroys and gray turtlenecks; a similar ensemble worked with brown and beige; and a third with navy and light blue. Occasionally, when feeling especially rakish, I mixed and matched (black corduroys, beige turtleneck), or threw in an earthy necklace. No one seemed to notice. Except, finally, my kindly female colleague, who ventured some advice. "You know," she said, although clearly I did not, "the students don't want you to look just like them. You're young and female. That creates enough problems establishing authority. Try some skirts. Saks is having a sale."

This was news to me. My previous student course evaluations had been reasonably kind and diplomatically silent on my wardrobe, or lack thereof. But I could see her point. So I bought some skirts. In gray, black, and beige. In a burst of daring, I added one that was tweed, along with a few more unmemorable accessories. For formal occasions, I fell back on clichés, a conventional little black dress and string of pearls. I assumed that other guests had more important things to notice than my unvarying attire. If they didn't care, why should I? My view was similar to that expressed by an infamously frumpy family in a Victorian novel by Elizabeth Gaskell: "'What does it signify how we dress at Cranford, where everybody knows us?' And if [we] go from home... 'What does it signify how we dress here, where nobody knows us?'"

Occasionally, however, I had the discomfiting sense that one of my outfits had crossed the line from understated to downright dowdy. I was beginning to resemble the female professor that Randall Jarrell portrayed in *Pictures at an Institution*: "When well dressed women met Flo they looked at her as though they couldn't believe it. She looked as if she had waked up and found herself dressed as if her clothes had come together by chance and involved her, an innocent onlooker, in the accident."

My difficulties mounted once I became director of Stanford's Institute for Research on Women and Gender. I now had regular contact with high-level administrators, foundation officials, well-heeled donors, and feminists with a flair for fashion. After observing my attire at a number of meetings and conferences, the feminists came to a shared view. Emergency remedial shopping was in order. Although many university centers, including my own, lived in genteel poverty, directors were not supposed to advertise that fact, and I was pushing the envelope. Colleagues undertook my conversion with the zeal of Christian missionaries. They temporarily appropriated my credit card, supervised its use in approved retail settings, and quarantined the worst offenders in my wardrobe rotation. One of the best dressed in the group made a house call. Grimly surveying my closet, she singled out half the contents for the Salvation Army. In a vain effort to salvage one especially treasured item from certain destruction, I pleaded that it had been with me since high school. "Exactly" was the response. Staff at the Stanford institute greeted my refurbishment with such obvious relief that I got the message, as well as the clothing.

Or so I thought. But a term as chair of the American Bar Association's Commission on Women in the Profession several years ago made clear that dress codes for academics and prominent professionals were worlds apart. The disparity came home to me several weeks before the commission's annual luncheon honoring distinguished women attorneys. The event generally attracted national media and well over a thousand lawyers. My role was modest, but the event was projected on large video screens that made every defect in appearance painfully apparent. As the luncheon approached, I received a kindly message from one of the ABA's media consultants, who informed me that "tension was mounting" over the "look" I would project. Accordingly, the association would be "happy to pay for a professional makeup and hair stylist, as well as a personal shopper." Prior experience had taught me to accept such advice in the constructive spirit in which it was offered, although I insisted on personally footing the bill. If I hadn't learned to manage mascara by this point in life, that was my responsibility, not the association's. But surely I must own one outfit that might be acceptable.

What followed was a series of negotiations in which ABA public relations staff inventoried my entire wardrobe. They reviewed the possibilities in light of my "coloring," which they assumed had been professionally evaluated. Was I a "spring" or a "fall"? Did I have "appropriate accessories" to match? The irony, of course, was that all of this was in the service of a commission seeking to promote equality for women in the profession. I wondered if anyone had ever grilled the many male ABA commission chairs and presidents about whether they were a spring or a fall or had "appropriate" neckwear.

Finally the staff grudgingly conceded that I owned one ensemble that was barely serviceable. Rumor had it that there were still some disgruntled disclaimers after the event along the lines of: "Well, we offered to pay for a shopper, but she insisted...." It was, however, made perfectly clear that for the luncheon the following year, the shopper would be necessary. When I suggested that no one would notice if I wore the same outfit again in twelve months, the response was stunned silence. Then, as if speaking to a small child, one of the staff explained that "*everyone* would notice."

On the morning of the first luncheon, two impeccably dressed stylists descended upon my hotel room at an uncivilized hour. Clearly someone had warned them to allow extra time to get me into a presentable state. It was necessary to hire both of them because the event was on a Sunday, no salons were open, and no stylist of any stature did hair as well as makeup. The weather was typical for Chicago in the summer—hot and humid—the kind that signaled "bad hair day" from the get-go. But my stylist was unfazed. He teased and sprayed up a storm. I estimated the survival time of his creation at about fifteen minutes once out of the heavily air-conditioned room. The makeup, however, was ladled on with enough layers to outlast any climate challenge. When I made a feeble plea for something understated, I was led to understand that I was out of my depth and might as well shut up and let the artist do her work. The result left me looking like the stereotypical "cheap hooker" in an expensive outfit.

As predicted, the hair drooped on first contact with the air outside. "Christ," I overheard one of the commission staff mutter. "I could have done better than that for free." At least, I grimly concluded, others will agree, and next year I'll save several hours and several hundred dollars. But no, twelve months later, the whole ghastly ordeal was repeated only with a more expensive hair stylist and still more spray. The apparent assumption was that however badly it had turned out the first time, whatever I produced unassisted would be worse.

My point in revisiting this ludicrous experience is not to overstate its importance. As a happily married academic, I have been blissfully insulated from serious concerns about appearance. Nothing much turns on how I look. But the event does highlight the double standard of appearance for women and men, and the way that seemingly petty cultural expectations get in the way of women's lives. If men can manage to be presentable without shoppers, stylists, and related expenditures, why can't women?

There is, it turns out, a cottage industry of commentary on that question. The disproportionate attention to women's appearance has been variously attributed to biology, misogyny, the media, the cosmetic industry, and a host of others. When I became interested in the issue as a subject for research, I discovered even an academic literature on the appearance of academics. The consensus appears to be that college and university faculty are the worst dressed professionals by a considerable margin, although opinions differ about whether this is a problem, or even a topic worth discussing. The tradition of frumpiness has its origins in the robes that symbolized academics' life of the mind and their distance from worldly pursuits. These black tent-styled garments covered a multitude of aesthetic sins, and helped to preserve the dignity of scholars who couldn't afford, couldn't recognize, or couldn't be bothered to acquire more tasteful alternatives. That tradition was gradually supplanted by the stereotypical tweed sport coat with patched elbows. Women, of whom there were historically few, had analogous tweedy ensembles, only with rumpled skirts and no patches.

The modern dress code is more eclectic, with wide regional and disciplinary variations. What is appropriately artsy for most art departments would raise eyebrows in my law school, and the flip-flops and piercings that pass unnoticed in Santa Cruz would not play well in Peoria. But in any field in any region, physical unattractiveness matters; deviance from local fashion norms carries a cost. Scholarly studies find that attractive teachers do better on student evaluations, and anecdotal experience confirms that fashion foibles are widely noted. A website, RateMyProfessors.com, gives students the option of ranking not only their teachers' clarity, but also their attractiveness.

Few of us escape unscathed, but what, if anything, can be done about it is another matter. The closer we look, the more complicated appearance issues become. On this subject, women are deeply divided and frequently ambivalent. For some of us, the pursuit of beauty is primarily a source of pleasure, self-expression, and escape. For others, particularly women of a certain age, it is often more trouble than it's worth. As the years have passed, I have moved increasingly into that latter camp and have grown more resentful of the double standard that divides the sexes. Although men are by no means exempt from appearance-based prejudice (ask any male under 5 feet 8), becoming minimally presentable is just a lot more trouble for women. My husband travels with a spare shirt, clean underwear, and antiperspirant. He takes a morning shower, shaves, and is good to go. I have all this stuff to cart around and still risk looking even more bedraggled than I feel.

There is also the age-old age problem, which is much more of a problem for women than men. The point came home to me one Christmas, when my then four-year-old niece confronted me before the family's pickup basketball game. "Aunt Deborah, you're too old to play," was her candid assessment. Her uncle, the same age, received no similar diagnosis. Silver hair and furrowed brows allow aging men to look "distinguished." That is not the case with aging women, who risk marginalization as "unattractive" or ridicule for efforts to pass as young. This double standard leaves women not only perpetually worried about their appearance, but also worried about worrying.

When someone complimented Gloria Steinem at midlife on how young she looked, she responded that "this is what fifty looks like." But as an accompanying photo made abundantly clear, it isn't. Most of us in our fifties don't look anything like that. And the lingering question is, why should we care? And why are we still spending so much on products that experts dismiss as "cosmetic hoo-hah"?

The title of Nora Ephron's latest best seller acknowledges *I Feel Bad about My Neck*. The book recounts how much time and expense she and her friends spend on what she euphemistically defines as "maintenance," including "astronomical sums" for useless antiaging products, "testaments to [our] gullibility." All of this fuels my interest. Why does someone as talented as Nora Ephron fuss about her neck? Why was Sarah Palin's campaign paying more for her makeup expert than her foreign policy advisor? Why is Oprah

Winfrey, the most successful female entrepreneur in America, perennially preoccupied with her weight? Why, in a country where more than a sixth of the population lacks access to basic health care, are cosmetic procedures the fastest-growing medical specialty, with women accounting for ninety percent of the patients? Why has the contemporary women's movement made so much progress on other issues of gender inequality but so little headway on unforgiving standards of appearance? *The Beauty Bias* reflects my search for partial answers and promising responses.

Acknowledgments

. . .

This book owes many debts. David McBride, at Oxford University Press, provided invaluable editorial suggestions, as did many colleagues: Laurence Friedman, Laura Rosenbury, Abigail Saguey, C. Barr Taylor, Malena Watrous, and Marilyn Yalom. I also benefited from exceptional research assistance by Stanford Law students Mariko Hirose, Foster Johnson, and Rachel Velcoff, and Columbia Law Student Katherine Scully. Mary Tye and Wendy Realmuto helped prepare the manuscript with extraordinary skill, patience, and good humor. I was also blessed by superb assistance from the Stanford Law Library, particularly its director, Paul Lomio, and library staff Sonia Moss, Rich Porter, Sergio Stone, George Vizvary, Erika Wayne, Kate Wilko, George Wilson, and Sarah Wilson. The book is dedicated to my sisters-in-law, Robin Broad, Madelynn Azar Cavanagh, and Caitlin Wold, who have helped me see the good side of appearance, and whose support has sustained me in this and all my other work. And as always, my deepest debt is to my husband, Ralph Cavanagh, whose love, support, and editorial insight has meant more than I can ever adequately acknowledge.

THE BEAUTY BIAS

CHAPTER ONE

Introduction

"Tenth circle. Ladies' shoes."

Glen Le Lievre, *New Yorker*, September 24, 2007, 124. Reprinted with permission.

"IT HURTS TO be beautiful" is a cliché I grew up with. "It hurts not to be beautiful" is a truth I acquired on my own. But not until researching this book did I begin to grasp the cumulative cost of our cultural preoccupation with appearance. Over a century ago, Charles Darwin concluded that when it came to beauty, "[n]o excuse is needed for treating the subject in some detail."[1] That is even truer today; our global investment in appearance totals over $200 billion a year.[2] Yet when it comes to discrimination based on appearance, an excuse for discussion does seem necessary, particularly for a scholar specializing in law and gender. Given all the serious problems confronting women—rape, domestic violence, poverty, inadequate child care, unequal pay, violations of international human rights—why focus on looks? Most people believe that bias based on beauty is inconsequential, inevitable, or unobjectionable.[3]

They are wrong. Conventional wisdom understates the advantages that attractiveness confers, the costs of its pursuit, and the injustices that result. Many individuals pay a substantial price in time, money, and physical health. Although discrimination based on appearance is by no means our most serious form of bias, its impact is often far more invidious than we suppose. That is not to discount the positive aspects of appearance-related pursuits, including the pleasure that comes from self-expression. Nor is it to underestimate the biological role of sex appeal or the health benefits that can result from actions prompted by aesthetic concerns. Rather, the goal is to expose the price we pay for undue emphasis on appearance and the strategies we need to address it.

What compounds the problem is our failure to recognize that it *is* a significant problem and one to which law and public policy should respond. Compared with other inequities that the contemporary women's movement has targeted, those related to appearance have shown strikingly little improvement. In fact, by some measures, such as the rise in cosmetic surgery and eating disorders, our preoccupation with attractiveness is getting worse.

Injustices related to appearance fall along a spectrum, and involve everything from debilitating discrimination and social stigma, to the costs of conformity in time, expense, and physical risk. Even relatively minor inconveniences can cumulatively exact a substantial price, which is partly what launched this book.

THE PERSONAL BECOMES POLITICAL: THE TROUBLE WITH SHOES

It started with shoes. Like many American women, I have had more issues with appearance than I care to recall. Happily, however, I have landed in an occupation with undemanding standards. As this book's Preface noted, academics are known for relentlessly unattractive apparel.[4] I am a case in point. My fashion instincts veer toward frumpy, but one compensation is that they have freed me from the footwear fetishes of many otherwise sensible women. In many professional contexts, I am surrounded by colleagues tottering painfully on decorative footwear. Some of the nation's most distinguished female leaders hobble about in what we described in high school as "killer shoes." During my term as chair of the American Bar Association's Commission on Women in the Profession, I was struck by how often some of the nation's most prominent and powerful women were stranded in cab lines and late for meetings because walking any distance was out of the question.

But inconvenience is the least of the problems. High heels are a major contributor to serious back and foot problems, and four-fifths of women eventually experience such difficulties.[5] In an interview with the *Wall Street Journal*, one owner of a marketing firm acknowledged that her taste in footwear was partly responsible for her herniated disk. But about half of her clothes only "look[ed] good" when accompanied by four- to five-inch heels, so she had become resigned to pain: "There is a price to pay for beauty and high heels is one of them."[6] Now that designers are offering stilettos topping out at six inches, and several models wearing them have fallen on Milan runways, some stores have started to offer "Heel Walking Workshops."[7]

This is not, of course, a new problem. As chapter 2 notes, Chinese footbinding is the most obvious, but by no means the only case in point. Although comfortable choices have clearly improved, shoe design may be the last politically acceptable haven for closet misogynists. Typical fashion profiles feature not a single item suitable for actual movement. Most have spindly heels and flesh-biting designs, on the apparent assumption that "if the shoe pinches, wear it."[8] All around me, smart accomplished women are doing just that, and ignoring the risk that heels this high will catch in grates, flatten arches, breed blisters, and hurt like hell on any extended walk. A startlingly large number of women are even willing to undergo painful and risky foot surgery for the sake of better "toe cleavage" that will fit fashionable styles.[9] Women account for about 80 percent of all foot surgery, much of it related to high heels.[10]

Some years ago, in a fit of pique, I wrote a semisatirical *New York Times* op-ed on footwear as a feminist issue.[11] Never have I touched such a responsive chord on issues involving gender; my mail box was swamped. Podiatrists sent supportive research, progressive shoe manufacturers sent catalogs, women shared tales of woe, and men vented their frustrations with wives' dysfunctional choices. Not all responses were, however, complimentary. Some readers questioned why I had squandered this rare media opportunity on such a trivial problem. In a country where four million women annually are victims of domestic violence and twenty million live in poverty, why put the height of heels at the top of the women's agenda? The short answer was that I hadn't. I have been peddling earnest policy-oriented editorials on more serious topics for decades. This was the column the *Times* was interested in printing. But my broader point, then and now, has been to expose how appearance-related practices, even some that seem petty or benign, can cumulatively limit our lives. If men manage to be sexy without help from their footwear, why can't women? And why have we made so little headway, in law, politics, and public education, in addressing the injustices of appearance?

The chapters that follow take up these questions. Chapter 2 begins the discussion by surveying the consequences of attractiveness and the costs of its pursuit. That appearance matters comes as no surprise. What is less obvious is the extent of its influence on employment, income, self-esteem, and personal relationships. We often understate the price of our preoccupation, not just in money but also in physical and psychological well being, and in gender, class, and racial inequalities. Chapter 3 explores what drives this fixation, including biological, market, technological, and media forces. Efforts to counteract these pressures and to challenge the corrosive influences of appearance are the focus of chapter 4. Why have efforts by the women's movement been so divisive, and so often ineffectual? Chapter 5 considers why it matters. What exactly is wrong with discrimination based on appearance and what, if anything, could the law do to address it? To further explore those questions, chapter 6 examines the limitations of current legal frameworks and the effect of the few statutes here and abroad that explicitly prohibit appearance discrimination. Chapter 7 concludes with a road map for reform. In an ideal world, what would be the role of appearance and what individual, legal, and political strategies might help bring us closer?

THE COSTS AND CONSEQUENCES OF APPEARANCE

A threshold question is why we should care about any of these questions. What are the social consequences of physical appearance?

Chapter 2 looks at the significance of attractiveness and the price it exacts. Although most of us realize that looks matter, few of us realize how much, or how early its influence starts. Beginning at birth, those who are viewed as physically appealing are also more likely to be viewed as smart, likeable, and good. The ridicule and ostracism that unattractive children experience can result in lower self-confidence and social skills, which leads to further disadvantages in later life. Appearance also influences judgments about competence and job performance, which, in turn, affect income and status. Résumés get a less favorable assessment when they are thought to belong to less attractive individuals. These individuals are also less likely to get hired and promoted, and they earn lower salaries, even in professions such as law where appearance has no demonstrable relationship to ability.[12]

Given these advantages, it makes sense for individuals to be concerned about their appearance. Still, the extent of that concern is striking, as the overview in chapter 2 makes clear. In representative surveys, 90 percent of women consider looks important to their self-image, and over half of young women reported that they would prefer to be hit by a truck than be fat; two thirds would rather be mean or stupid.[13] More than a third of obese individuals are willing to risk death in order to lose just 10 percent of their weight; three quarters will assume the risk for 20 percent.[14]

People also spend more on appearance than the results often justify. Americans invest $40 billion annually on diets, which rarely result in significant or sustained weight loss. About 95 percent of dieters regain their weight within one to five years.[15] Of the $18 billion consumers spend on cosmetics, only 7 percent pays for ingredients. The rest subsidizes expensive packaging and marketing of products, including many that scientists find ineffectual.[16] Even investments that result in high levels of individual satisfaction raise issues of social priorities. Although almost a fifth of the United

States population lacks basic health care services, inessential cosmetic procedures have increased by 400 percent over the last decade and are the fastest growing area of medical expenditures. Liposuction is the world's most common form of surgery.[17]

Moreover, time and money are not the only costs. Substantial health risks accompany some appearance-driven practices, particularly those involving cosmetic surgery and yo-yo dieting. For many individuals, concerns about appearance also contribute to psychological difficulties such as depression and eating disorders. These difficulties are partly attributable to widespread stigma and discrimination. Bias based on attractiveness is largely unregulated and compounds other inequalities based on class, race, ethnicity, and gender. Prevailing beauty standards privilege those with white-European features and the time and money to invest in their appearance. Women face greater pressures than men to look attractive and pay greater penalties for falling short.

SURVEYING THE FOUNDATIONS: SOCIAL, BIOLOGICAL, ECONOMIC, TECHNOLOGICAL, AND MEDIA FORCES

What accounts for this premium on appearance? Chapter 3 begins exploring that question through theories of evolution. According to sociobiologists, we value attractiveness, especially in women, because it is a sign of health and fertility, which are key factors in reproductive success. Such theories help account for nearly universal preferences such as clear skin, facial symmetry, and hour-glass figures. But evolutionary imperatives alone cannot explain the variations over time and culture in what people perceive as attractive. The most obvious example is weight. Whether plumpness is prized or punished seems to depend largely on its role in signaling social status under different environmental conditions. Where food is scarce, fatness is a mark of wealth and prominence. Where food is abundant, the reverse is true. Our current cult of thinness makes no sense from an evolutionary standpoint; low body weight is linked to reproductive dysfunction.[18]

Chapter 3 reviews other explanations for the importance of appearance and variations in cultural preferences. How someone looks can express religious and political values, as well as convey class and cultural identity. Particularly in today's consumer-oriented culture, dress, grooming, and figure are crucial signals, as well as sources, of wealth. The body is a prime site for what sociologist Thorstein Veblan famously described as "conspicuous consumption."[19] Huge global industries turn on addressing problems that we haven't always known we have. Sags and bags that were once accepted as a normal consequence of aging now account for a multi-billion-dollar market in frequently ineffectual cosmetic responses.[20]

Advances in science and technology have created new opportunities for "self-improvement" and corresponding pressures to take advantage of them. For example, the dramatic escalation in cosmetic surgery reflects both the growth in effective techniques and physicians' efforts to market services not subject to insurers' cost constraints. Other appearance-related products, now cloaked in a veneer of pseudo science, promise effortless perfection. "Space age slenderizer" and "poly-u collagen peptides."offer to shed consumers' unwanted pounds and wrinkles overnight.[21] The media in general and advertisers in particular have played an important role in magnifying the importance of appearance and the pressures to enhance it. Women's magazines pitch an endless array of cosmetic advice and exhortation. Judging from their tables of contents, readers' most urgent concerns are on the order of "thinner thighs in thirty days." Televised makeovers and beauty pageants fuel implausible aspirations and unhealthy practices. "Reality" programs involving weight loss and cosmetic surgery are anything but realistic; careful editing omits anything inconsistent with a happily-ever-after ending. The public's repeated exposure to airbrushed, surgically enhanced fashion models and Hollywood celebrities further reinforces unrealistic standards. Only five percent of American women are in the same weight category as models and actresses, and efforts to replicate their figures often lead to eating disorders and related psychological dysfunctions.[22]

The media's sexualized portrayals of prominent women, including everyone from athletes to politicians, also carries a cost. Overemphasis of their appearance deflects attention from their performance and reinforces sex-based double standards. That the highest paid member of Sarah Palin's vice presidential campaign was her makeup "artist" speaks volumes about our misplaced priorities.

FEMINIST CHALLENGES AND RESPONSES

Chapter 4 reviews efforts to challenge these priorities. In the United States, the nineteenth-century social purity crusade against cosmetics, the African-American campaign against skin whiteners and hair straighteners, and the feminist struggle for dress reform all set the terms for modern debates. During the Victorian era, religious and community leaders insisted that "respectable" women did not rouge. Prominent African Americans denounced cosmetic and grooming practices designed to replicate white norms. And suffragists such as Elizabeth Cady Stanton and Amelia Bloomer attempted to popularize alternatives to the corsets and crinolines that endangered women's health and constricted their movement.

None of these efforts were particularly successful. It took the rise of the contemporary women's movement in the 1960s to mount a broader and more sustained challenge to the beauty industry. That campaign kicked off with the infamous "bra-burning" protest at the

1968 Miss America pageant. Although no lingerie was in fact incinerated, the label stuck and battle lines were drawn. In most media portrayals, the activists were frumpy fanatical feminists, unhappy about standards of attractiveness that they could not hope to meet.

Gradually, however, the mainstream women's movement supplied more tempered and influential critiques. Naomi Wolf's bestselling *Beauty Myth* exposed many products as what dermatologists labeled "cosmetic hoo-hah."[23] A cottage industry of commentary on eating disorders and cosmetic surgery has made clear the medical risks of other appearance-driven practices. As critics have noted, even physically harmless preoccupations divert time and money to self-improvement rather than social action. Sexualized portrayals of prominent women—Hillary Clinton's cleavage, Sarah Palin's beehive, Michelle O'Bama's upper arms—have underscored the double standard that channels attention to women's appearance instead of their accomplishments.

Responses to these critiques have taken several forms. Commentators within and outside the women's movement have defended appearance-related efforts as either a satisfying form of self-improvement and self-expression, or a necessary concession to cultural expectations. From their standpoint, the "personal may be political" but it is also personal. As long as women are subject to a double standard, they might as well do what they need to do and get on with their lives. The beauty industry has made analogous efforts to respond to feminist critiques by co-opting feminist principles. In the world of Madison Avenue marketers, diet and cosmetic products are a way for women to "be all they can be" and express who they "really are."[24]

Yet what is it that women want to be and how much time and money do they want to spend to get there? For many women, there are no easy answers, and issues of appearance remain a source of anxiety and ambivalence. That is particularly the case for women of a certain age, when cosmetic procedures, hair tints, and weight loss regimes begin to seem like necessary alternatives to "letting themselves go." Even feminists who see these options as oppressive often feel shamed by their inability to escape them, or discomfited by the trade-offs. After all, as Susan Brownmiller ruefully notes, "sensible shoes aren't sexy."[25]

Chapter 4 concludes with some ways around this standoff. Whatever their other differences concerning appearance, most women would agree on several key points. The pursuit of beauty should be a source of pleasure, not a response to shame or social pressure. Women should be able to choose whether or not to dye their hair or use Botox without being viewed as politically incorrect or professionally inadequate. They should neither be held to a higher standard of appearance than men, nor ridiculed as vain for their efforts to measure up. If men can seem eminent as they age without cosmetic enhancement, so too should women.

APPEARANCE DISCRIMINATION: SOCIAL WRONGS

AND LEGAL RIGHTS

We are, however, a far distance from this ideal world, and chapter 5 explores what stands in the way. Discussion centers on two fundamental questions. Are any of the disadvantages resulting from discrimination based on appearance unjust? If so, do they call for some legal remedy?

The clearest argument for condemning appearance discrimination is that it offends principles of equal opportunity and individual dignity. As with other forms of prejudice, bias based on appearance often rests on inaccurate stereotypes. Assumptions that overweight individuals are lazy, undisciplined, or unfit are a case in point. Appearance–related discrimination also may stigmatize individuals based on factors at least partly beyond their control, and may encourage unsafe cosmetic and dieting practices.

A related concern is that such bias reinforces other inequalities based on race, ethnicity, class, age, and gender. A widely publicized example of sex-based double standards in appearance involved the grooming policy at Reno's Harrah's Casino. It required female beverage servers to wear makeup and nail polish, and to have their hair "teased, curled, or styled." Male servers needed only short haircuts and fingernails that were "neatly trimmed."[26] Darlene Jespersen, a bartender with an outstanding performance record, challenged the policy on the grounds of sex discrimination. She felt that being "dolled up" was degrading and interfered with her ability to handle unruly customers. A federal appellate court rejected her challenge because she had not introduced proof that the standards imposed disproportionate burdens of time and expense on women, a fact that presumably would be obvious to reasonable jurors. Does anyone, except apparently some federal judges, really need expert testimony comparing the average time required for cleaning fingernails with applying makeup and styling hair? And as one dissenting judge pointed out, cosmetics "don't grow on trees."[27] Such makeup and manicure requirements may seem trivial, but the broader principle is not. As another dissenting judge noted, the assumption underlying the casino's policy was that "women's undoctored faces compare unfavorably to men's."[28] Holding only women to sexualized standards diverts attention from competence and perpetuates gender roles that are separate and by no means equal.

A final objection to discrimination based on appearance is that it restricts rights to self-expression. How individuals present themselves to the world may implicate core political values, cultural identity, and religious beliefs. Frequently litigated examples include hair length, hair styles, headscarves, and yarmulkes that employers have been unwilling to accommodate.

Although many individuals dismiss such discrimination as inconsequential, it occurs more frequently than they assume. Anywhere from 12 to 16 percent of workers believe that they have been subject to such bias, a percentage that is in the same vicinity, or greater, than those reporting gender, racial, ethnic, age, or religious prejudice. So too, almost half of surveyed Americans believe that obese workers suffer discrimination in the workplace, a figure that is higher than for other groups, such as women and minorities, who are protected by antidiscrimination laws. When asked about legal remedies, the public splits almost evenly for and against prohibitions, with a majority of women and minority groups favoring a ban.[29]

What stands in the way? Chapter 5 reviews the major arguments against making appearance discrimination unlawful. One concern is that for some goods and services, employees' attractiveness can be an effective selling point. Many bars, restaurants, and department stores have imposed hiring and grooming standards that enforce a certain "brand" look: "slender," "hot" "young and trendy" or "not too ethnic."[30] As one Hooters spokesperson explained, "A lot of places sell good burgers. Hooters Girls, with their charm and all-American sex appeal, are what our customers come for."[31]

Yet that is an argument that courts have generally rejected in other discrimination contexts, and with reason. Consumer preferences often reflect and reinforce precisely the attitudes that society is seeking to eliminate. So, for example, unless sex is a business necessity, employers may not select workers on that basis. The same should be true of sexual attractiveness. Hooters' customers who want cleavage with their burgers are no more worthy of deference than the male airline passengers in the 1970s who preferred stewardesses in hot pants.[32]

To some courts and commentators, however, a ban on appearance discrimination asks too much. From their perspective, even if such discrimination is unfair, the law is incapable of eliminating it and efforts to do so will result in unwarranted costs and corrosive back-lash. Stanford law professor Richard Ford voices a common objection: "a business community united in frustration at a bloated civil rights regime could become a powerful political force for reform or even repeal."[33] Many judges bristle at the prospect of clogging the courts with petty disputes over makeup, weight, and grooming standards. But it is by no means self-evident that prejudice based on appearance is harder to eradicate than other forms of bias. In fact, considerable evidence suggests racial, gender, and disability biases are also deeply rooted, but nonetheless subject to change through legal prohibitions. Moreover, as discussion below notes, none of the few local and state prohibitions on appearance discrimination currently in force have triggered the exorbitant costs or backlash that critics have predicted.

Chapter 5 closes with examples of how bans on appearance discrimination could contribute to progressive social change. By expressing aspirations, establishing appropriate standards, deterring violations, and raising public awareness, such legal remedies could nudge us closer to a just society. In cases where victims of appearance discrimination have brought suit, the result has often been to raise public awareness of the costs of bias and to secure workplace or policy changes that help prevent it. Even litigants who lose in court may win in the world outside it. Harrah's casino changed its policy after the lawsuit.[34] But Darlene Jespersen paid too high a price. She lost a job at which she excelled and was blacklisted when she sought another. As her lawyer noted, when it comes to the casino business, "Reno is a small town."[35]

LEGAL FRAMEWORKS

Jespersen's experience is all too typical; the overview of law in chapter 6 suggests why. On the whole, the legal regulation of appearance has an unbecoming history. Its Anglo-European foundations date to thirteenth-century sumptuary laws, which reserved certain fashions only for aristocrats. Early American legislation focused more on preventing "indecency" than reinforcing class privilege. To that end, some jurisdictions banned "unsightly" individuals or women without corsets from appearing in public.[36]

Contemporary law has banished such archaic prohibitions, but it has also given wide latitude to businesses and employers to impose their own restrictive grooming requirements and to discriminate on the basis of appearance. In general, such discrimination is illegal only if it involves other characteristics that civil rights law protects, such as sex, race, religion, or disability. So, for example, weight and grooming standards can be struck down if they impose unreasonable, disproportionate burdens on one sex. Grooming codes may be impermissible if they fail to make reasonable accommodation for religious expression, or selectively target practices associated with a particular racial group. Disability law has been held to prohibit weight discrimination in a very small percentage of cases involving extreme obesity that has a biological basis and that appears to impair normal functioning.

Even in these contexts, however, many courts have taken a restrictive view of what counts as discrimination. A representative example is the Harrah's casino decision, which found no disproportionate burden resulting from hair and makeup rules. Judges have also been unsympathetic to African American women's desire to wear cornrows, and Sikh employees' wish to wear turbans or beards, even when the employer presents no convincing business justification for banning them.[37] Narrow interpretations of state and federal disability law also exclude from protection the very individuals who need it most: those who are only moderately overweight and who are not impaired in their job performance. Such employees can be dismissed at will even if employers can show no demonstrable competence or health-related reasons.

These dismissals seem particularly unjust when the job involves no customer contact. As an attorney for an obese man denied a job as a fast-food cook put it, "The only thing that should matter to McDonald's...[is] how he cooks, not how he looks."[38] Cases where individuals in such positions have lost their jobs occasionally have prompted public protests and policy responses, including some of the local ordinances that ban discrimination based on appearance. Chapter 6 provides the first systematic empirical evidence of how those ordinances work in practice.

One state and six cities or counties prohibit some form of appearance discrimination: Michigan, San Francisco, the District of Columbia, Santa Cruz (California) Madison (Wisconsin), Urbana (Illinois), and Howard County (Maryland). These laws vary in coverage and in the frequency of enforcement, but no jurisdiction has experienced the flood of frivolous claims that commentators have anticipated. Hypothetical examples such as Jewish deli owners forced to hire cashiers with swastika tattoos have made for provocative journalism, but they are nowhere to be found in reported cases.[39] Santa Cruz, the poster child for critics of appearance prohibitions, has had no complaints in fifteen years. Urbana has had none in seven, and San Francisco has had only two in eight years. The average number of annual complaints for the other jurisdictions has ranged between one (the District of Columbia) and thirty (Michigan). Most have included allegations of other forms of bias (race, sex, and religion). Although some of these claims seem frivolous, they could have been brought without an appearance law, so it is not clear that the law has added significantly to businesses' legal expenses.

Few appearance complaints have resulted in litigation or an unqualified victory for the complainant. For example, Michigan has averaged fewer than one lawsuit a year, and no final judgments of discrimination. However, a substantial number of cases have ended up with reasonable negotiated settlements, and the existence of the laws may have deterred unjust bias. Moreover, the grievances that have obtained some legal remedy demonstrate the need for such protection. A representative example involved a waitress fired when she was six to seven months pregnant, despite a doctor's letter indicating that she was still able to work. The manager's professed concern for maternal health was inconsistent with statements that she made to other workers about the effect of the waitress's appearance on the restaurant's image.[40]

Chapter 6 also places the American experience in a broader international context. European law is similar to that of the United States, and generally prohibits appearance discrimination only when it involves other forms of bias covered by human rights law (such as that involving race, gender, religion, age, disability, and sexual orientation). However, some countries, particularly France and Germany, extend greater protection to employee privacy, dignity, and self-expression; those interests prevail unless the employer can demonstrate a strong countervailing business justification.[41] So too, in Germany, grooming codes are often established through "codetermination" between management and elected worker councils, a process that accords significant weight to employee interests. Based on the information available, the Australian state of Victoria is the only jurisdiction outside the United States that has an explicit ban on appearance-related bias. It experiences few complaints that require a formal hearing.[42]

Part of the reason for the limited legal enforcement activity both here and abroad is that victims of appearance discrimination face significant costs and evidentiary obstacles; favorable decisions are unlikely in the absence of compelling undisputed facts. Many individuals are unwilling to assume the stigma and reputational damage of publicly airing complaints about their unattractiveness. Particularly in jurisdictions that do not authorize attorneys' fees or substantial financial damages, victims also may lack sufficient economic incentives to pursue a claim. Another deterrent is the extreme deference that some courts and commissions give to employer regulations. So for example, Wisconsin discount stores and pet supply outlets have been allowed to ban earrings for male sales personnel. Employers' desire to ensure a "pleasant shopping experience," and their unsupported assumption that jewelry on men is inconsistent with that goal, have been found sufficient justification for the restrictions.[43]

Yet despite these limitations, the existence of appearance discrimination laws can sometimes make a difference. Chapter 6 reviews examples in which victims of inaccurate stereotypes or invidious bias obtained reasonable remedies. When these cases also attracted significant publicity, they sent a message to employers, and raised public awareness of the costs of discrimination. A complaint before the San Francisco Human Rights Commission illustrates that potential. It involved Jennifer Portnick, a 240-pound aerobics instructor, who was denied a franchise by Jazzercise, a national fitness company. According to its lawyer, "One of the keys to success is extending franchises to instructors with a fit, toned body. Being able to portray this image inspires students... [and] is a necessary part of what students seek to achieve."[44] But Portnick was in fact fit. She worked out six days a week, taught back-to-back exercise classes, and had no history of performance problems or lack of students. She simply wanted to be "judged on my merits, not my measurements."[45] After a commission ruling in her favor and massive adverse publicity, the company changed its policy. The message that emerged in national media coverage was that full-bodied students can be inspired, not deterred, by an instructor their size who is fit and toned. Given recent evidence suggesting that fitness, rather than body mass, is the best predictor of health in most over-weight individuals, that is an important social message.[46]

Chapter 6 concludes by considering one final aspect in which more effective appearance-related laws and enforcement structures could make a difference: the regulation of false or misleading claims about beauty and weight-reduction products. Aggressive marketing of these products both encourages preoccupation with appearance and deludes consumers about effortless ways to enhance it. Although federal and state consumer agencies have authority to regulate fraudulent advertising, they lack the resources to keep up with the barrage of deceptive claims involving pseudoscientific "miracle methods." If promises about these products sound too good to be true, it's because they aren't true. No one, outside the fantasy land of Madison Avenue marketing, can "eliminate" fat through seaweed patches and Chinese herbal creams ("no will power required").[47] Yet consumers squander billions of dollars on such products, partly because a majority of the public wrongly assumes that manufacturers could not make these claims without solid scientific evidence for their validity.[48]

A ROAD MAP FOR REFORM

None of these problems connected with appearance are readily remedied. Our prejudices and preoccupations run deep, and multi-billion dollar industries have a stake in perpetuating them. Yet neither are we helpless to address some of the worst injustices, and chapter 7 explores strategies that could push us in the right direction.

As a threshold matter, we need greater clarity about our goals. At the cultural level, a central priority should be to promote more attainable, healthy, and inclusive ideals. Our standards of attractiveness should reflect greater variation across age, weight, race, and ethnicity, and our grooming requirements should reflect greater tolerance for diversity and self-expression. Judgments based on appearance should not spill over to educational and employment contexts where they have no socially defensible role. More support should also be available for strategies that promote healthy lifestyles, which could also help reduce the weight-related concerns that prompt discrimination.

Law can assist that agenda by combating appearance bias and by providing greater protection from restrictive grooming regulations and misleading advertising claims. One obvious strategy would be to prohibit discrimination based on appearance that is not justified by substantial business needs. A fair and accessible dispute resolution process, with the potential for judicial review, could increase the likelihood that victims would raise concerns as well as minimize the cost of addressing them.

In the absence of specific prohibitions on appearance discrimination, some progress is possible through broader interpretations of current discrimination and disability law. When evaluating sex-specific grooming and dress codes, courts should take a realistic view of what constitutes disproportionate burdens on one sex, and should disallow rules that reinforce gender stereotypes, like the makeup requirement of Harrah's Casino. Customer preferences should not constitute a justification for discrimination unless sexual attractiveness is a business necessity. So too, disability law should be interpreted more broadly and should encompass discrimination based on weight whether or not it involves extreme obesity with a physiological cause.

Law is, of course, only one of the strategies necessary to promote cultural change, and it is most effective when joined with other approaches. Litigation and policy initiatives can often raise public awareness about the appearance discrimination as well as the broader societal efforts necessary to address it. To achieve such reform, activists need to be strategic in how they coordinate legal, media, and political strategies. A textbook example is the work of fat activists in San Francisco after a local fitness center ran an advertisement featuring a space alien and a caption, "When they come, they'll eat the fat ones first." Protesters showed up at the center in alien costumes wearing signs that said "Eat Me" and "This Gym Alienates Fat People." Activists also demanded hearings before the San Francisco Human Rights Commission to explore examples of discrimination. The result was enactment of the city's ordinance prohibiting discrimination based on height and weight.

Another masterful coordination of legal and media tactics involved a sex discrimination suit by two former "Borgata Babes," cocktail waitresses at the Atlantic City's Borgata Hotel and Casino. As chapter 5 notes, two "Babes" agreed, as part of their employment contract to keep a hourglass figure, and be height and weight appropriate." The policy contributed to widespread eating disorders and related mental and physical health difficulties.[49] Widespread media coverage led not only to a substantial settlement, but also to greater public awareness of the health issues at stake.[50] The terms were confidential, but the impact was not. Commentators drew analogies to another celebrated lawsuit involving the Sand Hotel. There, a cocktail waitress successfully sued for sex discrimination after being forced to wear a revealing uniform and high heels, and being told that her job was to "sell sex." That litigation prompted other Atlantic City casinos except the Borgata to offer uniforms including pants and flat shoes.[51]

These cases, along with others described in chapters 5 and 6, underscore the possibilities for social change. Lawsuits, along with public protests, have made a difference. Workplace policies have been modified, legislation has been passed, and employees have been reinstated or compensated. Yet the full potential of law has yet to be realized. We need more explicit prohibitions of appearance-related bias, and more expansive interpretations of existing antidis-crimination laws that could address it. Even if formal complaints remain infrequent, such legal mandates can play an important role in deterring and publicizing abuse, providing bargaining leverage for victims, and expressing social ideals.

Beauty may be only skin deep, but the damages associated with its pursuit go much deeper. Only through a better understanding of the injustices of appearance can we fashion more effective responses. The chapters that follow are a step in that direction.

CHAPTER TWO

The Importance of Appearance
and the Costs of Conformity

I'm tired of all this nonsense about beauty being only skin deep.
That's deep enough. What do you want, an adorable pancreas?

—Jean Kerr

· · ·

BEAUTY MAY BE only skin deep, but that is deep enough to confer an
unsettling array of advantages. Although most of us learn at early ages
that physical attractiveness matters, few of us realize how much. Nor
do we generally recognize the extent to which our biases conflict with
meritocratic principles. In a recent national survey, only a third of
employees believed that, in their workplaces, physically attractive
individuals were more likely to be hired or promoted.[1] Yet a cottage
industry of studies indicates that popular assumptions are wrong, that
bias is pervasive, and that people underestimate the extent to which
attractiveness skews their evaluations.[2] Appearance imposes penalties
that far exceed what most of us assume or would consider defensible.

DEFINITIONS OF ATTRACTIVENESS AND FORMS OF DISCRIMINATION

A threshold question is what exactly do we mean by "attractive"? The issue has long vexed theorists of aesthetics, and considerable debate has centered on whether beauty is a definable property or a subjective perception.[3] Social scientists generally have focused on a more pragmatic issue. Is attractiveness something that researchers can adequately identify and measure? Although conventional wisdom holds that beauty is in the eye of the beholder, in fact most beholders agree about the appeal of certain characteristics. As chapter 3 indicates, sociobiologists see an evolutionary basis for these preferred features. Facial symmetry, unblemished skin, and an hour-glass figure have been widely viewed as evidence of health and fertility.[4] To be sure, some preferences, particularly those regarding weight and grooming, have varied considerably across time and culture. But today's globalization of mass media and information technology has brought an increasing convergence in standards of attractiveness.[5]

Researchers on appearance have achieved a substantial measure of reliability through a "truth in consensus" method.[6] In essence, subjects rate a photograph or an individual on a scale of attractiveness, and those ratings are then averaged to produce an overall assessment. Such methods yield a strikingly high degree of agreement even among individuals of different sex, race, age, socioeconomic status, and cultural backgrounds.[7]

Research on weight discrimination also relies on widely shared measures, although some terminology is controversial. Studies use clear verbal descriptions, visual portrayals, or government definitions.[8] The United States Centers for Disease Control and Prevention (CDC) define overweight and obesity based on a body mass index (BMI), a ratio of height to weight. Overweight is intended to designate the point at which individuals face an increased risk of disease because of excess body mass; obesity is intended to signify an increased risk of death, and is generally defined as 20 percent over ideal body weight. In 1998, the CDCs lowered the cutoff points for health risks. By the revised standards, about a third of American adults are overweight and another third are obese.[9] How accurately these standards predict increased risk is a matter of considerable dispute, as subsequent debate indicates. Related controversies involve use of the terms overweight and obese. The National Association to Advance Fat Acceptance (NAAFA) prefers the term fat, which its members believe carries less stigma and fewer contested connotations of abnormality.[10] However, in conventional usage, fat is generally taken as more offensive than overweight.[11] And for many researchers, fat appears less precise and less consistent with social science and legal terminology. This book follows the preferences of these different constituencies in describing their work. Obesity and overweight are used to discuss social science findings and legal rulings, and fat is used to discuss the efforts of activists.

A related issue is what we mean by "discrimination based on appearance." Such bias falls along a continuum. At one end is discrimination based on characteristics that are difficult or impossible to change, such as height and facial features. Although sex, race, and ethnicity have such an effect on appearance, they implicate identity in a more fundamental sense than other traits and are generally considered separately in legal and theoretical discussions of discrimination. At the other end of the continuum are purely voluntary characteristics, such as clothing and grooming. In between are mixed traits, such as obesity, which have both biological and behavioral foundations. Social science research on appearance generally does not distinguish among these forms of bias; what makes a given individual attractive may reflect both innate and voluntary characteristics. However, as subsequent discussion suggests, discrimination based on factors beyond personal control generally raises the most significant concerns of social injustice, and may sometimes justify different legal treatment than other forms of appearance-related bias.

INTERPERSONAL RELATIONSHIPS AND ECONOMIC OPPORTUNITIES

The significance of appearance begins early. Even infants stare longer at attractive faces.[12] Eleven percent of surveyed couples would abort a fetus genetically predisposed to obesity.[13] Parents and teachers give less attention to less attractive children, and they are less likely to be viewed as good, smart, cheerful, likeable, and socially skilled than their more attractive counterparts.[14] Children themselves quickly internalize these judgments. They ascribe better personality traits to good-looking individuals and prefer them as friends.[15] The teasing and ostracism that unattractive and over-weight children experience can lead to mental health difficulties and discourage healthy athletic activity.[16] During adolescence, many teenagers' self-esteem becomes dependent on appearance. By age twelve, girls place greater emphasis on attractiveness than compe-tence, and their frequent dissatisfaction with their looks can result in anxiety, shame, eating disorders, and related dysfunctions.[17]

In essence, individuals' unattractiveness in their early years can set off a chain of developmental difficulties that ultimately become self-reinforcing. Ridicule and marginalization often lessen self-confidence and social skills, which then translate into less satisfac-tory interpersonal and career experiences in later life.

That attractiveness matters for adults comes as no surprise, but the extent of its importance is greater than is commonly assumed. A wide array of research documents a phenomenon that psycholo-gists describe as "what is beautiful is good." Less attractive individ-uals are less likely to be viewed as smart, happy, interesting, likeable, successful, and well-adjusted.[18] They are less likely to marry and to marry someone well off.[19] Weight similarly matters; surveyed college students would prefer a spouse who is an embezzler, drug user, or shoplifter than someone who is obese.[20] For men, height signifies a wide range of positive attributes: a high IQ, competence, trustworthiness, even kindliness.[21] Among racial and ethnic minorities, those with darker skin color and non–Anglo-European features have lower marriage rates and social status.[22] Unattractive individuals receive less favorable treatment in a variety of settings, including higher sentences and lower damage awards in simulated legal proceedings.[23] Not only are the less attractive treated worse, their unfavorable treatment can erode self-esteem, self-confidence, and social skills, which compound their disadvantages.[24]

Appearance also skews judgments about competence and job performance. In studies where subjects evaluate written essays, the same material receives lower ratings for ideas, style, and creativity when an accompanying photograph shows a less attractive author.[25] Résumés get a more favorable assessment when they are thought to belong to more attractive candidates.[26] Overweight individuals are subject to similar bias; they are seen as less likeable and less well adjusted, and as having less self-control, self-discipline, effective work habits, and ability to get along with others.[27] Good-looking faculty receive better course evaluations from students, just as good-looking students receive higher ratings on intelligence from teachers.[28]

Unsurprisingly, the importance of looks varies across occupations and geographic locations. Attractiveness matters most in metropolitan areas and in jobs relying on influence and image rather than physical labor.[29] On the whole, however, less attractive individuals are less likely to be hired and promoted, and they earn lower salaries despite the absence of any differences in cognitive ability.[30] The penalty holds even in fields such as law, where appearance bears no demonstrable relationship to job performance.[31] In politics, some research finds that attractive candidates receive more than twice as many votes as unattractive candidates, even though three quarters of surveyed voters deny that their views are influenced by appearance.[32]

Other factors, particularly age and weight, play a similar role, and sex-based double standards amplify the disadvantages for women. Failure to maintain a youthful appearance can impose significant career costs, particularly for female employees.[33] About 60 percent of overweight women and 40 percent of overweight men report experiences of employment discrimination.[34] Researchers consistently find a significant income penalty for being overweight, particularly among women, and a bonus for attractiveness in both sexes.[35] Obese women are also more likely to be in poverty, even controlling for major employment-related characteristics.[36] For men, height is a key factor: short males are penalized in hiring, promotion, and earnings, and are underrepresented in leadership positions.[37] For racial and ethnic minorities, skin color and Anglo-European features play a similar role; those with dark skin and nappy hair have lower income and occupational status, even controlling for socioeconomic background.[38] In one survey of over 1600 minority professionals, sterling credentials were sometimes overshadowed by racially identified grooming practices including everything from cornrows and ethnic jewelry to certain kinds of manicures.[39]

SELF-ESTEEM, STIGMA, AND QUALITY OF LIFE

Given these consequences, it makes sense for individuals to be concerned about their appearance. Still, the extent of that concern is striking. In one representative survey, three-quarters of women ranked appearance as one of the main factors affecting their self-image, and a third ranked it as the most important quality, above job performance and intelligence.[40] In another poll of some sixteen thousand American women, almost half were very or moderately unhappy with their body, a percentage slightly larger than twenty-five years ago.[41] Women are less satisfied with their appearance than with any other important life dimension except financial success.[42] Even a bad hair day can lower self-esteem.[43]

These concerns about appearance are partly fueled by ridicule, shame, guilt, and discrimination. Stigma is particularly great for the overweight, whose condition is often attributed to laziness and self-indulgence.[44] In multiple surveys, close to 90 percent of obese individuals reported humiliating comments from friends, family, or coworkers.[45] Ninety percent of formerly obese individuals would rather be blind than return to being fat.[46] Bias is pervasive even among health professionals, including those who specialize in treating obesity.[47]

How much influence appearance has on overall quality of life is open to debate. Some research suggests that obese individuals are at greater risk for depression, anxiety, low self-esteem, and other mental health problems, although the extent to which overweight is a cause or consequence of other problems is subject to dispute.[48] Much may depend on how individuals feel about their bodies and whether they blame themselves for any bias they experience or attribute it to prejudice in others.[49] Other factors may also mediate the importance of appearance. For example, women who were pretty when they were young are less likely to feel satisfied in middle age than counterparts who were not.[50] Dark skin is generally associated with lower self-esteem among women of color, but not if they have other forms of self-validation such as high income.[51]

Yet paradoxically enough, despite the importance of appearance, focusing on its improvement is generally not the most effective way for individuals to enhance their quality of life. Like other forms of consumption, investments in appearance often do not yield enduring satisfaction.[52] Once their novelty wears off, or one "problem" seems fixed, new forms of self-expression or self-improvement seem necessary. Social scientists refer to this pattern as a "hedonic treadmill."[53] The more one has, the more one needs to have. Desires, expectations, and standards of comparison increase as rapidly as they are satisfied. As chapter 3 notes, advances in technology and marketing pressures are pushing the standards of physical perfection ever upward. In this context, enduring satisfaction is more likely to come from being comfortable with who we are than from constantly attempting to upgrade our image.[54] Much of the effort and concern that individuals now invest in their appearance could be better spent on relationships with family and friends, and on paid or volunteer work that leads to personal growth or makes a meaningful social contribution.[55]

GENDER DIFFERENCES

By virtually any measure, appearance is more important to women than to men. Women's self-worth is more tied to physical attractiveness and their attractiveness matters more in sexual relationships.[56] Overweight women are judged more harshly than overweight men and experience greater income penalties.[57] Obese women are 20 percent less likely to marry than those of average weight, a figure twice as high as for obese men.[58] Attractiveness does not affect how often men date, and their status is enhanced by being seen with an attractive companion of the opposite sex. Women, by contrast, are penalized for unattractiveness and get no boost from the appearance of a partner.[59] When considering potential partners, women care less than men about appearance and more about earning capability; as chapter 3 suggests, those preferences may be rooted in evolutionary imperatives that traditionally made family survival dependent on a male provider.[60]

Research also confirms what cultural critic Susan Sontag described as a "double standard about aging [that] denounces women with special severity."[61] Unlike men, who can "gain in gravitas" as they age, women are likely to become more socially marginal and, in novelist Carolyn Heilbrun's phrase, "invisible to the male gaze."[62] Studies of media bias reviewed in chapter 3 make clear the obstacles confronting women of a certain age. "This is not to say," Sontag noted, "that there are no beautiful older women. But the standard of beauty in a woman...is how far she retains or how she manages to simulate, an appearance of youth." The result is to entrap women in a ceaseless enterprise of "trying to close the gap between the imagery [of attractiveness] put forth by society...and the evolving facts of nature." A "vast array of products and...professionals exist to stave off, or mask, developments that are entirely normal biologically."[63]

So too, in employment contexts, women face a standard more difficult to satisfy; they can lose by being either too attractive or not attractive enough. Unattractive women are disadvantaged in female-dominated occupations, such as receptionist or secretary. But in upper-level positions that historically have been male-dominated, beautiful or "sexy" workers are subject to the "bloopsy effect": their attractiveness suggests less competence and intellectual ability.[64] Women with exceptionally large breasts are particularly likely to be judged lower in intelligence and effectiveness.[65]

For men, as feminist Susan Brownmiller has noted, "plumage" generally matters less, and too much attention to looks can appear "foppish."[66] German Chancellor Gerhard Schroeder sued tabloids that claimed he dyed his hair.[67] Almost no men subject themselves to the kind of decorative, structurally unsound footwear that causes such problems for women.[68]

However, recent trends suggest that men are becoming more concerned about some aspects of appearance.[69] Male consumers, particularly gays, account for an increased share of cosmetic products and procedures.[70] Gay men are more dissatisfied with their bodies than both straight men and straight women, and are particularly likely to face disadvantages in sexual relationships as they age.[71]

Despite these trends, American women still spend a third more time than men on daily grooming, and vastly more time and money on appearance-related goods and services.[72] Female consumers account for 80–90 percent of purchases in this ever-expanding market.[73] So too, about nine out of ten cosmetic surgery patients are women, and they incur the vast majority of costs and risks that accompany these procedures.[74]

THE PRICE OF UPKEEP: TIME AND MONEY

The costs of our cultural preoccupation with appearance are substantial. In financial terms, the annual global investment in grooming totals at least $115 billion: an estimated $38 billion for hair, $24 billion for skin care, $20 billion for cosmetic surgery, $18 billion for cosmetics, and $15 billion for perfume.[75] Americans also spend some $40 billion on diets, and slightly more on fitness, which is often driven by concern about weight.[76] Much of this expenditure fails to deliver; 95 percent of dieters regain their weight within one to five years, and many cosmetic purchases have no scientifically demonstrable benefits.[77] That is particularly true of antiaging products. "No matter how much money you spend," notes Alex Kuczynski in her recent account of *Beauty Junkies*, "time's winged chariot will catch up to you and march all over your face."[78]

Investments in time are similarly substantial, although impossible to quantify with precision. American women spend an average of three-quarters of an hour a day just on basic grooming, and significant additional time on shopping, exercising, and consuming services ranging from pedicures to cosmetic surgery.[79] For some of these women, upkeep of appearance can become a third shift. In calculating the time spent putting a "finger in the dyke," Nora Ephron notes that it takes some of her friends an hour a day to wash and style their hair, the equivalent of "nine work weeks a year."[80] The more time women spend on elaborate grooming, the more time many men spend waiting for the results. A survey of British husbands estimated that they would spend an average of twenty weeks over their lifetime waiting for their wives to "get ready for an evening out."[81]

Whether the scale of such expenditures makes sense is a matter of controversy.[82] From an individual standpoint, their rationality depends both on what consumers are hoping to achieve and how well informed they are about their investments. Most appearance-related expenditures deliver some benefits in terms of how people feel about themselves and how they are perceived by others. But much of the investment falls short of its intended effect or is induced by fraudulent or misleading claims.

The weight loss industry offers a case in point. In the fantasy land of diet marketers, miracle products abound. Product claims that the Federal Trade Commission (FTC) has targeted in consumer protection actions include:

- gel•ä•thin™ topical gel reduces fat and cellulite deposits on contact;
- Ultra LipoLean diet pill results in as much as four pounds of weight loss a week without the need to diet;
- Siluette Patch, made from seaweed, eliminates fat deposits and causes rapid weight loss without dietary changes;

- Xena RX diet pill with green tea extract blocks up to 40 percent of the absorption of fat;
- Fat Seltzer Reduce dietary supplement eliminates fat without diets or exercise;
- Hanmeilin Cellulite Cream with Chinese herbs causes up to ninety-five pounds of weight loss and eliminates fat and cellulite with "No Will Power Required";
- Himalayan Diet Breakthrough, a pill containing Nepalese Mineral Pitch, causes as much as thirty-seven pounds of weight loss in eight weeks without diets or exercise.[83]

Equally inventive are the ads for "cosmeceuticals," cosmetic products that include chemicals and druglike ingredients that aren't regulated by the Federal Food and Drug Administration. As the following discussion notes, some have undisclosed medical risks, and many carry pseudoscientific names and pedigrees. Consider StriVectin wrinkle cream, marketed as "Better than Botox?" selling at $135 a tube, and endorsed by Dr. Daniel B. Mowrey, director of the manufacturer's scientific affairs. Dr. Mowrey's degree is in experimental psychology, not medicine, a fact that the company says it is not obligated to disclose because its ad does not state otherwise.[84] Such claims are particularly problematic because a majority of Americans believe, incorrectly, that they cannot be made without "solid scientific evidence to support them."[85]

Even when advertising is not misleading, its expense often inflates the price of products well beyond what their contents justify. Over ninety percent of the cost of cosmetics goes to packaging and marketing; the remainder goes to ingredients that are often of minimal value.[86] A *Consumer Reports* study found no correlation between the price and effectiveness of anti-wrinkle creams.[87] Moreover, from a societal standpoint, the scale of investment in cosmetics raises serious concerns. This nation spends more money on grooming than on reading material.[88] And while almost a fifth of the United States population lacks a usual source of health care, nonessential cosmetic procedures are the fastest growing area of medical expenditures.[89]

HEALTH RISKS

The price we pay for appearance includes not just time and money, but also physical risks. Particularly when viewed from a historical and cross-cultural perspective, that price has often been substantial.

The most notorious example is footbinding. The practice began with Chinese court dancers in the tenth century, spread to the aristocracy, and persisted for nearly a thousand years. In an effort to produce the legendary three-inch "golden lotus," the feet of small girls were bound and broken at the arches so that the toes turned under. The flesh mortified and the bone and muscle structure was permanently deformed. This painful and crippling condition restricted women's mobility and reinforced their dependency. Wives who had to crawl or be carried were unlikely to stray.[90] By the fourteenth century, fashions for the European aristocracy were also deforming the foot and hobbling wearers. Women tottering on eleven-inch Chopine platforms needed the help of a man even to walk without falling.[91] As chapter 1 noted, the sexualization of footwear has contemporary echoes; high heels help account for women's grossly disproportionate experience with foot problems and surgeries.

Another appearance-related practice that has posed severe physical risks involves female genital mutilation (FGM). The extent of risks varies, depending on the type of the procedure and the conditions under which it is performed. In its most benign form, the practice resembles male circumcision, which has little effect on sexual performance or pleasure.[92] In its most severe form, FGM involves removal of the clitoris and labia and stitching of the vagina to leave only a small opening for urination and menstruation. The result is a severe inhibition of sexual responsiveness. When performed under unhygienic circumstances, the consequences may be sterility or death.[93] Although fifty nations have signed a protocol against FGM, and some reports suggest that it is declining, the World Health Organization estimates that more than one hundred million women have had some form of FGM and an estimated two million girls undergo the practice each year, primarily in Africa but also in some areas of Indonesia, Malaysia, and the Mideast.[94]

In western societies, one of the most obviously injurious practices involved corsets. Beginning in the fourteenth century, these undergarments exaggerated the breasts and narrowed the waist. Depending on the season's style, the woman's endurance, and the corset's design, it could exert as much as eighty pounds of pressure on internal organs. The results could include bent or fractured ribs, displacement of the liver and uterus, digestive disorders, and constriction of movement.[95] Yet defenders of corsets, such as the author of one 1889 advice manual, *How to Be Beautiful*, blamed such effects not on the garment but on its misuse: "If tight lacing has wiped off the face of the earth a few brainless women," so be it.[96]

Full skirts also limited mobility and posed other risks, such as catching in fire grates and carriage wheels. In nineteenth-century American winters, women wore an average of thirty-seven pounds of street clothes. Even those in the most demanding household or factory occupations often worked in highly impractical hoop skirts with as many as eight petticoats.[97] "In one way or the other," historians note, women's skirts "have hemmed them in or tripped them up."[98] In 1867, three thousand women burned alive and twenty thousand suffered severe injuries from flammable petticoats.[99]

Makeup has also posed longstanding risks. What the classic Roman poet Ovid described as "medication for the soul" has often had toxic effects for the body.[100] In the first century AD, early church fathers, such as Clement of Alexandria, warned women not to pursue the "pernicious arts of luxury [and]...furrow the flesh with poisons...thus blighting their own beauty."[101] Such warnings had little apparent effect. For two thousand years, women resorted to high-risk products that, in the words of a leading nineteenth-century American beauty manual, seemed "necessary to keep Time at bay."[102] Mercury, one of the most popular treatments for removing freckles, removed the outer layer of skin as well, and sulfuric acid and turmeric made some women bald. Ceruse, a cosmetic whitener, was composed of deadly combinations of lead oxide, hydroxide, and carbonate. With frequent use, the toxic bleaches accumulated in the body and sometimes resulted in premature death.[103]

Although government regulation now provides protection from the most risky appearance-related practices, safeguards remain inadequate. In the United States, a major problem is the absence of any requirement that regulators approve cosmetics before marketing.[104] As a consequence, 80 percent of the ten thousand ingredients used in cosmetics and personal care products have never been assessed by the Federal Food and Drug Administration.[105] An Environmental Working Group survey found that nearly four hundred products sold in the United States contained chemicals that are prohibited in other countries, and that more than four hundred had contents considered unsafe by American industry standards; one in thirty failed to meet industry or federal requirements.[106] Experts are divided over whether even widely used products such as lipsticks contain enough toxic material to pose potential health risks after prolonged exposure.[107] Moreover, many products that are too risky for sale in the United States can still be exported to countries with less rigorous regulatory structures. So, for example, skin bleaches that can lead to disease and disfigurement are marketed in many parts of Africa, Asia, and the Caribbean.[108] Humans are not the only victims of toxic cosmetics. Unlike the European Union, which in 2009 began barring products tested on animals, the United States permits such testing, and procedures for some products, such as Botox, result in the death of half of animals tested.[109]

Cosmetic surgical procedures pose other risks. Almost half are performed in office facilities that are not subject to the same state and federal regulations as hospitals and freestanding outpatient surgical centers.[110] Nor are these offices prepared to deal with complications such as those resulting from general anesthesia.[111] Some procedures run exceptionally high risks. About 40 percent of breast augmentations result in complications within three years, and the underground unapproved practice of injecting silicone directly into the body can cause death.[112]

In many states, doctors who perform surgical procedures in offices rather than surgical facilities need not be board certified.[113] Few patients are aware of what certification means; many are misled by their physician's membership in associations with names similar to the official certifying association, the American Board of Plastic Surgery.[114] The problem is compounded by the inadequacy and inaccessibility of data concerning the risks of procedures in various settings, consumers' tendency to understate risks, and the lack of ethical standards by the American Medical Association and the American Academy of Cosmetic Surgery about when doctors should decline assistance.[115] Individuals suffering from body dysmorphic disorder, a preoccupation with slight or imagined imperfections, can often undergo multiple procedures carrying substantial expense and risk with little objective benefit.[116] As one surgeon candidly acknowledged, too many patients have "too much money and too little sense."[117] Yet a widespread view among physicians is that it is not their place to pass judgment on patients' preferences. "If it's doable," explains one surgeon, "I don't stop them. I don't really discuss it with them."[118]

Other risky behaviors involve body size. Illegal use of steroids to create a "buff look" poses significant concerns, particularly in male adolescents.[119] More widespread practices involve weight reduction. About 30 percent of American adults and 60 percent of female adolescents are on diets, and some of their efforts lead to serious health problems.[120] Eating disorders carry the greatest risks. Anorexia nervosa, which results in severe weight reduction and distorted body image, was first named and identified as a medical problem in the 1870s, although records of the dysfunction date back to at least the seventeenth century.[121] Bulimia, which involves binging and purging, was recognized as a disorder in the 1920s but practiced much earlier in Byzantine and Roman cultures.[122] Although such disorders are believed to have a strong genetic component, their dramatic increase over the last half century is clearly tied to cultural forces. Estimates suggest that slightly under 1 percent of Americans will suffer from anorexia and slightly over 1 percent from bulimia; about four percent will experience a binge eating disorder (binging without purging).[123] Anorexia can result in organ compromise and heart and kidney failure; 90 percent of sufferers end up with bone loss.[124] Bulimia can lead to heart and gastrointestinal problems, and damage to the teeth, throat, and esophagus.[125] Binge eating without purging is associated with cardiovascular problems as well as an increased incidence of diabetes and gallbladder disease.[126] Treatment is costly and often ineffective or inaccessible, and many who lack adequate care have associated mental health difficulties.[127]

Eating disorders, as well as more general concerns about appearance, can result in depression, anxiety, or low self-esteem.[128] Whether being overweight of itself impairs psychological function is in dispute. Findings are mixed, and where a relationship exists, causality may run in either direction. Individuals may be depressed because they are grossly overweight, or they may become overweight because they use food as compensation when they are depressed.[129] As noted earlier, much may depend on how individuals respond to appearance-related stigma, and whether they blame the culture or themselves. However, for a significant number of people, shame and embarrassment related to appearance has a significant negative effect on psychological well-being.[130] Those with eating disorders have significantly elevated risk of depression, anxiety, and substance abuse. Anorexia has the highest rate of death among psychiatric disorders; estimates range between 10 and 20 percent, and the suicide rate for anorexics is fifty-seven times higher than for women of the same age in the general population.[131]

Many weight reduction techniques, whether or not associated with eating disorders, also raise concerns. A recent *New Yorker* cartoon parodies the extent to which dieters are often prepared to go: an oarsman on a galley slave ship boasts to another: "I dropped twelve pounds the first week and kept it off!"[132] For some women, smoking is the functional equivalent. Fear of weight gain is a major deterrent to quitting. Three-quarters of surveyed female smokers are unwilling to put on more than five pounds as a result of stopping; nearly half will not tolerate any increase.[133] Bariatric surgery, which involves reducing the stomach's capacity in order to control appetite, is one of the only effective procedures for the extremely obese, but it poses significant risks of complications.[134] Moreover, patients sometimes replace compulsive eating with other addictive behavior such as smoking or alcohol abuse.[135] Yo-yo dieting, the pattern of losing and regaining weight, is by far the most common experience of dieters, and a growing body of evidence suggests that it may impose even more risks than remaining moderately overweight. Such weight cycling is linked to clogged arteries, loss in bone density, congestive heart failure, and other serious health problems.[136] Over fifteen studies associate yo-yo dieting with increased rates of mortality.[137] Many "miracle" diet drugs like olestra and fen-phen also have created more medical problems than solutions.[138]

Indeed, from a health perspective, the current obsession with weight is misdirected. Many experts believe that except at extreme levels, body mass is less important than fitness in preventing disease and prolonging life.[139] Recent research finds that moderately overweight individuals have the lowest mortality rates of any weight group; thin individuals who match cultural ideals have the highest rates.[140] Low body weight compromises reproductive and work capacity, and predicts a greater frequency of sickness.[141] This is not to deny the health benefits in preventing the poor diets and sedentary lifestyles associated with obesity, which are explored more fully in chapter 7.[142] Nor is it to undervalue the importance of weight reduction for individuals with certain conditions such as hypertension, osteoarthritis, and diabetes.[143] But it is to suggest that our culture would be healthier if the focus were less on "thunder thighs" and more on nutrition and fitness.

BIAS

Many of the mental health difficulties associated with appearance are the product of widespread social stigma and discrimination. Beginning at early ages, children develop an aversion to individuals who are overweight or unattractive, and those individuals are teased, ridiculed, and ostracized.[144] By age nine, anywhere from 50 to 80 percent of girls want to lose weight.[145] Unlike other forms of bias, reports of weight discrimination are increasing and at a rate that cannot be explained by a rising rate of obesity.[146] Obesity carries as much stigma as AIDS, drug addiction, and criminal behavior.[147] Stigma often leads to stress, which is a risk factor associated with many diseases.[148] Yet as noted in chapters 5 and 6, discrimination based on appearance is common and generally legal. Weight bias is a particularly serious problem, even in health care settings, which both discourages overweight individuals from seeking medical treatment and compromises the quality of care they do receive.[149]

Such discrimination reflects deeply rooted cultural attitudes. About two-thirds of surveyed Americans believe that people are fat because they lack self-control.[150] The problem, according to pop cultural accounts like *The Fat of the Land*, and *Fat Land*, is "sloth and gluttony."[151] Yet experts generally agree that weight is not simply a matter of willpower. Weight reflects a complex interaction of physiological, psychological, socioeconomic, and cultural factors.[152] Genetically determined set points work to keep bodies within a predetermined range; when dieters reduce their caloric intake and increase their exercise, their metabolism slows down to compensate and makes any weight loss difficult to sustain.[153] The problems are compounded by sedentary occupations and "toxic environments" that lack recreational opportunities and encourage unhealthy food choices.[154]

A related and equally unfounded assumption is that the stigma associated with being overweight serves a legitimate function by shaming individuals into shedding unhealthy pounds. According to Michael Fumento, author of *Fat of the Land*, bias against fat people is a "helpful and healthful prejudice for society to have."[155] In fact, such bias is counterproductive; around 80 percent of those enrolled in weight loss programs respond to stigma by eating more or giving up their diets.[156]

Obesity is particularly problematic from a class standpoint. As one expert puts it, there is some "evidence that poverty is fattening," and an even "stronger case...[that] fatness is impoverishing."[157] Many urban and rural poor communities are "nutritional deserts"—areas with no readily accessible grocery stores that sell fresh fruits and vegetables.[158] These communities also tend to lack public recreational facilities and schools with adequate physical education programs.[159] What they often have instead are high concentrations of fast-food restaurants that make unhealthy eating an easy response to poverty-related constraints and stress.[160] The bias that their overweight residents face then compromises their educational and employment opportunities. Those living below the poverty line are nearly 15 percent more likely to be obese than the general population.[161]

Minorities also experience disproportionate rates of obesity and its corresponding stigma, as well as other forms of appearance-related discrimination. According to data from the Centers for Disease Control and Prevention, blacks have a 51 percent higher rate of obesity, and Hispanics a 21 percent higher rate, than non-Hispanic whites.[162] So too, although images of beauty are growing more diverse, they still reflect a legacy of racial privilege. As noted earlier, light skin, straight hair, and Anglo-European features have long defined the ideal that minorities have been encouraged to accept.[163] Cosmetic surgery has reflected similar assimilationist pressures.[164] The first Americans to seek such surgery in significant numbers were Jews who wanted less distinctive noses, along with individuals who wanted to avoid being mistaken as Jewish.[165] After World War II, Japanese women had transformer coolant injected into their breasts to please American GIs.[166] Among contemporary Asian Americans, a common desire is for eye procedures that will produce a more Anglo-European look.[167] African Americans seek narrower noses and lips.[168] Although minorities are significantly underrepresented among the groups with substantial discretionary income in the United States, they have similar rates of cosmetic surgery (around 20 percent), much of it oriented toward obtaining a more Anglo-European appearance.[169] Part of the reason is that minorities who look "too ethnic" rarely become media icons. In commenting on the absence of diversity on fashion runways, a *Washington Post* story put the take away in the title: "Once Again, White is the New White."[170]

Finally, appearance discrimination also compounds gender inequality by reinforcing a double standard and double bind for women. They face greater pressure to be attractive and greater penalties for falling short. Overweight women are judged more harshly than overweight men.[171] As a consequence, women's self-worth is more dependent than men's on physical attractiveness.[172] Yet even as the culture expects women to conform, it mocks the narcissism in their efforts.

"It is only the shallow who do not judge by appearances," quipped Oscar Wilde.[173] In contemporary societies, it is questionable whether anyone remains that shallow. What is not questionable, however, is the need to reduce the price of our preoccupation.

CHAPTER THREE

The Pursuit of Beauty

A WIDELY CIRCULATED cartoon by Nicole Hollander features her main character, Sylvia, having a drink with a male friend. He wants her to "Admit it Syl. You need us. Can you imagine a world without men?" Her response: "No crime and lots of happy fat women." Underlying that quip are more serious questions about where our preoccupation with attractiveness comes from and what costs it imposes. To what extent are current standards a function of deeply rooted sexual drives, market forces, technological advances, or media pressures? Only by understanding what fuels our concerns about appearance can we effectively challenge their adverse consequences.

SOCIOBIOLOGICAL FOUNDATIONS

In sociobiological frameworks, evolution is the dominant explanation for the importance of appearance. From this perspective, our aesthetic preferences are to large extent hardwired, based on circuits in the brain shaped by millions of years of sexual selection. Over time, individuals whose genes survive are those who choose mates with characteristics conducive to reproductive success. Attractiveness is one such characteristic because it signals health and fertility, particularly in females.[1] Evolutionary imperatives similarly encourage parents to favor children who are attractive because they are likely to have greatest reproductive potential.[2]

Not all aesthetically appealing features are common to both sexes. Some that are, such as facial and body symmetry, are thought to hold appeal because they reflect population averages that signify healthy physical development and screen for abnormalities and vulnerabilities to diseases that reduce fertility.[3] Other traits, and their relative importance, reflect differences in the sexes' reproductive roles. Women's fertility is more tied to youth and physical health than is men's. Particular significance attaches to cues about female age, health, and hormonal balance, such as firm breasts, clear skin, lustrous hair, and hourglass figures.[4] By contrast, men's reproductive success is linked more closely to ability to support a family. For them, relevant characteristics have historically been those that suggest access to resources, including physical dominance, such as height and muscles, as well as factors unrelated to appearance that affect the provider role.[5]

These sociobiological theories offer only a partial explanation of the role of appearance. They obviously help account for the universality of certain aesthetic preferences. As chapter 2 noted, some preferences have shown considerable consistency across time and culture, such as those concerning facial and body symmetry, clear skin, youth in women, and height in men. Even members of tribes insulated from the mass media share these preferences, and infants as young as three months prefer faces that are attractive in geometric proportions.[6] Sociobiological frameworks also may help to explain some research findings that women attach greater importance than men to financial capacity in potential long-term mates, and that men attach greater importance than women to youth and physical appearance.[7]

Yet these frameworks cannot account for variations across time and culture in other perceptions of attractiveness. Weight is the most obvious example. As chapter 1 noted, plumpness has sometimes been prized and sometimes penalized, and much seems to depend on its role in indicating status under differing environmental conditions. In societies where food is scarce, a well-endowed body is a sign of wealth and social prominence. In developed societies where food is abundant, the reverse is true; a slender body is associated with high socioeconomic status.[8] From a purely evolutionary standpoint, the contemporary cult of thinness for women is perverse, because low weight, particularly in extreme forms, leads to reproductive dysfunctions.[9] Moreover, sociobiological frameworks cannot explain why concerns about appearance that are adaptive for selecting sexual partners should be so significant in such a wide array of other settings. These frameworks may help us understand why women do well in the marriage market, but not why attractive men get an edge in running for presidency of the American Economic Association.[10]

To account for these broader patterns, researchers note that evolutionary forces do not work in isolation but rather interact with the natural and social environment.[11] Changes in that environment can sometimes produce dysfunctional results. Weight is again a prime example. For centuries, evolution selected for the ability to eat and store substantial quantities of fat as protection against periodic famines resulting from natural disasters and local scarcities. Such biological propensities are ill suited to contemporary societies marked by abundant food and sedentary living patterns. The result, as subsequent discussion notes, is a rise in obesity despite the health concerns and social penalties that accompany it.

CULTURAL VALUES, STATUS, AND IDENTITY

Appearance, and efforts to enhance it, serve a range of functions apart from reproduction. The urge to improve on nature is common to every known society; cosmetics have been in use for at least forty thousand years.[12] Adornment often expresses aesthetic, religious, and political values. It reflects and reinforces socioeconomic status and can signify group identity or individual resistance to cultural norms.[13]

For women, appearance has also played a part in perpetuating gender hierarchies. In contexts where a woman's primary identity has been her domestic role, her status has been dependent on her physical attractiveness to a marriage partner, and on his socioeconomic position. Men, who have not been so limited, have had other ways of attracting a spouse and of establishing social and economic status.[14] Such differences in gender roles help explain why attractive women, but not men, have tended to "marry up" the socioeconomic ladder.[15] "Trophy wives" are common; trophy husbands are not.

Social status is also a major influence on appearance. Adornment and body size have long been a means of establishing wealth and privilege, and distinguishing the leisure from the laboring class.[16] When necessary, the law has also kicked in to reinforce socioeconomic hierarchies; for several centuries, European sumptuary statutes reserved certain garments, colors, and fabrics for aristocrats.[17]

Multiple social and economic forces have reinforced the importance of appearance. Among the most significant have been the market, technology, the media, and advertisements. Taken together, they lay the foundations for discrimination based on appearance and the personal costs that it imposes.

MARKET FORCES

The rise in consumer-oriented cultures has increased the significance of appearance as a source, as well as signal, of wealth. With
the growth of economic prosperity, individuals not born to beauty
have been more able to pursue it. Although this trend has come at a
particular cost for women, they have also been major beneficiaries.
In countries such as the United States, the beauty business was
initially built largely by women for women. In the nineteenth and
early twentieth century, when few other commercial avenues were
open to them, women founded beauty schools, salons, correspondence courses, and mail-order companies. Female entrepreneurs
also developed the first marketing strategies involving direct sales
and celebrity endorsements.[18] As Helena Rubenstein put it, "Here
[women] have found a field that is their own province—working for
women, with women, and giving that which only women can
give—an intimate understanding of feminine needs and feminine
desires."[19] Yet that field has also given individual women an
increasing stake in perpetuating the preoccupation with appearance
that works against their collective interest in gender equality.

Of course, women were not the only ones to see the potential of
this market, and its growth accelerated in response to trends in other
fields. The rise of department stores, mass marketing, and shopping
malls helped reinforce a consumer ideology that made attractiveness
seem a matter of choice, not chance, and provided opportunities for
recreation and female bonding.[20]

The growth of weight reduction products in the early twentieth
century also emerged largely in response to market forces. As historians note, its evolution had little to do with health and everything
to do with money.[21] In recent decades, the diet industry has received
a further boost from insurance companies concerned about the
health costs associated with obesity and from doctors interested,

both economically and professionally, in its treatment.[22] As growing numbers of health professionals have become researchers or coinvestors in weight reduction clinics and products, they have lent scientific credibility to industry campaigns. Their financial involvement has also created obvious conflicts of interest. The most egregious problems arise when doctors peddle unproven diet foods, therapies, and potentially habit-forming drugs.[23] Less visible conflicts involve industry funding of research and organizational activities that result in policy initiatives. In a sense, the business model of the entire weight-loss industry reflects an underlying tension between corporate and consumer interests. The buyer benefits when the diet works; when the weight stays off rather than cycles up and down. Businesses benefit from repeat purchases; the fact that 95 percent of dieters do not sustain weight loss is lucrative as long as enough buyers keep making the effort. Prominent British expert Susie Orbach puts it bluntly: diet companies' "profitability depends on failure... and failure [is what] happens."[24]

So too, the rise of managed health care and eroding profitability of some medical specialties has encouraged more physicians to offer cosmetic procedures that are "cash cows." A medical practice concentrating on those procedures is among the most lucrative in the profession.[25] Through physicians' entrepreneurial efforts, natural characteristics such as wrinkles have become "deformities," and surgical correctives have become normalized. In 1923, Americans wondered why Fanny Brice, a Ziegfeld Follies star, had bobbed her nose. Four decades later, when Barbara Streisand played Brice on Broadway, Americans wondered why she had not.[26]

The market in cosmetic procedures has grown over 400 percent in just the last decade, spurred by ever more creative marketing strategies: "surgeon and safari" getaway vacations and Botox house parties, with a physician on hand to inject the guests.[27] Los Angeles' Aesthetica offers the "perfect" "Say It with Liposuction" Valentine's

Day gift "for the woman who has everything." This "ultimate cosmetic surgery experience" comes complete with stretch limousine travel, a twenty-four-hour private nurse, Dior robe, Godiva chocolate, and the "fixative" procedure of her choice.[28] An international tourist company based in Dubai offers a similar opportunity: cosmetic surgery and "post- operation rest and recuperation in stellar resorts and even summer camps for patients' children."[29] No area of the body is beneath notice. A 2009 *Wall Street Journal* article captured recent trends in liposuction under the lead: "For the Body-Conscious, It's Now the Ankle that Rankles...Women Wage Costly Fight against 'Cankles.'"[30]

In recent decades, the beauty industry has widened its scope and increasingly targeted girls and men. Female adolescents have been a particularly inviting market because most are unhappy with their bodies and vulnerable to media messages.[31] By the early twenty-first century, about half of six- to nine-year-olds were wearing lipstick, around two-thirds of preteens wanted to lose weight, the number of adolescents receiving breast implants had quadrupled over the preceding decade, and over 90 percent of female teenagers reported shopping as their favorite activity.[32] A hot-selling t-shirt for teens captures prevailing priorities. The slogan blazoned across the chest reads: "Why have brains when you can have these?"

Moreover, aggressive marketers no longer wait until adolescence. Thongs, makeup, and "Jail Bait" T-shirts are available for seven-year-olds; "youth spas" offer "minifacials" for six-year-olds; Charles Dior makes lace bras for preschoolers; a $3 billion dollar industry capitalizes on the princess craze; and makeover and "Darling Diva" parties target girls beginning at age four, offering makeup, hairstyles, and manicures.[33] And, of course, there is Barbie, and her even sexier Bratz competitors. Over the past half century, Barbie's pursuits have widened from Shopper Barbie to Astronaut

Barbie, but her wildly implausible hourglass proportions have remained the same. Her figure, for a woman of average height, would work out to 36, 15, 33, which would require removal of a bone and allow insufficient fat to permit menstruation and pregnancy.[34] In commenting on the appearance of Dr. Barbie, comedian Rita Rudner notes that in addition to her stethoscope, she has a "short, tight skirt and nine-inch heels. So she's a doctor. And a prostitute on the side."[35] The Bratz line offers more of same. Its "Wicked Twins" wear low-slung skirts, high-heeled boots, and tight black T-shirts that say "Bad Girls." As an American Psychological Association task force noted, such products encourage girls to evaluate themselves in terms of their sexual appeal rather than other less superficial qualities.[36]

For men, the primary market efforts begin later, and confront additional challenges. During some historical periods, men of means were subject to elaborate fashion requirements, including corsets, wigs, and face powder. However, the rise of industrial capitalism in the nineteenth century brought more austere standards stressing comfort and functionality.[37] Too much attention to appearance was thought effeminate, and a diversion from more important, masculine pursuits. President Martin Van Buren's 1830 reelection bid ran aground after toiletries such as Persian Essence were discovered on his dressing table.[38] In the late twentieth century, marketers made increasing inroads on that mindset. Although male products still account for less than 10 percent of the global grooming market, they represent a growth industry particularly among younger and gay consumers.[39] Men's representation among cosmetic surgery patients has also increased. In the United States, it has grown more than 200 percent during the last decade, and the range of procedures has similarly expanded to include everything from reshaping pecs to enlarging the penis.[40] Marketers are also peddling unrealistic body images for boys: GI Joe has grown increasingly muscular, and current proportions, translated in a man of normal height, would work out to a 55-inch chest, 27-inch biceps, and a 29-inch waist.[41]

TECHNOLOGY

Technological advances have also increased individuals' concerns about appearance by enhancing their abilities to improve it. As the renowned anthropologist Margaret Mead noted, "Once there is a possibility that [a] defect can be remedied, our attitudes change. Something should be done. Whatever is wrong that can be fixed, should be fixed."[42] Cosmetic surgery is the clearest example. Reconstructive procedures date to 600 BC in India and were used sporadically in Europe, beginning in the fifteenth century for disfiguring diseases, accidents, and birth defects.[43] However, no anesthetics were available until the nineteenth century, and the shock and loss of blood that often accompanied the procedures made them risky as well as painful. Advances during the Crimean and World Wars for injured soldiers proved transferable to cosmetic patients, and by the early twentieth century, a profitable specialty had begun to develop. The emergence of photography and close-up cinematography fed desires for greater facial attractiveness, and recent advances in photoshopping have enabled consumers to envision how surgery could achieve it.[44] Research in other areas also has improved the products available for skin, nail, and hair care, and laid the foundations for pseudoscientific claims that marketers have adeptly exploited.[45] In the 1950s, only about 7 percent of women dyed their hair. With the development of inexpensive, fast, and effective coloring products, the number has jumped to 60 percent.[46]

The internet also has made available a vast range of websites that reinforce the importance of beauty and body image. One winner in a survey of the "world's lamest social networks," is Beautiful People, with 120,000 members who vote each other membership based solely on appearance. The website, which features "hot singles events," operates on the premise that "Looks matter. It may not be politically correct but it's honest."[47] Also available are "thinspiration" websites supporting anorexics and bulimics who believe that they are making lifestyle choices rather than experiencing eating disorders. The sites post pictures of extremely thin celebrities, provide tips for weight loss, and support blogs for group discussion.[48] For young girls, a "Miss Bimbo" website helps them create a virtual doll, keep it "waif thin" through diet pills, and upgrade its appeal through breast implants and face-lifts.[49]

Marketing opportunities on the internet also have vastly increased public exposure to advertisements and media celebrities, which reinforces the significance of appearance. So does the accessibility of visual images through teleconferencing and networking websites such as Facebook.com. Technologies for airbrushing and photoshopping those images further promote unattainable ideals. Beauty may be only skin deep, but that's what's instantly and incessantly available in our electronic age; and it is increasingly out of touch with the bodies that nature offers.

THE MEDIA

The media have also had increasing influence on both the importance and definition of attractiveness. Although publications for women long included tips for "beautifying" products, their audience expanded significantly with the rise of women's magazines in the late nineteenth and early twentieth centuries. In these magazines, the lines between advice and advertisements have often blurred. Commentators have seldom been shy about endorsing products touted in ads, and sellers increasingly have demanded "compatible copy" surrounding their products.[50] As early as 1934, a prominent exposé, *Skin Deep: The Truth about Beauty Aids*, called editors to task for peddling unnecessary and ineffectual products. For example, columnists who were in "kindly cooperation with the advertising department" declared it "quite improper [for women] to appear on the tennis court without a certain shade of nail polish," and insisted "that another is needed for cocktails, still another for the theatre."[51]

Fashion, figures, food, and furnishings have been the main staples of women's magazines, and have often yielded ironic juxtapositions. Endless variations of the "last chance diet" have run back to back with recipes for "new ways to sin." A contemporary cover story on model Cybill Shepherd, "At Home with Cybill, and Yes, She's Lost 25 Pounds," featured not only diet tips but also a favorite desert (toasted banana bread with ice cream).[52]

A common refrain of these publications has been the importance of self- improvement. Estee Lauder captured the prevailing wisdom: "There are no homely women, only careless women. You have to want [beauty] very much and then help it along."[53] The *Ugly-Girl Papers*, an 1875 collection from *Harper's Bazaar*, made a similar point in chapters titled "Women's Business to Be Beautiful," and "Hope for Homely People."[54] One hundred and thirty five years later, the basic message remains the same. A recent sample of leading women's magazines reveals cover features including: "Get a Sexy Body" (*Cosmopolitan*); "The Cost of Looking Good" (*Vogue*); "Swallow This: New Beauty Pills" (*Marie Claire*); "Look Younger by Morning" (*Harper's Bazaar*); "Wynonna's Weight Loss Secrets" (*Ladies Home Journal*); "Easiest Ways to Lose 10lbs: No Diet, No Exercise, Seriously" (*Good Housekeeping*). Even niche magazines often have a liberal sprinkling of such assistance. Evangelicals get "Pray Your Weight Away," and "More of Jesus, Less of Me;" older women learn "Top Tricks to a Flawless Face" and "59 Ways to More Radiant Skin."[55]

Beauty pageants are another media staple. The tradition is long-standing. Published accounts date back at least twenty-four centuries to Persian Queen Vashti's celebrated refusal to reveal her beauty to the king's drunken companions; he held a beauty contest that replaced her with Queen Esther.[56] For centuries, many European festivals and May Day celebrations featured a beauty competition, as did their later American counterparts.[57] The popularity of these events increased greatly in the late nineteenth and early twentieth centuries when mass-circulation newspapers and magazines began holding their own photographic contests. These events, together with a growing number of carnival and seaside resort competitions, helped to legitimize the concept. In 1921, Atlantic City business owners launched a bathing beauty contest to extend their season and to lure tourists from other resorts. The result was the Miss America pageant, which eventually inspired an international network of spin-off extravaganzas. Women of color, excluded from the Miss America competitions, held the first "Miss Bronze America" in 1927. By the turn of the twenty-first century, some 7,500 pageants were operating under franchises by Miss America or Miss USA, joined by several thousand other local contests ranging from beach bikini to Miss Budweiser competitions.[58] One and a half billion viewers were tuning into the Miss World competition.[59]

Initially condemned as "indecent and exploitative," many pageants have consciously cultivated an image of wholesome respectability.[60] Miss America competitions carefully monitor contestants' morals as well as attire, including the precise amount of skin (in inches) that their bathing suits can reveal and, in some states, the exact number of pounds that they can gain without losing their crown (two for Miss Texas).[61] To combat critiques of sexual objectification, Miss America pageants began awarding scholarships, changed the label of their swimsuit contest to a "physical fitness" competition, and demanded displays of "talent" as well as "issue platforms" demonstrating a commitment to some widely accepted social cause. However, many contests resist this facade. Miss Universe and Miss USA pageants dispense with talent and issues competitions. And local bikini and wet bathing suit contests are, as one pageant participant put it, explicitly and exclusively about "boobs and bounce."[62] Even the Miss America pageant ran up against the limits of public tolerance for substance over sexuality when some contestants lobbied to eliminate the bathing suit competition. Viewers had a chance to vote on the issue and about three quarters opted to retain it.[63]

Although the standards of beauty reflected in these competitions have grown somewhat more inclusive, they still reflect a legacy of racial and ethnic bias. Over the course of seventy-five years, only one Jew and four African Americans have won the Miss America title. It was not until 1970 that black contestants entered the pageant, and the first Hispanic winner in 1985 was sent to language classes to reduce her Spanish accent.[64] African- American women who have won the title generally have had light skin, Anglo-European features, and straight hair, and have avoided talent choices that appear "too black."[65]

In the United States, opportunities for competition begin at startlingly early ages, and have spread to countless other educational and employment settings. Since the 1960s, a billion-dollar youth industry has emerged, involving an estimated three thousand pageants for girls between five and ten years old. Over the last decade, these events have become more professionalized and more sexualized. Small children receive extensive coaching and appear with elaborate makeup, hair extensions, and even false teeth and eyelashes.[66] Less formal contests have sprung up in many schools and workplaces where women are not always willing competitors. For example, in 2008, anonymous bloggers at Skadden, Arps, Slate, Meagher & Flom, a prominent Wall Street law firm, conducted a highly publicized survey to determine its "Hottest Female Associate." Women's names and pictures were circulated without their consent. After an embarrassed leadership suspended the poll as "inappropriate" and inconsistent with Skadden values, it was resurrected at Gawkers.com. Comments from disgruntled associates raised questions about how widely the firm's professed values were shared. "I don't see how anyone could find this particularly offensive unless they have no lives"; "So who complained? Humorless partners or attention deprived plain women who felt neglected?"[67]

A related phenomena involves reality television shows in which contestants either compete to lose weight (*The Biggest Loser, Celebrity Fit Club*) or receive full-body makeovers through diets, cosmetic surgery, hairstyling, and clothing (*The Swan, Extreme Makeover*). Before it expired in 2007, *Extreme Makeover* promised potential contestants "a truly Cinderella-like experience" in which they could transform their "life and destiny" and "make [their] dreams come true."[68] Although male makeover candidates were welcome, they constituted only 4 percent of the applicant pool.[69] And they have been excluded from other events that exalt such reconstructive efforts, such as a Miss Plastic Surgery contest, in which women from all nations vie to improve on nature.[70] Here again, reality television's display of competition begins early. *Toddlers and Tiaras*, a TLC show, follows two-year-old pageant contestants as they "strut and swagger" with full makeup and styled hair.[71]

This prime-time landscape is littered with irony. Surrounding weight-reduction contests are many of the very food advertisements that make the competitions necessary; Baskin Robins' Oreo sundaes and "all you can eat" breakfasts at Applebee's.[72] These reality programs approximate "reality" in only the loosest sense. Editing omits anything that is not part of the "new and better you" story line: "bad results...complications, and lengthy recovery time."[73] Watching these programs—the functional equivalent of "infomercials"—has been linked to lower self-esteem and higher dissatisfaction with body image, as well as greater desire for cosmetic surgery.[74]

Similar results occur from repeated exposure to fashion models and other celebrities who reflect increasingly unattainable ideals. Playwright Eve Ensler's *The Good Body* notes the influence of this "blond, pointy breast, raisin-a-day-stomached girl....She is there every minute, somewhere in the world, smiling down on me, on all of us. She is omnipresent. She's the American Dream, my personal nightmare."[75] A central problem involves weight. In 1894, the United States' average female model was 5 feet 4 inches tall and weighed 140 pounds. A century later, these proportions reflected the average American woman, but the average model was 5 feet 10 inches tall and 110 pounds, and she has been growing thinner ever since.[76] Only 5 percent of American women are now in the same weight category as actresses and models.[77] Comparable changes have occurred in other cultural icons. *Playboy* centerfolds have dropped in weight every year since the magazine began, and Miss Americas have followed suit.[78] In top-rated prime-time television programs, overweight female characters seldom appear, and rarely in appealing roles.[79] In women's health and fitness magazines, nonslender bodies are entirely absent, except as "before" pictures in successful weight-loss sagas.[80] Yet as medical experts note, "[t]he current ideal of female beauty, a thin, well-toned, yet big-breasted woman—rarely occurs without restrictive dieting, excessive exercise, and cosmetic surgery."[81] Women who internalize this ideal end up with unrealistic aspirations and unhealthy habits. About three quarters of women who are at or below normal weight believe that they should lose some.[82]

For men, cultural expectations have traditionally been less demanding. However, male concerns have recently been increasing, partly in response to media messages. "Torch Your Bodyfat" and

"Train Your Way to Megamass" are recurring refrains in men's magazines and advertisements.[83] Male icons have grown larger and more muscular in virtually all media portrayals, except in fashion.[84] There, designers have insisted that emaciation makes male as well as female models "look good in the clothes."[85]

On the whole, however, the focus on weight reduction is much greater for women than for men. Articles and ads on weight loss in women's magazines have been rising as women's ideal weight has been falling; such magazines average about ten times as many diet advertisements and seven times as many diet articles as publications targeting men.[86] Much of this material is unhelpful, unrealistic, and, for younger readers, unhealthy. "I Was a Hopeless Fatty, Now I'm a Model" has long been a dominant theme.[87] Many studies show that frequent exposure to media images and diet articles is associated with heightened anxiety and unhappiness concerning appearance, as well as eating disorders, particularly in female adolescents.[88]

The power of the media was dramatically illustrated by the introduction of television in Fiji in the 1990s. This was a culture that had long valued robust bodies and had almost no incidence of eating disorders. Within three years after television viewing became common, such disorders dramatically increased. Many female adolescents quickly became intent on replicating the figures they saw; "I want their body" was a common refrain.[89] That desire is, of course, widely shared in Western countries such as the United States, where half of girls age nine to eighteen consider themselves fat and two-thirds of college-age women are dieting.[90]

The media's focus on the appearance of prominent women reinforces these desires. Hillary Clinton is a textbook case. As first lady, she was ridiculed as "frumpy"; "Fashion stayed home" was a representative description of one of her European trips.[91] During her Senate campaign, panelists on CNN's *Larry King Live* show described her as "fat," "bottom heavy," and "short legged." No one made even a pretense of explaining why her "bad figure" was relevant.[92] During Clinton's presidential bid, her slight show of cleavage on the Senate floor merited *Washington Post* coverage, and Rush Limbaugh asked his estimated fourteen million listeners whether Americans "will want to watch a woman get older before their eyes on a daily basis?"[93]

If they don't, part of the reason is the absence of attractive older women in the media who actually look their age. Studies of film, television, and print media repeatedly find that older women are grossly underrepresented and rarely unreconstructed.[94] News anchors such as Walter Cronkite and Tom Brokaw retain their influence, and male movie stars can play romantic leads well into their later years. In his sixties Sean Connery earned one of *People* magazine's annual awards for the "sexiest man alive." Women, by contrast, are expected to play opposite men thirty years their senior, and to bow out gracefully or have "work done" when the signs of age become pronounced. Even those who make the effort risk comments like the one from a *Boston Herald* columnist about an overly made-up politician: "There seemed to be something humiliating, sad, desperate and embarrassing about Katherine Harris, a woman of a certain age trying too hard to hang on."[95] The "certain age" was 43.

Even when more skillfully managed, such refurbishing efforts reinforce implausible ideals. In commenting on an airbrushed, surgically enhanced image of a woman, "probably in her seventies," Betty Friedan noted, "She doesn't look old. The problem is, she doesn't look real either."[96] *Boston Globe* columnist Ellen Goodman made a similar point about a photo of Elizabeth Taylor at sixty, "nipped, tucked, and lifted out of her peer group.... Looking 35 and holding." But the prevalence of such images only gives women "an extension on aging. They are not being given permission to age gracefully." The culture generally, and the media in particular, is "telling women they can be younger longer. It is not welcoming old women."⁹⁷

This special scrutiny of female appearance puts prominent women in a no-win situation: it penalizes them for caring too much or not enough and diverts attention from their qualifications and performance. The media had a field day with Sarah Palin's Beehive Beauty Shop hairdo and the disconnect between her "hockey mom" rhetoric and $150,000 designer wardrobe, financed by the Republican National Committee.⁹⁸ On Condoleezza Rice's first day as national security adviser, the *New York Times* ran a profile discussing her dress size (6), taste in shoes ("comfortable pumps"), and hemline preferences ("modest"). After becoming secretary of state, her appearance in high boots when visiting troops in Germany inspired portrayals as a dominatrix in political cartoons and comedy routines.⁹⁹ San Diego mayor Donna Frye's change of hairstyle and makeup after her election earned her the nickname "surfer chick."¹⁰⁰ Harriet Miers, President Bush's White House counsel and unsuccessful candidate for a Supreme Court appointment, was described on Jon Stewart's *Daily Show* as a "friend of the president and a Talbot's frequent shopper."

Male candidates have also been on the receiving end of such treatment. Al Gore's weight and wardrobe choices were cause for comment, as were John Edward's $400 haircuts and John Kerry's possible Botox use. But the scrutiny of women is more intense, the standards more exacting, and the risks are greater of paying too much or not enough attention to their appearance. When Katie Couric became the first female anchor of network nighttime news, the comments on her image were unremitting. Many wondered whether she was up to the job or had gotten it for the "right reasons." After all, noted the *New York Times*, "Unless CBS designs a new anchor desk, Ms. Couric's well-toned legs will no longer be on prominent display."¹⁰¹ In fact, when Couric had briefly substituted for Jay Leno several years earlier, the network staff cut a hole in the desk to expose her legs.[102]

Yet women who have all the substantive qualifications for such a position, but lack the right age, ethnicity, or "look," face even greater hurdles.[103] When a female meteorologist lost her position on a weather show for appearing too "matronly" and "dowdy," television host Conan O'Brien described her problem as "partly saggy with a chance of menopause."[104]

Recognition of these disabling stereotypes seems part of what mpted the extraordinary outpouring of support for British singer Susan Boyle. Some 114 million viewers replayed her performance on England's *You've Got Talent*. As *Ms* editor Letty Pogrebin suggested, what moved many of them to tears may have been the "years of wasted talent, the career that wasn't.... If someone with a voice like Julie Andrews spent decades in a sea of frustration and obscurity [because she didn't look the part], how many other women (and men) must be out there...in the same boat?"[105]

Even the most successful celebrities can be hobbled by our cultural obsession with appearance. On a 2009 cover of her magazine, a full-sized Oprah looks at a recreation of her trim 2005 body and asks, "How did I let this happen again?" In the story inside, one of the world's most successful entrepreneurs confesses that she felt "completely defeated" by her hardly atypical experience of yo-yo dieting. "I give up. Fat wins."[106]

Such mea culpas are consistent with most media portrayals, which frame fat as a failure of personal responsibility and a sign of moral laxity.[107] Such accounts are partly responsible for the assumptions discussed in chapters 2 and 5: that overweight individuals are too lazy to exercise and too self-indulgent to diet. Occasionally there are other villains in the story. The fast-food industry exploits our weaknesses, invades our schools, and blocks appropriate policy responses; technology spawns "telly tubbies" and "couch potatoes";

and feminism encourages "careerism," which leaves working women with too little time to provide home-cooked meals and to ensure healthy lifestyles for their children.[108] No one faults working fathers.

A final example of the media's preoccupation with appearance and sexual double standards involves the coverage of female athletes. Those who are attractive receive vastly disproportionate attention, and much of it highlights sex rather than sports. A study of *Sports Illustrated* found that only 10 percent of the photos were of women, and half of those were in provocative poses. Many female Olympic athletes manage to achieve coverage only in the swimsuit issue.[109] The alluring Anna Kournikova received an eight-page spread in the magazine and became the highest-earning female tennis player in the world without ever winning a professional singles tournament. The far-less-photogenic Wimbledon winner, Lindsay Davenport, got barely a mention.[110] Playboy.com has featured "babes of the LPGA," and *Gear* magazine pictured Brandi Chastain wearing only her soccer cleats, balancing soccer balls on her breasts and crotch. Even the normally staid *New York Times Sunday Magazine* offered a sexualized photo spread of the Russian women's tennis team under the title "Court-esans." For these women, one portrayed with racket, spike heels, and a low-cut "Louis Vuitton minidress," the subtitle ran "love is just another four letter word." "How practical is a stiletto on the court?" asked the photo caption. Answer from Anna Chakvetadze: "Those heels would destroy the courts."[111] But who cares? Product endorsements often take a similar tack. Anna Kournikova's Berlei Bra ad ran under the slogan, "Only the balls should bounce."[112]

Defenders of such displays claim that they benefit women's sports by appealing to potential male viewers and dispelling any stereotypes that make strength and sweat seem unfeminine. But if so, the price is to objectify athletes who deserve the attention on other grounds and to suggest that, whatever their accomplishments, their sexual appeal matters just as much. Male athletes encounter no such expectations. No one is posing Tiger Woods with golf balls foregrounding his crotch.

ADVERTISING

A final influence on appearance involves advertising. In 1887, the manufacturers of Pear soap marketed their product with a drawing of a celebrated beauty over the caption, "I am fifty today and thanks to Pears soap my complexion is only seventeen."[113] Contemporary consumers get endless variations on that theme. Estimates vary regarding the number of ads that an average American encounters daily, from 625 to more than 3,000.[114] But whatever the figure, no one disputes their power. As Stewart Ewen famously put it, advertisers are "captains of consciousness," not simply commerce; they create social meaning and shape individual desires and identity.[115] Nowhere is their impact greater than in matters of appearance, where they have founded multibillion dollar industries on needs of their own construction.

Marketing strategies take several forms but often begin by encouraging or exploiting a sense of inadequacy and then identifying a convenient commercial cure. For example, 95 percent of the women pictured in women's magazines are rated as beautiful or very attractive.[116] "By inviting women to compare their unimproved reality with...[this] airbrushed perfection, advertising erodes self-esteem, then offers to sell it back—for a price."[117] In this sense, the beauty industry resembles the medieval church, which instilled "profound anxieties about the body...and then present[ed] itself as the only instrument able...to take away the very guilt and shame it [had] itself produced."[118]

Cellulite is a textbook case. In 1978, two German dermatologists published a widely read paper, "So Called Cellulite: An Invented Disease," which described the "essential normality" of dimpled fat deposits in adult women and "the near futility of treatment."[119] Their prognosis did not deter the legions of entrepreneurs who discovered "gold in them thar thighs"; the result was a $3 billion market in products such as creams and massagers that have almost no demonstrable success in their intended use.[120] And of course, thighs are only a small part of the challenge. The average American woman lives in constant struggle in the "beauty contest of life," fighting excess pounds, encroaching wrinkles, unruly hair, unsightly cuticles, and fashion blunders. At every turn, she receives reminders of the consequences of neglect. "If your hair is not beautiful, the rest hardly matters." "Why aren't your feet as sexy as the rest of you?"[121] Why indeed?

Part of what distinguishes modern marketing is the ability to co-opt criticism. Although feminists have long advocated a standard of beauty that reflects women's natural state, marketers have created a world in which "[o]nly a handful of women have the Natural Look naturally."[122] Most require a large supply of "natural" products to achieve the healthy glow that nature must have intended. So too, marketers have reappropriated the very concepts of choice and empowerment that feminists claim are undermined by manipulative ads. In the universe that Madison Avenue portrays, women have a "right to romance."[123] The quest for beauty is a form of self-expression—a "commitment to yourself."[124] Or as a L'Oreal slogan put it, "Because I'm worth it."[125] In a world where much of life seems shaped by institutions that individuals cannot control, advertising presents the body as a welcome site for self-expression and self-respect.[126]

Unlike the choices that the women's movement serves up, which typically require hard work and sensible footwear, marketers offer "effortless extravagance," "glamour," "luxury," "indul-gence," and "uncompromising elegance," all of which women have "earned."[127] In the fact-free fantasy land of diet marketing, it is possible to "Lose Weight While You Sleep"; "Lose Fat and Calories Even If You Eat More"; and "Lose Up to Five Pounds in Five Minutes, Five Inches in Five Hours" with a "Space Age Slenderizer."[128]

Cloaked in a veneer of pseudoscience, skin-care ads often list ingredients that Nobel laureate chemists have been unable to iden-tify, and make claims on the fringes of fraud:

- "Advanced Filgrinol Complex and AQUAXYL...actually binds critical moisture within the skin's surface layers."
- "Perfectionist (CP+) with Plyu-Collagen Peptides...and BiSync Activating™ Complex, this anti aging phenomenon helps reduce the look of deep wrinkles faster than ever before."
- "Capture R60/80 Eye Cream offers a visible transformation, which thanks to 'Bi-Skin' instantly reduces the appearance of wrinkles around the eyes."[129]

Investment in such products "doesn't just give you a new face; it gives you a whole new point of view in life."[130]

The problem is that this point of view draws on myths of perfec-tion detached from biological and social realities. Products such as Evian Water promise that with "[t]he proper diet, the right amount of exercise...you can have, pretty much, any body you desire."[131] Would that it were true. But the assumption that our ideals of beauty are easily and equally available ignores the constraints that most of face in slimming down and shaping up, constraints that have different impacts across class, race, ethnicity, age, and gender. The ads sound self-empowering, but their effect is anything but. They set us up to fail, and to fault ourselves for falling short.

THE CULTURE OF BEAUTY

Should we try to learn to live with what we are left with? wonders Doris Grumbach in her memoir of aging, *Coming into the End Zone.* Contemporary Western societies make that difficult. Our genes, history, and market structures are stacked against it. A $200 billion global industry is heavily invested in fueling anxieties over appearance and a need for self-improvement. Technological advances have expanded our opportunities, and media images are an ever-present reminder of the gap between our aspirations and achievements. Our appearance is in constant need of renovation, and our spiffed-up selves need a wide range of commercial assistance to keep them that way.

Although some of the effort can be satisfying, it can also be an unwelcome burden and a source of shame, frustration, and unnecessary expense. Particularly for women, the priority we place on appearance presents ongoing challenges, with profound personal as well as political dimensions.

CHAPTER FOUR

Critics and Their Critics

"WHEN SHE ASKS How She Looks, Any Answer Could Get Ugly," is Dave Barry's title for a column on gender differences regarding appearance. According to Barry, "[m]ost men form an opinion of how they look in seventh grade," often as "irresistible stud muffins," and they "stick to it for the rest of their lives." Most women, by contrast, think they will never be "good enough," partly because a multibillion dollar industry reinforces that view and holds women to impossible standards. As an example, Barry cites an Oprah Winfrey program in which supermodel Cindy Crawford coached women in applying makeup that would never leave them looking anything like Crawford, "who is some kind of genetic mutation." Barry observes:

> I'm not saying that men are superior. I'm just saying that you're not going to get a group of middle aged men to sit in a room and apply cosmetics to themselves under the instruction of Brad Pitt in hopes of looking more like him. Men would realize that this task was pointless and demeaning. They would find some way

to bolster their self-esteem that did not require looking like Brad Pitt. They would say to Brad: "Oh YEAH? Well what do you know about LAWN CARE, pretty boy?"

Moreover, Barry concludes, "men don't even notice 97 percent of the beauty efforts [women] make anyway. Take fingernails. The average woman spends 5000 hours per year worrying about her fingernails; I have never once, in more than 40 years of listening to men talk about women, heard a man say, 'She has a nice set of fingernails.'"[1]

Barry joins a long line of critics, ranging from conservative Christians to radical feminists, who have mocked or denounced cosmetic pursuits. In 1792, Mary Wollstonecraft's *Vindication of the Rights of Women* launched the classic feminist critique: "Taught from their infancy that beauty is woman's scepter, the mind shapes itself to the body, and roaming around its gilt cage, only seeks to adorn its prison."[2] In a similar vein, Samuel Johnson's influential 1751 essay, *The Rambler*, consoles a woman who has lost her looks to smallpox: "Consider yourself...as a being born to know, to reason, and to act....You will find that there are other charms than those of beauty and other joys than the praise of fools."[3] Some two centuries later, Pope Pius XII maintained that cosmetic surgery was "morally unlawful" if sought to enhance the "power of seduction" or to "satisfy vanity or the caprice of fashion."[4] Somewhat unlikely allies were leading feminists, who denounced a wide range of cosmetic practices as perpetuating the objectification and subordination of women.

Yet that position has attracted its own share of critics who invoke feminist principles to justify their cosmetic choices. And millions more women who are not active participants in the debate cannot help but take a stand in their day-to-day decisions. Virginia Woolf, in her 1929 classic, *A Room of One's Own*, maintained that every woman needed to consider "what your beauty means to you...and what is your relation to the ever changing and turning world of gloves and shoes.[5] In today's universe of escalating opportunities for cosmetic "enhancement," the issues surrounding appearance have posed more complex challenges. Underlying these issues are fundamental questions concerning personal choice and political priorities that have long been central to the women's movement.

NINETEENTH- AND EARLY-TWENTIETH-CENTURY CRITICS

Contemporary challenges to appearance-related practices draw on two lines of argument that defined nineteenth-century debates. From conservatives came concerns about "painting," a practice initially associated with prostitutes. And from women's rights activists came dress reform. The conservatives campaign won respect but not victory; the feminists achieved neither in the short run, but eventually at least partial success.

During America's first two centuries, the conventional wisdom was that "[w]hen a woman wears cosmetics, it is...prima facie evidence that her character is frail."[6] In some states, a man could have his marriage annulled if he had been seduced into marriage by his wife's use of paints or powders during courtship.[7] An influx of Parisian fashions during the mid-nineteenth century briefly helped to liberalize these traditional views, but within a few decades, the social purity movement had marshaled its forces, and "respectable" women did not "rouge." They might ingest chalk, vinegar, or even arsenic to achieve a fair complexion, or kiss rosy crepe paper to redden their lips, but any detectable use of paints or powders put their reputations at risk. Beauty and virtue were intertwined, and reliance on cosmetics was corrosive to a "chaste soul" and a sign of moral depravity.[8] Some black women's leaders similarly condemned anyone who wanted to whiten her skin: "Why does she wish to improve her appearance? Why not improve her real self" through education and cultural activities?[9] On hair, many leaders echoed the advice of Marcus Garvey: "Don't remove the kinks from your hair! Remove them from your brain."[10]

Market forces, however, kept putting temptation within ever-easier reach, and by the early twentieth century, much of the stigma surrounding cosmetics had eroded. "We can't all be born beautiful," reasoned one purchaser.[11] So too, as more women entered the labor market, they began seeing makeup as a way to increase their employment opportunities. Cosmetics also served as a form of self-expression and an emblem of emancipation, as well as a means of moving up in the marriage market. According to Zelda Fitzgerald, "paint and powder" were a way for women to "choose their destinies—to be successful competitors in the great game of life."[12] By the early twentieth century, suffragists advocated lip rouge as a symbol of women's rights and incorporated its use in public rallies.[13]

Although some activists in this "first wave" of feminism also attempted to link dress reform with other feminist causes, their initial campaigns had little success. In 1851, Elizabeth Cady Stanton and Amelia Bloomer launched their crusade against corsets and crinolines by wearing shortened skirts over Turkish-styled pantaloons, a style quickly labeled "bloomers." A few other suffragists joined the effort, but soon dropped out after journalists viciously caricatured the costume and spectators jeered and stoned women who wore it.[14] However, many doctors, educators, editors of women's magazines, and authors of advice manuals supported at least some reform, and "sensible dress" apart from bloomers gradually emerged.[15] The increasing popularity of the bicycle and other forms of physical exercise, as well as women's entry into the paid labor market, ultimately reinforced the demand for functional fashions.

THE CONTEMPORARY WOMEN'S MOVEMENT

In the 1960s, the emergence of a "second wave" of feminism brought a more fundamental and sustained challenge to the beauty industry. In 1968, protestors at the Miss America pageant announced a boycott of all products related to the competition, and unceremoniously deposited bras, girdles, curlers, false eyelashes, and women's magazines into a "Freedom Trash Can." Although no undergarments were burned, the label "bra burner" stuck as an all-purpose pejorative to characterize "radical" feminists. Among that group were authors of a statement accompanying the protest, which explained, "Women in our society are forced daily to compete for male approval, enslaved by ludicrous beauty standards that we ourselves are conditioned to take seriously."[16] Building on the premise that the "personal is political," activists shed a range of conventions along with their undergarments. Unshaved legs and unadorned faces became a symbol of "liberation."

The public reception was not unlike the response to early dress reformers. Feminists were seen as "dowdy," "frumpy" "moralizers," who hated men because they could not attract them.[17] Because radicals gained disproportionate media attention, the early feminist movement in general, and its critique of beauty in particular, was often dismissed even by those who accepted most of its other egalitarian principles. In *The Sceptical Feminist*, Janet Radcliffe Richards voiced a common concern: "The image of the movement comes from the individuals in it. If large numbers of them are unattractive the movement as a whole is bound to be so too."[18]

Despite the presence of glamorous leaders such as Gloria Steinem, right-wing commentators such as Rush Limbaugh have often insisted that "feminism was established to allow unattractive, homely women access to mainstream society."[19] Christina Hoff Sommers hasn't gone quite that far, but she has pointed out that "there are a lot of homely women in women's studies."[20] But of course, women's studies, and the organized women's movement, by no means reflect a single view on issues related to appearance. Nor do their members necessarily speak for the vast majority of contemporary American women who do not identify themselves as feminists but who share basic feminist commitments to equal opportunity.

Indeed, over the last quarter century, as the feminist movement has grown increasingly fragmented, different subcultures have differed sharply on matters of appearance. Beginning in the late 1960s, fat activists have sought to challenge discrimination on the basis of weight and to make tolerance for all body sizes a social priority. Beginning in the 1990s, a group of young activists, self-labeled as "third-wave feminists," has focused on interlocking categories of oppression and ways of encouraging sexual agency.[21] For some of these women, that has involved reclaiming conventional emblems of femininity—sexualized clothing and stiletto heels. For others, such as those in punk rock subcultures like Riot Grrrls, it has meant rejecting traditional images of femininity and asserting deviant styles—green hair or shaved heads.[22] And for aging second-wave feminists, the challenge has been finding ways to reconcile their personal attachment to femininity with their political commitments.

CRITIQUES

Despite their other differences, many contemporary feminists have shared certain concerns about appearance along the lines set out in chapter 2. The most obvious is cost. In her widely publicized account, *The Beauty Myth*, Naomi Wolf noted that women's absorption with appearance "leeches money and leisure and confidence."[23]

Because women are held to unattainable ideals, their task is boundless. Almost all areas of the female body are in need of something. The result is to focus women's attention on self-improvement rather than social action.[24]

Prevailing beauty ideals also objectify women. According to many feminists, "gender hierarchy is sustained by beauty norms that define women's power...and worth in terms that [reinforce] male dominance.... Feminine beauty is defined primarily for men's pleasure. So the woman who strives to achieve an aesthetic ideal does so not for self-actualization or accomplishment but for masculine approval."[25] When the first black Miss America lost her crown after *Penthouse* magazine published photographs depicting her in sexually provocative poses, the coalition "Women Against Pornography" denounced her forced resignation as hypocritical. "The Miss America pageant differs from *Penthouse* in degree not kind. Like *Penthouse*, the pageant judges women on the basis of conformity to a sexist ideal."[26]

Although women may experience pleasure or self-expression through their appearance, theorists such as Sandra Bartky view these "satisfactions of narcissism" as "repressive," a response to "false needs, indoctrination...guilt [and] shame."[27] Kathryn Morgan similarly sees women who opt for cosmetic surgery as coerced by husbands and family, or duped by promises from male surgeons of "beauty that will last a lifetime."[28] "Choice" under these conditions is the "choice of conformity" to oppressive ideals.[29] Nathaniel Hawthorne anticipates the point in his haunting 1846 short story "The Birthmark." In it a beautiful young woman is untroubled by a birthmark on her cheek until after her marriage. Then she discovers that her husband, a "man of science," sees the discoloration as a "frightful...symbol of imperfection," a reminder of death and decay. She comes to hate it even more than he, and resolves to have him remove it, "at whatever risk."[30] He prepares a potion that causes the birthmark to fade but that kills her in the process. Having "rejected the best the earth could offer," the couple falls victim to the folly that Hawthorne captures in his closing line—man's inability to find the "perfect...in the present."[31]

To many contemporary feminists, what underlies such follies are complex cultural forces in which women no less than men have a substantial stake.[32] Over two-thirds of college students majoring in advertising are women, and they are well represented among the leaders of cosmetic, fashion, weight-reduction, and modeling industries.[33] From critics' vantage, these industries serve to reinforce gender inequality in the ways that chapter 3 describes. The overemphasis of attractiveness diminishes women's credibility and diverts attention from their capabilities and accomplishments. In the long run, these are more stable sources of self-esteem and social power than appearance.[34] Prevailing beauty standards also place women in a double bind. They are expected to conform, yet condemned as vain and narcissistic for attempts to do so. Neither should they "let themselves go," nor look as if they were trying too hard not to.[35] Beauty must seem natural, even, or especially, when it can only be accomplished through considerable unnatural effort.[36] As Germaine Greer notes, an older woman feels "a duty to go on 'being attractive' no matter how fed up she is with the whole business."[37]

Feminists are in a particularly problematic situation. Those who defy conventional standards are ridiculed as homely harpies; those who comply are dismissed as hypocrites. Jane Fonda's decision to have breast implants and other surgical procedures seemed to "contradict everything she advocates" concerning health and fitness.[38] When confronted by the contradiction, Fonda responded, "I never asked to be a role model....I don't pretend to be different from any other woman. I'm subject to the same foibles and pressures."[39] Even conservative women who resist cosmetic upgrades are not immune from critique. Despite her matronly appearance and untinted hair, former first lady Barbara Bush was mocked for claiming indifference to beauty concerns. "What you see is what you get," was her favorite self-description, yet critics noted that she had a hairdresser constantly on call, sometimes three times a day.[40]

Most disturbing of all is the toll that these criticisms take on individuals' own self-esteem. Many women who recognize beauty norms as oppressive feel humiliated by the inability to escape them. They are ashamed for feeling ashamed.[41] Writing about her resort to electrolysis to eliminate unsightly facial hair, Wendy Chapkis confesses: "I am a feminist. How humiliated I then feel. I am a woman. How ugly I have been made to feel. I have failed on both counts."[42] With self-deprecating irony, Eve Ensler's *The Good Body* recounts her own struggles: "What I can't believe is that someone like me, a radical feminist for nearly thirty years, could spend this much time thinking about my stomach. It has become my tormentor, my distractor; it's my most committed relationship."[43]

RESPONSES

Responses to these critiques have proceeded on multiple levels. As chapter 3 noted, marketers have attempted to co-opt feminist messages by pitching products as a source of health, pleasure, and luxury, and assuring women that they "deserve to be 'all they can be.' "[44] A typical cosmetic surgery ad suggests: "look like the person you really are."[45] Women themselves also stress self-determination. As one beauty pageant contestant put it, "I'm here because I want to be.... [Competitions] help you improve as a person...to be the best you can be."[46] Cosmetic surgery patients similarly describe their decision as "the independent choice of a liberated woman" and deny that they are pressured by others.[47] In sociologist Kathy Davis's study, nearly all of the women who had breast implants reported that their family and friends had attempted to discourage them.[48]

At the same time, many women in Davis's and other studies have acknowledged ridicule, humiliation, and shame as driving their decisions. Some have spent years trying to accept how they looked before resorting to surgery. One female patient expressed a common view: "I wish I could have said 'To hell with it. I am going to love my body the way it is,' but I had tried to do that for fifteen years and it didn't work."[49] For these women, the goal has been not beauty but normalcy—fixing an aspect of their appearance that they "just really hate."[50] To some, this flaw has assumed disproportionate significance: it has come to represent "everything that was wrong in their lives."[51] Others simply have not "want[ed] to look [their] age," or have felt embarrassed by "secretarial spread," "flabby" thighs, or "sagging knockers."[52] Hillary Clinton, who has had a number of minor makeovers, captured these views when she told *Elle* magazine, "Cosmetic surgery may be just as important for someone's state of mind and well being as any other kind of surgery."[53]

The vast majority of women patients achieve at least some measure of well-being. In most studies, at least 85 percent report substantial satisfaction with cosmetic procedures, and almost as many would be willing to have additional surgery.[54] Patients consistently report a reduction in self-consciousness, anxiety, and depression connected with appearance and frequently experience improvements in self-confidence and sexual relationships.[55] As one woman noted, "It made a difference in how I felt about myself as a person."[56] In Davis's study, even patients who experienced disfigurement or painful side effects generally did not regret their decision.[57] So too, other studies of women's reliance on makeup, salons, spas, find considerable satisfaction with such purchases. Cosmetics make many individuals feel more "credible" and "professional."[58] Time spent shopping or in spas and salons provides pleasure and opportunities for female bonding.[59] Even high heels can boost self-esteem. As a features editor for *Marie Claire* put it, they can bring women up to "eye level to male superiors. Don't underestimate that 'leg up.' "[60]

In one widely circulated *Playboy* article, Jan Breslauer, a former Yale feminist theory professor further insisted that having a "boob job" expressed feminist principles—"a woman's right to do what she wants with her body." It "made me focus on how far I've come.... I have arrived at the point where I can go out and buy myself a new pair of headlights if I want.... And if somebody asks if they're [mine, I can] tell them, 'Yes, I bought them myself."[61]

Moreover, some women see little if any difference between widely accepted beauty rituals and the surgical procedures that critics deplore. Cosmetic surgeons are quick to point out that most of these procedures have low risks; some, like liposuction, may be healthier than the disordered eating, yo-yo dieting, and excessive workouts that women may use to achieve the same results.[62] With surgical options becoming cheaper and safer, growing numbers of consumers wonder: "What is the difference between highlighting your hair and having a facelift?"[63] As chapter 3 noted, about two-thirds of American women color their hair.[64] For some, it may seem a professional necessity. Of the sixteen female United States senators between ages forty-six and seventy-four, not one has visible gray hair; nor do 90 percent of the women in the House of Representatives.[65] The reasons for tinting are not unlike those that motivate users of Botox. As Susan Brownmiller observed two decades ago, the face-lift is "a logical extension of every night cream, moisturizer, pore cleanser and facial masque that has gone before it."[66]

But to many feminists, that analogy seems unpersuasive. Women don't suffer severe complications, disabling injuries, or disfigurement from moisturizers. The worst that is likely to result from a botched tint job is the discovery that blondes do not necessarily have more fun. The financial as well as physical costs of cosmetic surgery are also on a different order of magnitude than those associated with over-the-counter skin products. Moreover, as Carolyn Heilbrun argued in a celebrated essay "Coming of Age," makeup or hair tints are a form of temporary "camouflage" that can be shed at will. Surgery reflects a more significant attempt to alter the body, and the efforts may be only "briefly if at all effective. Worse, they increase the fear of age. . . . [O]ne should encourage youth, not try to be it." Freedom in midlife can only come in understanding that "who I am is what I do" not how I look.[67] Eve Ensler makes the same point about diets and other appearance-related regimes: "LOVE YOUR BODY: STOP FIXING IT."[68]

PERSONAL INTERESTS AND POLITICAL COMMITMENTS

In 1975, Nora Ephron noted: "Once I tried to explain to a fellow feminist why I liked wearing makeup. She replied by explaining why she does not. Neither of us understood a word the other said."[69] Three decades later, a similar impasse occurred in testimony before the Federal Drug Administration as women squared off over whether to ban silicone breast implants. For several days, the FDA heard from those who claimed that implants had "either ruined their lives or restored their self-worth."[70] The agency ultimately decided to temporize. Until more data on safety become available, it allowed the product only for those needing reconstructive surgery after a disfiguring disease such as breast cancer. But such debates persist, as do disputes about other forms of implants, and expose the fault lines in contemporary attitudes toward appearance.

While women remain divided over cosmetic practices, they often share discomfort about the culture that produces them. Appearance is an opportunity for self-expression and self-determination, but many women recognize that their options are far too "limited by circumstances not of their own making."[71] In one study of makeup in the workplace, virtually all the participants believed that they had a choice about whether to use cosmetics. But they also believed that women who decline to wear makeup "do not appear healthy, heterosexual or credible."[72] Other participants expressed ambivalence about whether to "age with dignity" or to "fight back any way [they] can." One woman bought Clinique's Turn Around cream when she was "feeling old" but hadn't yet "turned around" because the jar sits unopened in her bathroom cabinet.[73] So, too, even the women in Davis's study who were satisfied with their decision to have cosmetic surgery were often highly critical of the culture that had led them to take that step. It was simply "the lesser of two evils."[74] Cosmetic surgery was "symptomatic of an unjust social order in which women had to go to extremes" just to look acceptable.[75] To Katha Pollitt,

> what is most of this starving and carving about but accepting that woman is basically just a body...with a rather short shelf life? You can postpone the expiration if you "work" at it...or you "have work done," as if the body were some sort of perpetual construction site. But basically you are suffering a lot to please people...and disguising that fact from yourself with a lot of twaddle about self-improvement and self-esteem.[76]

Not all women are, of course, under such illusions. Many also recognize that in the long run, their efforts to conform to conventional ideals carry "heavy costs for them and for all women."[77] But this seems like the price for success in the short run, which requires "making do with a culture that they believe judges and rewards them for their looks."[78] Why insist that individual women "ignore their personal advancement for a distant dream of collective gender equality?"[79] For decades, those who have heeded the call have made little impact on the culture generally and undermined the image of feminism in the process.

Many women who self-consciously opt for conformity remain unapologetic about their choice. In 1954, when an obscure socialist journal, *Militant*, ran an article condemning the cosmetics industry for selling useless products, the astonished editor received a barrage of unhappy letters, "the kind of response that only an important issue deserves."[80] Many readers were incensed by the journal's romanticization of working women's natural beauty. "There is nothing beautiful in the dishpan hands, the premature wrinkles, the scraggly hair, the dumpy figures in dumpy housedresses," wrote one reader. Another explained: "I wish to improve and enjoy my physical appearance and at the same time improve and develop all the other sides of my personality. And I think all women have a right to both those things."[81]

Some contemporary feminists make similar claims. In her youth, Angela Neustatter viewed cosmetic surgery patients as "more to be pitied than despised" but reversed course in midlife. After deciding to "tidy up" rather than "stand proud" with the "crumples and rumples" around her eyes, she explained that what had changed was not her principles but her "time frame." "I am a midlifer in today's world and I don't think I have time to reeducate society for the greater good."[82] "Plastic surgery," she acknowledged, "is a bit of a sellout, but I don't think it means I have to skewer myself on the feminist spike.... The personal may be political, but the personal is also personal.... I know that ageing naturally is the more honorable way to go but I'm not there to be honorable to my gender. I've done quite a lot of that in my life."[83] Jan Breslauer defends her implants along similar lines. Sexism "isn't going to change any time soon. Here's the choice: you can rail at an imperfect world or go get yourself a great pair of bazongas."[84] As long as "women are judged by their jugs... it's sometime better to acknowledge that the injustice exists and get on with your life."[85]

British singing sensation Susan Boyle's decision to get a make-over provoked similar arguments. Initially Boyle herself resisted suggestions that she should spruce up her image. "Why should it matter as long as I can sing?" she asked one British interviewer. "For now I'm happy the way I am—short and plump.... What's wrong with looking like Susan Boyle? What's wrong with that?" But after watching her television performance, her question no longer seemed rhetorical. "I realized how frumpy I was."[86] So she invested $57 to have her hair cut and tinted and her eyebrows shaped.

This set off a frenzy among British tabloids and bloggers. Should she or shouldn't she? Could she afford to abandon her principles and the "look" that had helped make her famous in the first instance? Angela Holton, one of the judges of *Britain's Got Talent* insisted that Boyle "needs to stay exactly as she is because that's the reason we love her. The minute we turn her into a glamour puss is when it's spoiled." This advice, columnist Ellen Goodman noted, came from someone "blonde, Botoxed and burnished," a glamour puss herself. What concerned Goodman about the debate was that "in our cultural ambivalence about appearance, we look too hard for someone (else) to be a stand-in army, a one-woman resistance force. Women who are both fighting and succumbing to the beauty standards that have seemed both relentless and powerful want to see someone hit just the right note. They also want to see someone happy in their unadorned cellulite-marked skin. That's an awful lot of pressure to put on one middle aged woman who is about to face a second round of talent scrutiny in the full spotlight."[87] As it turned out, that pressure, together with her second-place finish in the next round, was enough to cause Boyle to check into a clinic for "stress."

These experiences underscore the discomfiting dilemma that many feminists face between personal interests and political commitments. As Lynn Chancer puts it:

[83]

Conventional beauty standards have failed to wither away, and ironically feminism may have even added a second set of standards against which we can...find ourselves wanting: those of the model feminist. The model feminist haunts us with her lack of concern over being attractive. Her self-confidence gives her beauty, never the other way round. And above all, she never wishes to just pass.... To a lingering sense of feminine inadequacy, we thus added shame for our supposed failures as feminists.[88]

Even leaders of the women's movement who try to set the right example frequently fail to achieve the inner peace that their principles demand. As a matter of principle, Susan Brownmiller stopped shaving her legs, but years later she "had yet to accept the unaesthetic results."[89] Patricia Williams makes a similar confession about her attachment to "power point" footwear—shoes with spindle heels and narrow toes that are unsuitable for actual walking.[90] Such ambivalence is scarcely surprising, given the deep-seated cultural forces and market pressures that underpin conventional ideals. "Is it any wonder," asks Wendy Chapkis, "that we sometimes feel ourselves to be unattractive, ridiculous, and generally inadequate even while expressing pride in our principled stand? Or that we come to echo the punishing judgment of our culture demanding we choose between principles and pleasure."[91]

So where does that leave us? "Has feminism failed women?" Karen Lehman wonders. "Have women failed feminism? Or has society failed them both?"[92] Perhaps more to the point, are those helpful ways of framing the question? Or as this book argues, isn't a better way forward to avoid looking back and to get beyond blame? Can't we criticize appearance-related practices without criticizing the women who find them necessary?

Underlying these questions are deeper, more vexed issues of false consciousness, free "choice," and the "authentic" or "autonomous" self.

Much of the early work on appearance by contemporary feminists underscored the need to link the personal with the political. From this perspective, a "choice" to engage in practices that objectified women as a group or imposed undue costs on individuals seemed irreconcilable with feminist principles. When women experienced themselves as autonomous consumers, making pleasurable decisions, that was simply evidence of the power of repressive ideologies. The only answer was to raise women's consciousness and to demand that they value their authentic unreconstructed selves. They should accept their ies as they "really" are, and please themselves, not others, with the way that they look.[93]

By contrast, most contemporary feminist theorists, influenced by postmodern perspectives, see no universal, uncontested standpoint from which consciousness can be declared "false" or identities considered "authentic." Yet they also emphasize the link between the personal and political. Choices are never wholly "free" or solely "personal." Cultural practices inevitably shape individuals' preferences, and their individual responses in turn help sustain or alter those practices. According to critics such as Susan Bordo, that entails viewing the body as a site not simply for self-expression but also for political struggle.[94]

Yet to many activists, such theoretical formulations offer too little guidance on personal choices that have broader implications. As Katha Pollitt notes, the failure to take a stance on practices that subordinate women as a group lead all too easily to a "You go, girl" approach, in which "[a]nything is feminist as long as you 'choose' it." It has now become "unsisterly, patronizing, infantilizing and sexist to question another woman's decision.... There's no social context and no place to stand and resist; there's just a menu of individual options and preferences."[95] An *Onion* parody makes a similar point. Under the title, "Women Now Empowered by Everything a Woman Does," a woman's studies professor explains that "fortunately for the less impressive among us, a new strain of feminism has emerged," in which almost any activity—shopping for shoes, or gaining weight—is "championed as the proud bold assertions of independence.... Only by lauding every single thing a woman does...can you truly go, girls."[96] It was "so much simpler," Pollitt observes, when feminism could just "tell women to use their famous agency to pull up their socks and say, *Screw you.*"[97]

To other feminists, however, that earlier era may have been simpler, but its approach to appearance was profoundly misguided. According to Harvard psychologist Nancy Etcoff,

> The idea that women would achieve more if only they didn't have to waste time on beauty is nonsense. Women will achieve more when they garner legal and social rights and privileges, not when they give up beauty.... We will only make our world a drabber place by not enjoying it, as long as we are not limited to it.... Rather than denigrating one source of women's power, it would seem more useful for feminists to attempt to elevate all sources of women's power.[98]

Nancy Friday, in *The Power of Beauty*, echoes similar themes. "Feminists should stop debunking...beauty." They should instead learn from it, and master ways to enjoy and cabin its influence.[99]

BEYOND THE IMPASSE

"What do women want?" Freud famously asked, as if the preferences of half the world's population could be captured in some universal standard. When it comes to appearance, what women want is not always the same or always compatible. Many women who opt for cosmetic enhancement feel well-served by the result. But the cost is to reinforce standards that make it harder for other women to opt out. Moreover, on broader but related issues about the role of gender in an ideal world, many individuals are agnostic or ambivalent. Do we want a society in which sex is like eye color, a biological characteristic irrelevant in determining dress and grooming codes? To borrow Barbara Risman's phrase, how much "gender vertigo" are we prepared to embrace?[100]

Most social science research suggests that attempting to eliminate all nonbiological markers of gender difference is an implausible ideal. Humans are hardwired to categorize by sex and to rely on appearance-related cues about sexual identity in structuring their social interactions.[101] Yet to acknowledge the inevitability of some gendered grooming practices is not to acquiesce in the extent or form they currently take. Nor do we need a fully developed or widely shared vision of the relationship between gender and appearance in an ideal world to build consensus about what needs changing in this one.

Whatever their other disagreements on these issues, most women appear to share certain core values. Appearance should be a source of pleasure, not of shame. Individuals should be able to make decisions about whether to enhance their attractiveness without being judged either politically incorrect or professionally unacceptable. Our ideals of appearance should reflect diversity across race, ethnicity, age, and body size. In this ideal world, the importance of appearance would not be overstated. Nor would it spill over to employment and educational contexts in which judgments should be based on competence, not cosmetics. Women would not be held to higher standards than men. Neither would they be subject to sexualized grooming requirements unless sex is the commodity being sold. Women's self-esteem would be tied to accomplishment, not appearance. In order for appearance to be a source of enjoyment rather than anxiety, it cannot dictate women's self-worth.[102]

So how do we get from here to there? There are no easy answers, but refocusing the feminist critique is an obvious place to start. It has not helped feminists' political agenda or public image to denounce widely accepted beauty practices and women who won't get with the program. Greater tolerance is in order, along with recognition that women are not all similarly situated in their capacity for resistance. Those who write about women's issues need to recognize that not everyone has the luxury of being able to say "screw you" to the cosmetics industry. In my job as a law professor, no one cares whether I use mascara. For television's legal commentators, such as Greta Van Susteren, the circumstances are far different, and the condemnation she received for her surgical upgrade seemed misdirected. "From Plain Greta to Foxy Babe," ran a headline in the *New York Daily News*, and almost two million viewers tuned in to check out her first post–eye lift performance.[103] But why center criticism on her choice rather than on the preferences of viewers and network executives that made the choice seem necessary?

Yet Van Susteren herself missed an opportunity to make that point. Rather, she took the opposite tack. In attempting to put a better face on her face-lift, Van Susteren commented, "I've made it safe for other people."[104] But she also made it less safe for those who want media limelight without "fixing" their features. Still, denouncing her decision is unlikely to alter the norms that encourage it, or to enlist participants in that reform effort. Focusing attention on personal decisions rather than collective practices asks too much of individuals and too little of society.[105]

This is not to imply that we should suspend critique. It is rather to suggest that we reframe the inquiry. When it comes to cosmetic surgery, the key issue is not whether it is hypocritical for feminists to have face-lifts. It is rather whether such practices are sufficiently safe and well-regulated, and whether a nation that leaves millions without basic health care is well served when the fastest growing medical specialty is cosmetic surgery. Do we want such a rapidly increasing portion of our scarce health dollars spent on enabling women to fit into designer shoes or fill out a D cup? If the goal is altering current priorities, it makes sense to concentrate critiques less on individual decisions and more on the culture that encourages them.

To that end, we need a broad range of initiatives along the lines that chapters 6 and 7 describe. Individuals should educate themselves and others about the risks of cosmetic practices and offer more support for women who resist them. Schools should do more to discourage appearance-related biases and unhealthy practices regarding weight and related issues. The media needs to offer more diverse and natural images of beauty, and to avoid promoting unrealistic and fraudulent appearance-related advertising. The law should more effectively regulate product safety and misleading claims, and should also prohibit appearance discrimination and sexualized grooming codes. Whatever their views about makeup and "sexy" apparel, women can agree that the choice should be theirs, not their employers, unless it is demonstrably related to job performance.

Feminists claim to speak from the experience of women. But that experience counsels tolerance for the different ways that appearance is perceived by different women under different constraints. *Fat Is a Feminist Issue,* declared the title of Susie Orbach's widely circulated critique. So are implants, Botox, stilettos, cornrows, and a host of other appearance-related concerns. Women need better ways of talking to rather than past each other on issues that continue to shape their opportunities and identities.

CHAPTER FIVE

. . .

The Injustice of Discrimination

"Not to worry — I'm going to put our best-looking people on the job."

Trevor Hoey, *New Yorker*, October 12, 2009. Reprinted with permission.

THE COSTS AND disadvantages associated with appearance raise two fundamental questions. Are any of these consequences unjust? If so, do they call for some legal remedy or other societal response? In considering these questions, it often makes sense to distinguish among various aspects of appearance. At one end of the spectrum are physical attributes that are difficult or impossible to change such as height and facial features. Although sex, race, and ethnicity are generally considered to be such immutable traits, they implicate identity in a more fundamental sense than other characteristics and are therefore considered separately in most discussions and policies concerning discrimination. At the other end of the continuum are purely voluntary characteristics involving fashion and grooming. These are likely to prove problematic only in certain contexts or for certain groups: examples include long hair or earrings for men and makeup or high heels for women. In between are mixed traits, such as obesity, which have both biological and behavioral foundations. Our concern is likely to be greatest with discrimination in the public sphere that is based on factors that are at least partly beyond an individual's control and that are not critical to performance.

In general, American law prohibits discrimination on the basis of race, sex, ethnicity, religion, age, and disability, but not appearance. As chapter 6 notes, only one state and six cities or counties prohibit some form of appearance discrimination. In the rest of the United States, such bias is unlawful only if it is linked with characteristics that other antidiscrimination laws cover, such as race, sex, or disability. So, for example, weight and grooming standards are impermissible if they impose unreasonable, disproportionate burdens on only one sex. Disability law prohibits weight discrimination in a very limited number of cases involving extreme obesity that impairs normal functioning. For the most part, however, bias based on appearance is lawful in the United States, and the same is true in other nations.[1] Whether it should be is a question demanding closer scrutiny.

Justifications for banning appearance discrimination rest on three basic claims. The first is that such discrimination offends principles of equal opportunity; individuals should be judged on merit and performance, not irrelevant physical characteristics. A second rationale is that appearance-related bias reinforces group subordination; it exacerbates disadvantages based on gender, race, ethnicity, class, age, and sexual orientation. A third justification is that some decisions based on appearance unduly restrict self-expression and cultural identity. Although opponents of prohibiting appearance discrimination raise legitimate concerns, these can be met through well-designed statutory schemes. Moreover, the barrage of meritless claims and business backlash that critics have predicted have not in fact materialized in the few jurisdictions that have prohibited appearance-related bias.

ENSURING EQUAL OPPORTUNITY: CHALLENGING STIGMA AND STEREOTYPES

The clearest argument for banning discrimination based on appearance is that it offends principles of equal opportunity and individual dignity. Many of the costs associated with appearance are the product of widespread prejudice. Educational and employment settings reveal frequent examples of bias. Short men are penalized in hiring, advancement, and earnings.[2] Overweight individuals of both sexes suffer corresponding disadvantages and stigma. A National Education Association report found that for these individuals, the "school experience is one of ongoing prejudice, unnoticed discrimination, and almost constant harassment."[3] The lower grades and college enrollments of obese female students have been at least partly attributed to stigmatization and the resulting disengagement and loss of self-esteem.[4] In several surveys, close to 90 percent of obese individuals reported humiliating comments from friends, family, or coworkers.[5] Overweight workers lose job opportunities and endure offensive jokes, cartoons, and nicknames.[6] In controlled experiments, these individuals are seen as less desirable colleagues and supervisors and are stereotyped as lazy, sloppy, and lacking in competence, self-discipline, and emotional stability.[7] Social critics denounce the "pathological slothfulness" that being overweight reportedly reflects.[8] Employers worry about customer, client, and coworker responses. Particularly for upper-level positions, fat is a "sure-fire career-killer. If you can't control your own contours, goes the logic, how can you control a budget and staff?"[9]

Concerns about health risks also play a role even when they have no basis in fact. For example, some commentators characterized Supreme Court nominee Sonia Sotomayor as "quite overweight," and worried that she might not "last too long on the [C]ourt because of [her] health." Yet as the research summarized in chapter 2 indicates, Sotomayor is nowhere near the extreme weights at which increased risks of mortality appear.[10]

Discrimination on the basis of appearance carries both individual and social costs. It undermines self-esteem, diminishes job aspirations, and compromises merit principles. As Princeton political philosopher Anthony Appiah notes, "Equality as a social ideal is a matter of not taking irrelevant distinctions into account."[11] When, as is typically the case, appearance bears no relationship to competence, discrimination on that basis undermines values of both efficiency and equity.[12]

Philosopher Michael Walzer's concept of spheres of justice illustrates the point.[13] Characteristics such as attractiveness that may justify decisions in one sphere, such as intimate personal relationships, are unjust when they spill over to other spheres, such as education or employment. Advocates of a Santa Cruz, California ordinance prohibiting appearance discrimination made precisely that claim: such a prohibition would force employers to judge workers "on the basis of real criteria," namely, "their ability to perform the job."[14] "What this ordinance is really saying," one city council member explained, is "hire the best-qualified person."[15]

Of course, as subsequent discussion notes, whether attractiveness is a relevant qualification is sometimes subject to debate. But in many contexts, discrimination based on appearance, like other forms of bias, rests on inaccurate stereotypes. Assumptions that overweight individuals are lazy, undisciplined, or unfit are a case in point. In one all-too-typical example, an obese woman failed to receive a job as an airport bus driver because a company doctor concluded that her weight would prevent her from effectively protecting passengers in an accident. The doctor subsequently acknowledged that the woman had no health problems and that he had performed no agility tests; he simply assumed that she was unfit because he had watched her "waddling down the hall" to her exam.[16] What makes such stereotypes objectionable is not only that they reflect overbroad or inaccurate generalizations; it is also that they can be self-perpetuating. Denying obese women jobs as bus drivers also denies them opportunities to challenge the assumptions of incompetence on which such bias rests.

In short, discrimination based on appearance unfairly stigmatizes individuals based on factors that often are at least partly beyond their control. As chapter 2 noted, that stigma can impose substantial financial and psychological costs, undermine individuals' self-esteem, and pressure them into burdensome and unsafe practices.

CHALLENGING SUBORDINATION BASED ON CLASS, RACE, ETHNICITY, GENDER, DISABILITY, AND SEXUAL ORIENTATION

A related justification for prohibiting discrimination based on appearance is that it reinforces group disadvantages. As constitutional scholars including Cass Sunstein and Jack Balkin have argued, practices that systematically stigmatize and subordinate groups prevent members from developing their full capacities.[17] The perpetuation of hierarchies also jeopardizes perceptions of fairness and legitimacy on which well-functioning democracies depend.[18] Like many other forms of discrimination, prejudice based on appearance compounds the disadvantages of already disadvantaged groups, particularly those defined by class, gender, race, ethnicity, age, disability, and sexual orientation.

In *The Case against Perfection*, Harvard philosopher Michael Sandel notes that one byproduct of the contemporary fixation on physical attractiveness is the exacerbation of economic inequality.[19] Appearance both reflects and reinforces class privilege. Prevailing beauty standards disadvantage individuals who lack the time and money to invest in their appearance. Fashion, makeup, health clubs, weight-loss products, and cosmetic procedures all come at a cost. Yet for many consumers, these are not "luxury goods." In a culture where appearance is so often linked to status and self-esteem, low-income individuals pay a substantial price when they cannot afford to meet conventional standards.

Minorities are also held to idealized norms that favor Anglo-American features and to grooming requirements that are unevenly applied.[20] A classic illustration involved an African American machine operator working in a company requiring a "neat and well groomed hairstyle." Her preference for "finger waves" was unacceptable to white supervisors, who found it too "eye-catching." They required her to submit new hairstyle choices for approval, and sanctioned her for wearing an unapproved ponytail above her head, even though it was "neat" and virtually identical to styles worn without objection by white female workers.[21]

Appearance discrimination also compounds gender inequality by reinforcing a double standard and double bind for women. As prior discussion noted, female employees face stricter standards than male employees and can suffer discrimination for being either too attractive or not attractive enough. Women who fail to conform to prevailing norms are often disadvantaged in female-dominated occupations. But in upper-level positions that traditionally have been male-dominated, a beautiful or "sexy" appearance may suggest less competence.[22] The preoccupation with female appearance encourages evaluation of women in terms of sexual attractiveness rather than character, competence, hard work, or achievement.[23] Although some women benefit from their beauty, it is not a stable form of self-esteem.[24] Nor does it generally produce the same social benefits as qualities related to merit.

These sex-based double standards impose disproportionate burdens on women along the lines described in chapter 2. They spend vastly more time and money than men on appearance.[25] So too, about nine out of ten cosmetic surgery patients are female, and they experience the disproportionate health risks that accompany these procedures.[26] A classic illustration of the different pressures facing male and female professionals emerges in political races. John Edwards's willingness to spend $400 on a haircut met widespread ridicule. By contrast, Republican National Committee officials and industry experts found it perfectly reasonable to spend more than $40,000 (about $750 a day) for a traveling hair stylist for Sarah Palin, and another $68,000 for her makeup artist.[27]

Female employees also disproportionately suffer from grooming standards that sexualize the workplace and focus attention on their looks rather than their competence. Some requirements of alluring apparel are of particular concern because they expose women to humiliation, harassment, or, in the case of high heels, physical injury.[28] But even less burdensome standards can reinforce demeaning stereotypes. Examples include the Midwest television station with requirements that its female anchor wear bows and ruffles; the Bikini Espresso, a drive-through coffee bar with waitresses wearing sheer babydoll negligees and matching panties; the Heart Attack Grill, with servers in "naughty nurses" costumes; the Nevada casino with "Barbie doll" dealers; the Little Saigon coffee shops with baristas in six-inch stilettos and fishnet lingerie; and the "Valet of the Dolls" valet parking service with a "wild" and "sexy" all-female staff.[29] As a parking competitor noted, "When people say that it's cute, I tell them to buy a puppy.... When you are dealing with people's cars, it's about your professional standards."[30]

A textbook case of double standards in appearance is the sex discrimination suit by two former cocktail waitresses at the Atlantic City's Borgata Hotel and Casino, noted in chapter 1. As part of their employment contract, the "Borgata Babes" agreed to keep a "clean smile" and an "hourglass figure" that was "height- and weight-appropriate." In implementing that policy, the casino prohibited more than a seven percent weight gain.[31] One of the "Babes" wore a dress size 4 when hired but had a thyroid condition that caused weight fluctuations. When she asked for a size 6 dress, she was told "Borgata Babes don't go up in size."[32] The only exception was for women who got breast implants, who were entitled to a paid recovery period and a bigger bustier.[33] The policy contributed to eating disorders and associated mental and physical health difficulties.[34] The case gained substantial and universally sympathetic media coverage. After interviews with the waitresses appeared on *Good Morning America* and in leading newspapers and magazines, the casino settled their $70 million lawsuit.[35] The terms were confidential, but the public impact was not.

Sexualized grooming standards also penalize gays and lesbians who reject conventional gender norms. A case in point involved Nikki Youngblood, a Florida high school senior who challenged a school board requirement that female students sit for yearbook portraits in a scoop neck dress. Youngblood was a lesbian who had never worn skirts or dresses while a student and wanted to pose in a suit comparable to those worn by male classmates. As her lawyer noted, she was not "a rebellious kid trying to destroy the sanctity of the school yearbook. She simply wanted to appear in her yearbook as herself, not a fluffed-up stereotype of what school administrators thought she should look like."[36]

Sexualized appearance standards reinforce gender stereotypes and gender subordination. In commenting on such prejudices, Victorian novelist Edith Wharton once observed: "Genius is of small use to a woman who does not know how to do her hair."[37] The legacy of those attitudes too often underpins contemporary grooming policies.

PROTECTING SELF-EXPRESSION: PERSONAL LIBERTY AND CULTURAL IDENTITY

A final objection to discrimination based on appearance is that it restricts individuals' right to self-expression. If, as cultural critic Susan Sontag once put it, our "manner of appearing *is* our manner of being," then requiring conformity to conventional norms may significantly restrict personal freedom.[38] The way individuals present themselves to the world often implicates core values and cultural identity. Most courts regard matters of grooming as relatively insignificant concerns, partly because they reflect voluntary characteristics that victims of bias have the power to change. Yet many of these individuals see such self-expression as central to their personal beliefs and religious, racial, or ethnic affiliations. Examples that employers and courts have sometimes failed to accommodate involve Muslim men who refuse to shave, Muslim women who wear headscarves, Jewish men who wear yarmulkes, and African American women who braid their hair.[39] Grooming codes that require women to wear makeup or skirts, prevent men from wearing earrings, and restrict transsexuals' ability to alter their gender identity also reinforce the stereotypes that contribute to gender inequality and homophobia.[40]

Prohibitions on grooming styles associated with particular racial groups, such as Afros, cornrows, or dreadlocks pose special concerns; at issue may be core values of cultural identity.[41] A prominent example is *Rogers v. American Airlines*. There, a female African American employee challenged the airline's prohibition on braided cornrows. In rejecting claims of race and sex discrimination, the court noted that the plaintiff had not demonstrated "that an all-braided hair style is worn exclusively or even predominantly by black people" and had herself adopted the style only "after [it] had been popularized by a white actress."[42] Yet it is not necessary to see braiding as the exclusive or dominant preference of black women to understand its racial significance. The practice has been common among African American women for more than four centuries and has often served as an expression of racial pride.[43] To the *Rogers* court, and others that have followed its approach, hairstyle has seemed "a matter of relatively low importance."[44] But that has not been the view of historians who have studied the issue, employees who have been willing to litigate it, and managers who have chosen to fight back.[45] "Why is this so important to you?" one can almost hear the judges asking the plaintiff in *Rogers*.[46] But if they had also questioned why it should be so important to her employer, the stakes might have been more apparent.

The same is true for other appearance-related choices that are not necessarily tied to racial or ethnic identity. Hair length, facial hair, earrings, tattoos, and piercings have been such issues, and they have accounted for longstanding controversies. Federal judges on both sides of these issues have denounced them as trivial. Some have ridiculed educators and employers who view such grooming choices as planting the "seeds of violence and rebellion."[47] Other judges have been frustrated by plaintiffs who clutter up the courts with claims that high school hairstyles have "constitutional signifi-cance."[48] Yet the sheer number of public and private institutions that have sought to regulate in the area, and the number of individuals and civil liberties organizations willing to spend scarce resources challenging those regulations, suggest the stakes to those involved. At issue have been cultural values and ideological commitments of considerable significance. Even when the particular requirement seems inconsequential, the broader principle is not. Why should Subway restaurants have the right to decide that one piercing on employees is acceptable but two are not?[49]

In short, individual examples of appearance discrimination often seem insignificant, but their cumulative effect is anything but. Such prejudice violates merit principles, undermines equal opportunity, exacerbates stigma, erodes self-esteem, restricts individual liberty, and reinforces disadvantages based on class, race, ethnicity, sex, and sexual orientation. Discrimination based on appearance compro-mises the same values of personal dignity and social equality as other forms of discrimination that are now illegal. What accounts for the difference in treatment?

THE RATIONALE FOR DISCRIMINATION AND RESISTANCE
TO PROHIBITIONS

Public tolerance of appearance-related prejudice may in part reflect inadequate understandings of its frequency or conse-quences. Such bias often operates at unconscious levels and neither the perpetrator nor the victim may be aware of its extent. Nor do most victims identify as a cohesive group. Unlike sex, race, or ethnicity, "unattractiveness" falls on a continuum and who even falls within that category can be open to dispute. Given the stigma involved, few want to claim that status.[50] Apart from the relatively small number of individuals involved in the "fat acceptance" movement, no organized constituency mobilizes around discrimination based on appearance. Nor are many legal scholars and policy makers sensitive to the causes and consequences of such bias. For example, in distinguishing among types of prejudice, one prominent constitutional law expert asserted: "Although aversions and attractions based on physical attractiveness are common, they usually neither derive from nor reinforce biases, ideals, or stereotypes."[51] Yet as the preceding summary made clear, all research is to the contrary.

Other commentators, such as Stanford Law Professor Richard Ford, take a comparative perspective. Appearance discrimination, he argues, "is rarely as explicit or as severe as racism. 'Fat' and 'ugly' people...don't think of themselves as a discrete social group," and "are spread pretty evenly across families and social classes, so the ill effects of bias against them are often ameliorated by other social advantages." Accordingly, "[w]eightism and lookism aren't problems of social order or of *social* injustice."[52] But why not? Women are distributed across classes in ways that reduce the effects of bias. That does not make the social injustice of gender discrimination any less pronounced. Moreover, Ford is simply wrong about the distributional consequences. Overweight individuals are the most common targets of appearance discrimination, and as prior discussion indicated, they are overrepresented among low-income and minority groups.

So too, discrimination based on appearance appears at least as widespread as other forms of prohibited bias, and many Americans believe that something should be done about it. In national surveys, between 12 and 16 percent of workers report that they have been subject to appearance-related discrimination.[53] That percentage is comparable to, or greater than those reporting other forms of discrimination, such as that based on sex (12–19 percent), race (12 percent), age (9–14 percent), or religious or ethnic bias (3 percent).[54] So too, almost half of surveyed Americans believe that obese workers suffer discrimination in the workplace, a higher figure than for groups that are protected by antidiscrimination laws.[55] When asked about legal remedies, the responses are close to evenly divided. Thirty-nine percent of workers think that employers "should have the right to deny employment to someone based on appearance, including weight, clothing, piercing... or hair style." By contrast, 33 percent believe that workers who are "unattractive, overweight, or generally look or dress unconventionally, should be given special government legal protection such as that given persons with disabilities."[56]

Yet framing the questions in those terms may have skewed the results. Experience with surveys on related issues indicates that people respond less favorably to strategies described as special treatment than those described as equalizing opportunities.[57] Asking whether the unattractive should get special protection is likely to get less support than asking whether workers should have the right not to be discriminated against because of their appearance. It also bears note that public opinion varies considerably by sex and race. Women are much less likely than men to agree that employers should have the right to discriminate based on looks (32 percent compared to 46 percent), and nonwhites are much less willing to allow discrimination than whites (24 percent compared to 41 percent). Such disparities may reflect the fact, noted earlier, that appearance-related bias has a disproportionate impact on already disadvantaged groups.

Among individuals who oppose a prohibition on such bias, a main concern is that appearance may be relevant to job performance. For example, obesity is widely assumed to reflect health and physical capabilities, which can affect absenteeism, effectiveness, and medical insurance costs. Yet in employment cases challenging weight discrimination, employees often have shown that their obesity caused no performance difficulties or additional expense.[58] As one leading expert has noted, "The extent to which overweight people have difficulty in obtaining work goes far beyond what can be justified by medical data."[59]

One of the few reported cases involving discrimination based on health costs concerned a woman who was denied employment by Xerox because the corporation's doctor determined that she presented a significant risk to the company's disability and life insurance programs. Yet the plaintiff had neither a history of health difficulties nor any previous performance problems. Although a New York court ultimately held that state disability law protected her from such discrimination, the outcome would have been different in other jurisdictions that lack such expansive statutory protections.[60] And the absence of such protections is hard to reconcile with rulings in other discrimination contexts that prevent denial of important individual rights on the basis of highly imperfect statistical correlations.[61] If the true concern is employee health not appearance, then, as research summarized in chapters 2 and 7 indicates, employers' focus should be on fitness, not simply weight.

To some commentators, however, when prejudice based on appearance involves seemingly voluntary characteristics, such as weight, it appears less offensive than other forms of discrimination. As one expert notes, "[W]e're running out of [groups] that we're allowed to hate and to feel superior to.... Fatness is the one thing left that seems to be a person's fault—[even though]...it isn't."[62] Permitting discrimination on that basis seems justifiable to those who believe that overweight individuals can and should modify their condition. In Ford's view, "obesity causes illness and exacerbates disease," and "losing weight...for most [people is] only moderately challenging."[63] He offers no support for that rosy view of dieting, and virtually all expert opinions and statistical surveys are to the contrary. Only about 5 percent of dieters manage to achieve long-term weight loss, and those who do frequently require surgical and lifestyle interventions that are anything but moderate.[64] Although the public health community is divided on other issues, there is nearly universal agreement that discrimination against fat people is a singularly unjust and ineffective way to deal with obesity; stigma is more likely to trigger than discourage overeating.[65]

A related business concern is that appearance will influence an employee's credibility and an employer's image. That was the rationale for a fitness company's denial of a franchise to Jennifer Portnick, a 240-pound aerobics instructor, in the case described in chapter 1.[66] Similarly, Sharon Russell, an obese nursing school student, was expelled not because of her record but because school administrators worried that she would provide a poor "role model [for] good health habits" when counseling patients about nutrition.[67]

Yet concerns about employee credibility often reflect more about the prejudices of the employer than about the behavior of customers or patients. We do not refuse medical education or doctors' licenses to individuals who smoke or are overweight on the assumption that they cannot counsel patients about health. Nor is nutrition counseling an integral part of most nursing positions. Russell went on to graduate from another school, to obtain sympathetic national news coverage, and to have a highly successful career as an administrator in a Florida children's hospital.[68] So too, we should not assume, in a country where two-thirds of adults are classified as overweight, that most aerobics students would be deterred rather than inspired by an instructor who looked like them, but was fit and toned. In fact, a growing number of fitness classes are expressly marketing themselves to full-bodied women.[69] Portnick also received sympathetic media treatment and went on to teach successfully at another organization. Her students realized what the company belatedly acknowledged when reversing its policy on appearance: "people of varying weights [can] be fit."[70]

For some goods and services, however, employees' attractiveness can be an effective selling point, and part of a strategy to "brand" the seller through a certain look.[71] According to a spokesperson for the Borgata Hotel Casino and Spa, its weight limits and periodic "weigh-in" requirements for "Borgata Babes" cocktail waitresses responded to market demands: "Our customers like being served by an attractive cocktail server."[72] Analogous assumptions evidently underpinned the order by a L'Oreal cosmetic store manager to "[g]et me somebody hot" for a sales position; Abercrombie and Fitch's notorious policy of hiring sexually attractive, "classic American," white salespersons; and the preference by certain bars and restaurants for staff that are "young" and "trendy" or not "too ethnic."[73] If an employee has the right to assert identity through appearance, why shouldn't an employer? As one owner of a Santa Cruz restaurant put it, "If someone has 14 earrings in their ears and their nose—and who knows where else—and spiky green hair and smells like a skunk, I don't know why I have to hire them."[74] Other commentators are similarly sympathetic to the elite hotels' desire for "elegance and refinement, not the…big hair and press-on nails" of the "working class."[75] "So You Want to Hire the Beautiful," ran the title of a *Business Week* column. "Well, Why Not?"[76]

Well, to start with, it may be illegal if employers' definition of beauty has anything to do with race, ethnicity, sex, age, or disability. Discrimination on the basis of those criteria is unlawful under federal and state statutes, as some of the businesses mentioned above have discovered.[77] Moreover, the reasons why antidiscrimination law generally does not permit customer preferences as a defense apply equally to bias based on appearance even if it does not involve race, sex, age, or disability. Those preferences generally reflect and reinforce precisely the attitudes that society is seeking to eliminate. During the early Civil Rights era, Southern employers often argued that hiring blacks would be financially ruinous; white customers would go elsewhere. In rejecting such customer preference defenses, Congress and the courts recognized that the most effective way of combating prejudice was to deprive people of the option to indulge it.

Sex has been treated somewhat differently. Federal discrimination law and its state analogues provide an exception from liability if sex is a "bona fide occupational qualification reasonably necessary to the normal operation of that particular business or enterprise."[78] But Equal Employment Opportunity Commission guidelines and court decisions have interpreted that exception narrowly and have not viewed customer preference as a business necessity except for a limited category of occupations requiring privacy, authenticity, or sexually explicit entertainment.[79] During the 1970s and 1980s, major airlines argued that passengers, particularly predominantly male business travelers, preferred attractive female flight attendants. According to the airlines, those preferences made sex a bona fide occupational qualification and exempted them from antidiscrimination requirements. In rejecting that claim, courts reasoned that only if sexual allure was the "essence" of the job should employers be allowed to select workers on that basis, and airlines were not flying bordellos.[80] Allowing sex-based preferences in broader circumstances would perpetuate the biases the statute aimed to challenge.

This approach is not without difficulty in some contemporary contexts involving appearance-related discrimination. For example, what is the "essence" of the job for television newscasters? How much does attractiveness matter and what if viewers set higher standards for women than men? In one celebrated case, a court rejected news anchor Christine Craft's claim that she was unlawfully terminated because she was "too old, too unattractive, and not deferential enough to men."[81] Under the court's analysis, viewer ratings were relevant to job performance.[82] By that logic, it would seem perfectly permissible for television media to require that women, but not men, look young and attractive, because viewers will accept a Walter Cronkite or Larry King, but not the female equivalent. Yet such double standards readily become self-perpetuating. Audiences expect youth and beauty in female newscasters in part because they lack frequent exposure to an alternative: women who gained those positions through merit-related qualifications. A true commitment to equal opportunity argues for rejecting customer preferences as a defense except where appearance is essential to the occupation, such as modeling, acting, or sexual entertainment. In contexts where the necessity of attractiveness is open to dispute, employers should have to demonstrate, not simply assert its importance.

Similar logic applies to grooming codes. As subsequent discussion reflects, courts have sometimes permitted sexually specific grooming codes if they reflect generally accepted community standards, involve no fundamental rights, or impose no disproportionate burdens on women or men. But such permission should be granted less frequently than is now the case. Customers of a "family restaurant" who want what a Hooters' spokeswoman described as a "little good clean wholesome female sexuality" are no more worthy of deference than the Southern whites in the 1960s who didn't want to buy from blacks, or the male airline passengers in the 1970s who liked stewardesses in hot pants.[83]

A similarly problematic justification for discriminating on the basis of appearance is that it may reflect other relevant traits. Grooming is often taken as a "good indicator" of virtues such as industriousness and sociability.[84] Yet what makes some grooming codes objectionable is not that they prescribe neatness, which could correlate with performance-related traits, but that they reinforce sex stereotypes and unnecessarily restrict self-expression. Neither empirical research nor common sense suggests that men who wear earrings or women who decline to wear nail polish or high heels are less industrious. Employers' justifiable concerns can be met by antidiscrimination provisions that permit regulation of health and hygiene, but that do not institutionalize gender inequalities. Judged on that basis, a policy preventing Santa Cruz employees from "smell[ing] like a skunk" stands on different footing than casino requirements of hourglass figures, teased hair, and makeup.[85] Only the latter reflects traditional sex-based stereotypes, imposes disproportionate burdens on women, and bears no demonstrable relationship to job performance. Indeed, in the case against Harrah's casino described in Chapter 1, the bartender who refused to wear makeup had consistently received glowing evaluations from supervisors and customers during her twenty-year service.[86]

Another way to accommodate employer concerns, reflected in the Santa Cruz ordinance, is to prohibit only discrimination on the basis of a "physical characteristic" that arises from birth, accident, disease, or other events outside of the individual's control.[87] The logic underlying this approach is self-evident. Bias against the unattractive seems most unjust when it involves features that people cannot readily alter. Yet American antidiscrimination law is not so restrictive. It protects individuals from prejudice based on religious affiliations that are chosen and on disabilities such as tobacco-related medical conditions that individuals have power to affect. Bias based on voluntary characteristics often offends principles of equal opportunity and personal liberty. Moreover, one of the most common forms of appearance discrimination involves weight, which has both biological and behavioral roots, and is far more difficult to control than is commonly assumed.

A final cluster of arguments against prohibiting appearance discrimination is pragmatic. To many commentators, the preference for attractiveness appears natural and immutable in a way that other forms of bias do not. Some cite sociobiological explanations reviewed in chapter 2. Attempting to ban discrimination based on such deeply rooted preferences strikes these observers as impractical and imprudent. In their view, "some aspects of what we consider physically attractive are...hardwired.... [T]he taste for physical beauty is unfair. But legal intervention is unlikely to eliminate it."[88]

It may also risk trivializing other more serious forms of bias. Some courts and commentators, for example, have worried that allowing appearance-discrimination claims under civil rights and disability laws will undermine these statutes' effectiveness in assisting individuals with more severe disadvantages.[89] Richard Ford voices a common objection:

> [T]here are practical limits of human attention and sympathy. The good-natured humanitarian who listens attentively to the first claim of social injustice will become an impatient curmudgeon after multiple similar admonishments.... And a business community united in frustration at a bloated civil rights regime could become a powerful political force for reform or even repeal.... The growing number of social groups making claims to civil rights protection threatens the political and practical viability of civil rights for those who need them most.[90]

Mario Cuomo put the point succinctly in debates over a proposed New York law banning discrimination based on appearance. This was "one law too many."[91] If the goal is ensuring merit-based employment decisions, where is the stopping point? As an editorial in *The New Republic* asked, should we ban "prejudice on the basis of a whiny voice?...What about 'grouch liberation'?"[92] Social critic Andrew Sullivan continued the parody in the London *Sunday Times*: "But by the time you've finished preventing discrimination against the ugly, the short, the skinny, the bald, the knobbly-kneed, the flat-chested and the stupid, you're living in a totalitarian state."[93] Other hypothetical candidates for the proverbial parade of horribles include a fast-food restaurant in a black neighborhood forced to employ a skinhead wearing a "White Power" t-shirt, a newspaper required to offer its "ace crime reporter" position to a transvestite, and workplace regulations banning "fat jokes."[94] According to law professor Michael Selmi, "Although most slippery slopes are not as slippery as they appear, this one actually [is]."[95]

Part of the problem is that attractiveness and grooming standards fall along a continuum. How would employers or courts determine what aspects of appearance are entitled to protection? As one judge put it, "No Court can be expected to create a standard on such vagaries as attractiveness."[96] "Will there be a national standard of attractiveness established by EEOC rulemaking?" wonders the author of "Civil Rights for the Aesthetically-Challenged." "Will beauty contest judges go on to find lucrative careers as expert witnesses in these cases?"[97] Commentators from all points on the political spectrum worry that appearance-discrimination statutes will result in "litigiousness run wild," impose "untold costs" on businesses, and erode support for other legislation prohibiting "truly invidious discrimination."[98]

If the objective is greater protection for employee appearance in the workplace, then skeptics also question whether the solution lies in transferring control "from one set of authority figures (employers) to another (judges, officials)."[99] An increasingly conservative federal bench has plenty of members such as Richard Posner who believe that the law on sex stereotypes has already "gone off the tracks" in reasoning "as if there were a federally protected right for male workers to wear nail polish...and mince about in high heels."[100] Another trial judge expressed similar views: courts "have too much to do" to become embroiled in petty disputes about where women can and can't wear pants.[101]

Critics also have questioned the willingness and ability of discrimination victims to take advantage of legal remedies. Won't the same stigma that underlies biased treatment also prevent individuals from challenging it? As one civil rights attorney notes, people are unlikely "to say they were wronged because they are ugly."[102] Another adds that most employers will be equally unlikely to acknowledge unattractiveness as the reason for an adverse decision; they will offer a "more neutral reason" that is hard to disprove.[103]

Although such concerns are not without force, neither do they justify the prevailing tolerance for appearance discrimination in contemporary legal doctrine and social practices. An initial difficulty lies in critics' assumption that prejudice based on appearance is more natural and harder to eradicate than other forms of bias. In fact, considerable evidence suggests that in-group favoritism—the preferences that individuals feel for those who are like them in salient respects such as race, sex, and ethnicity—are also deeply rooted.[104] *Plessy v. Ferguson*, the shameful 1896 Supreme Court decision that affirmed "separate but equal" racial policies, assumed that segregation was a natural desire.[105] Opponents of civil rights statutes in the 1960s similarly insisted that "you can't legislate morality" on matters like racial tolerance. But we can legislate conduct, and a half century's experience makes clear that changes in attitudes can follow. Providing legal forums to expose injustice and break down racial segregation has helped to transform cultural perceptions and practices. A half century ago, a majority of Americans surveyed thought that the Supreme Court's ruling in *Brown v. Board of Education* prohibiting school segregation had "caused a lot more trouble than it was worth."[106] Today, only 11 percent share that view, and the ruling is widely regarded as one of the Court's finest moments.[107] Legislation such as the American with Disabilities Act also has had powerful positive effects on attitudes about the capacities of disabled individuals.[108] And in less than a decade, views on gay and lesbian relationships have shifted dramatically, partly in response to laws that have helped to publicize injustice and normalize same-sex orientation.[109]

Similar initiatives on appearance discrimination could result in similar shifts in popular opinion and practices. The point is not to equate all forms of discrimination or to deny that bias raises greater concern when it is based on innate rather than voluntary characteristics. The point rather is that even forms of prejudice assumed to be hardwired have in fact been profoundly influenced by law. There is no reason to believe that appearance discrimination would be different.

Nor is there reason to believe that prohibiting such discrimination would erode support for other civil rights legislation. Jurisdictions with such ordinances, such as Santa Cruz, San Francisco, Madison (WI), and the District of Columbia, are not known for problems either of "totalitarianism" or backlash against antidiscrimination policies. There are, to be sure, limits to how far such policies can be extended without diminishing their moral force. But no evidence suggests that we have reached that limit. Neither is it likely that prohibitions on appearance discrimination would unleash a barrage of loony litigation. As the research summarized in chapter 6 indicates, jurisdictions that have such laws report relatively few complaints. Cities and counties average between zero and nine cases a year, and Michigan averages about thirty, only one of which ends up in court. Moreover, most complaints allege other violations in addition to from appearance discrimination, so they could be brought even without such ordinances. Given the costs and difficulties of proving bias, and the qualifications built into current legal prohibitions, their enforcement has proven far less burdensome than opponents have feared.

Of course, legal requirements that ask too much of human nature may lack moral authority and undermine the legitimacy of legal institutions. Prohibition is a textbook case. But for every one of these examples, there is always a counterexample. Many laws that have been widely ignored or resisted at the outset have gradually acquired legitimacy and reshaped public values. Indeed, much of American civil rights legislation is a case in point. By providing a forum to air injustice, law can be a powerful catalyst for social change. Although stigma and evidentiary difficulties will prevent most victims of appearance related bias from coming forward, the same is true in other discrimination contexts. Even laws that are notoriously underenforced can serve a crucial role in designating public norms, deterring violations, and affirming social ideals.[110]

THE PARALLEL OF SEXUAL HARASSMENT

In predicting the impact of expanded prohibitions on appearance bias, the nation's experience with sexual harassment is instructive. For centuries, women were harassed, but the law provided neither a label nor a remedy. In the mid-1980s, the Supreme Court agreed with the Equal Employment Opportunity Commission that sexual harassment was a form of sex discrimination that was actionable under federal civil rights law.[111] The initial reception was often less than enthusiastic. Many men who dominated the upper levels of employment, judicial, and policy circles were skeptical that sexual overtures and workplace banter constituted significant problems and that women were, or should be, offended. As one manager put it in a 1980s survey by the *Harvard Business Review*, "I have never been harassed but I would welcome the opportunity."[112] Conservative critics had a field day with the occasional frivolous case—women who were offended by photographs of a bikini-clad wife, copies of *Playboy*, or a Goya portrait of a nude.[113] So too, many federal judges were unpersuaded that courts were the appropriate forum to cope with sexual "horseplay." In their view, the civil rights law was not meant to be a "clean language act" or a remedy for the "petty slights suffered by the hypersensitive."[114] One trial judge expressed common views with uncommon candor: "So, we will have to hear [your complaint], but the court doesn't think too much of it."[115]

In fact, the principal problem with sexual harassment law has turned out to be underreporting, not overreaction. Only a small percentage of those experiencing abuse make any complaints, and far fewer can afford the financial and psychological costs of litigation.[116] Yet despite such underenforcement, the opportunity for legal remedies has made an enormous difference in deterring and redressing harassment. The public has grown more aware of the costs of such abuse both for employees and employers, including economic and psychological injuries, decreased productivity, and increased turnover.[117] Strategies designed to prevent litigation such as training programs and internal complaint procedures have all helped to reshape understandings of unacceptable conduct.

THE CONTRIBUTIONS OF LAW

Similar results might follow if more jurisdictions enacted prohibitions on appearance discrimination. Additional complaints like those involving the overweight nursing student and aerobics instructor could build public awareness of the injustice of such bias and challenge the stereotypes underlying it. The outcome in the Jazzercise case underscores the distinction between overweight and unfit. That distinction is important for the public to grasp in light of growing evidence indicating that unfitness is more predictive of health difficulties than weight alone.[118] So too, the adverse publicity concerning the Borgata Babes weigh-in policy focused useful attention on our culture's unrealistic female body images and their link to eating disorders. In some cases, employers have abandoned appearance requirements as a result of well-publicized legal claims. Both Harrah's Casino and Continental Airlines dropped their makeup mandates in the wake of unsympathetic media coverage.[119] Litigation forced other Atlantic City casinos to abandon requirements of revealing uniforms and high heels.[120] To settle the Florida graduation photo controversy, the local school board created an appeal process allowing students to show "good cause" why they should not have to follow the specified yearbook-picture dress code. Other schools also modified their codes to eliminate "ultra-feminine" requirements.[121]

But not everyone lives happily ever after. Nikki Youngblood lost her case in the trial court and had no photo in her yearbook; other students who lack free legal assistance or face uncompromising school boards remain subject to similar, often more restrictive daily dress codes.[122] The Borgata plaintiffs settled their case, but the casino's policy remained in force and other workers were unprotected.[123] Darlene Jespersen's refusal to "fix" her face cost her the job she loved. Such cases illustrate the need for a law banning such appearance discrimination in the first instance. Our prejudices run deep, and while law can never eliminate them entirely, it can do more to address at least the worst abuses.

CHAPTER SIX

Legal Frameworks

THE LEGAL REGULATION of appearance has a long and unbecoming history. Early regulation reflected class and gender bias. As noted earlier, European sumptuary laws prohibited all but the aristocracy from wearing certain fabrics, colors, and garments; other statutes punished women who used false hair, makeup, and high-heeled shoes to seduce a man into marriage.[1] In the United States, early legislation focused mainly on decorum; most jurisdictions banned public display of clothing (or lack of clothing) that was considered indecent.[2] Dress reform efforts by nineteenth-century women's rights advocates ran afoul of ordinances forbidding women from wearing divided "harem" skirts and "knickerbockers," or appearing out of doors without a corset.[3] A number of jurisdictions also prohibited "ugly" or "unsightly" individuals from appearing in public.[4]

Contemporary defenses of decorum are more limited, but have not entirely vanished. In 2005, the Virginia legislature considered a provision modeled on an earlier Louisiana statute prohibiting the intentional display of "below waist undergarments...in a lewd or indecent manner."[5] The legislation targeted male adolescents who wore sagging pants and female teens who flaunted thongs. Sponsors billed such measures as a "vote for character"; as one Louisiana legislator put it, "if we pull up their pants, we can lift their minds while we're at it."[6]

Yet those who welcome criminal penalties in support of propriety often oppose civil remedies in support of equality. Proposals to ban discrimination on the basis of appearance evoke visions of "litigiousness run wild."[7] Commentators from all points on the political spectrum worry that appearance discrimination statutes will impose "untold costs" on businesses and erode support for other legislation prohibiting "truly invidious discrimination."[8] Such "gauzy idealism" assertedly threatens the "practical viability" of more deserving civil rights claims.[9]

Yet such criticisms have proceeded without factual foundation. To assess their validity, this chapter offers the first systematic research on how appearance-related protections actually work. Its review of claims under both general antidiscrimination statutes, and more specific laws on appearance, undercuts critics' apocalyptic assertions.

THE LIMITATIONS OF PREVAILING LEGAL FRAMEWORKS

In jurisdictions that do not explicitly prohibit appearance discrimination, victims have occasionally sought relief under more general legal protections. The most common are: constitutional guarantees of free speech and religious expression; statutes banning employment discrimination based on sex, race, ethnicity, and religion; and legislation prohibiting discrimination based on disability. All have proven seriously inadequate.

Constitutional Challenges

Challenges to appearance regulation based on freedom of speech generally have been unsuccessful except when religion is involved. Even then, the results have been mixed and inconsistent. So for example, courts have found a sufficiently compelling interest to uphold bans on religious jewelry or clothing for police but not teachers; by contrast, other judges have struck down prohibitions on religiously affiliated hairstyles for police but upheld bans on head-scarves for teachers.[10] The extent of constitutional protection has been limited both by the requirement of state action and by the deference that courts typically extend to those acting on the state's behalf. The Due Process Clause of the Fifth and Fourteenth Amendments protects liberty interests only against regulation by the public, not the private, sector. The respect given to state decisions is apparent in a 1976 grooming case that set the tone for many to follow. In *Tardif v. Quinn*, a public high school official fired a teacher because he disapproved of the length of her skirt. She sued, claiming that her termination violated liberty interests protected under the Constitution's Due Process Clause. The trial court found that her skirt was within reasonable limits, was not lewd, and was no shorter than outfits worn by other professional women. Nor did it have any demonstrably "adverse effect on her students" or her teaching. Despite such findings, the court of appeals ruled that the government's interest in approving a teacher's image outweighed her personal interest in defining her own appearance.[11] What exactly that interest in image was remains unclear, given its lack of connection to classroom effectiveness. On similarly strained reasoning, other courts have sustained a school's ban on Muslims' head covering, a juvenile detention center's requirement of a "Brooks Brothers look for female staff," and police departments' prohibitions on long hair or on earrings worn only when officers are off duty.[12]

Underlying these decisions is an assumption similar to that expressed by the distinguished British philosopher H. L. A. Hart: "[T]he rules of...dress...occupy a relatively low place in the scale of serious importance. They may be tiresome to follow, but they do not demand great sacrifice: no great pressure is exerted to obtain conformity and no great alterations in other areas of social life would follow if they were not observed.[13] For an Oxford professor this may have been true. But for many Americans, the costs of conformity are more substantial. And prohibiting rules that objectify women is likely to have at least some influence on gender roles in other areas of social life.

Statutory Challenges Based on Sex, Race, and Religious Discrimination

A second line of challenges to appearance discrimination has involved sex-neutral grooming requirements applied on a sex-specific basis, often termed "sex-plus" requirements. Common examples include prohibitions on long hair or earrings only for men or requirements of makeup only for women. These challenges build on cases not involving appearance where disparate treatment has been viewed as discrimination on the basis of sex in violation of Title VII of the 1964 Civil Rights Act.[14] So, for example, a leading Supreme Court case held unlawful an employer's denial of job opportunities for women, but not men, with preschool children.[15] However, courts have generally allowed grooming rules applicable to only one sex on the assumption that Congress intended to protect "equality of employment opportunities," not to prevent regulations requiring both sexes to conform to "generally accepted community standards."[16]

On that premise, grooming codes have been permissible as long as they involve no immutable characteristics, no fundamental rights, and no greater burden for one sex than the other. Cases finding unequal burdens have included regulations that required only women to be thin and attractive or to wear uniforms.[17] But courts have also failed to perceive inequalities despite obvious differences in the effort and expense required for men and women to comply with appearance standards. The Harrah's Casino's makeup requirement is a case in point.[18] Courts have also failed to question the sex stereotypes underlying conventional "community standards" and to demand a reasonable business justification for employers' restrictions. Typical cases have upheld the termination of a male optometrist for wearing a small earring and casino dealers for wearing ponytails concealed inside their collars despite the absence of any evidence that these grooming preferences affected their work or customer relations.[19]

The problem with this prevailing approach to appearance regulation is not only that judges often seem clueless about the disproportionate demands that many codes impose on women. The difficulty is also that a framework comparing male and female burdens fails to capture all of what makes these regulations objectionable. Darlene Jespersen resisted Harrah's makeup requirement not because it took more time and money for her to be presentable than her male counterparts, but because she felt that being "dolled up" was degrading and undermined her credibility with unruly customers. Dress codes that require women to wear alluring outfits and high heels are problematic for similar reasons, regardless of the standards for men.[20]

In other contexts, courts have recognized that sexualizing women in the workplace can constitute sex discrimination. For example, where an accountant claimed that she was denied a partnership because of sex-based stereotypes, the Supreme Court viewed supervisors' references to her need to "'dress more femininely, wear make-up, have her hair styled, and wear jewelry'" as evidence of unlawful gender bias.[21] Courts' failure to apply the same analysis to grooming codes points up a serious inadequacy in prevailing law.[22]

Similar limitations are applicable to decisions involving appearance-related discrimination based on race or religion. Typical cases involve grooming requirements that have a differential impact on certain racial groups or that are inconsistent with religious beliefs and practices. As in the context of constitutional challenges, courts interpreting civil rights statutes have been most sympathetic to claims involving religion. So, for example, some employers have been required to accommodate Muslim employees' desire to wear head coverings (hijabs) or beards.[23] However, workers have generally not succeeded in challenging bans on dreadlocks or cornrows on grounds that they are racially discriminatory.[24] Moreover, many courts have been highly deferential to employers' business justifications for restrictions. Costco was allowed to ban facial piercings consistent with an employee's religious beliefs because of the undue hardship that accommodation would assertedly cause to the company's public image.[25] Sikh employees who claimed religious reasons for wearing turbans or beards could be denied supervisory positions on the ground that a family restaurant was entitled to project a " 'clean cut' image" and to worry that customers might find a bearded manager "unsanitary."[26]

Discrimination Based on Disability

One further basis for challenges to appearance discrimination involves the federal Americans with Disabilities Act (ADA) and Rehabilitation Act. They prohibit discrimination against "qualified" disabled individuals, defined as those able to "perform essential [job] functions" "with or without reasonable accommodation."[27] To qualify as disabled under these acts, individuals must be "substantially limit[ed]" in a "major life activit[y]" by a "physical or mental impairment," have "a record of…impairment," or be "regarded as impaired," whether or not the perceived impairment limits a major life activity.[28] States have comparable statutes, which vary in scope but typically define disability in similarly restrictive terms.[29]

Most appearance-related disability claims have involved overweight or obese individuals, and the vast majority of these have been unsuccessful. In a recent survey of weight-related cases in which the complainant received some relief, only 13 percent proceeded under the ADA and only 4 percent under other disability law.[30] The Equal Employment Opportunity Commission Interpretive Guidance on the ADA states that, except in rare circumstances, obesity is not a disabling impairment.[31] Only morbid obesity (100 percent over average weight), caused by a physiological disorder (such as a thyroid dysfunction) will qualify, a limitation that excludes over 95 percent of obese individuals.[32] Although a small minority of state and local laws offers broader protection than the federal statute, all but a few victims of weight discrimination fall into the "disability gap": they are "either too disabled to be qualified for their jobs or insufficiently disabled to merit statutory protection."[33] So too, although recent amendments to the ADA reverse some restrictive judicial interpretations of what constitutes a perceived impairment, these reforms are unlikely to address the major barriers to relief.[34]

The relatively rare cases of successful plaintiffs indicate why a remedy for weight discrimination is necessary. An example is Bonnie Cook, who, for five years, satisfactorily performed her work as an aide at a Rhode Island residential center for severely retarded children. A daughter's illness forced her resignation. When she reapplied for her former position, the center denied her application on the ground that her morbid obesity made her "susceptible" to a host of health problems. But her weight was the same as it had been during her prior period of satisfactory employment, a physical exam found no impairments that would interfere with her job performance, and her condition was the result of a metabolic dysfunction. Accordingly, a federal court ruled that the Rehabilitation Act entitled her to reinstatement and $100,000 in punitive damages.[35] In commenting on the verdict, the executive director of the American Civil Liberties Union office representing Cook noted: "'The irony...is that we have an agency that has worked hard to change public attitudes toward the mentally disabled and here they are discriminating against someone based on all the stereotypes of obesity.'" Cook herself drew a more straightforward lesson: "'[P]eople shouldn't judge others because of how they look. What's important is whether or not they can do the job.'"[36] In a similar case, a morbidly obese teacher was allowed to proceed against a college that refused to renew her contract. The court held that a jury could find that the college's reason involved not inadequate performance but stereotypical perceptions that overweight professors were "less disciplined and less intelligent" than those of average weight.[37]

In most cases, however, plaintiffs lose even when they present compelling evidence of weight discrimination. Victims are unsuccessful because they fail to show that they are substantially impaired in life activities or viewed as impaired, or that their condition is caused by a physiological disorder.[38] A typical example involved a morbidly obese woman who lost her job when her employer moved to a smaller office. Her supervisor explained that "there was no room" for such a "'big girl'" in the new location. However, according to the court's analysis, she was not entitled to reinstatement, given the absence of proof that obesity limited her life activities or that her employer perceived her weight as disabling.[39] Also unprotected are individuals who allege wrongful termination due to employers' perceptions that overweight employees do not fit their organization's "corporate image," or lack the discipline necessary to inspire "respect."[40]

As currently interpreted, federal and state disability laws offer a highly inadequate response to weight-related discrimination. By excluding all but the extremely obese, these statutes deny protection in contexts where the discrimination is most likely to be irrational—cases in which moderate obesity or overweight does not compromise job performance and impair major life activities. By limiting relief to complainants who can demonstrate actual or perceived impairment, these statutes leave unprotected many competent workers and leave unchallenged stereotypes of incapacity that give rise to discrimination.[41] Such stereotypes reflect the same forms of bias that prompted passage of disability statutes in the first instance, and that diminish the life opportunities of those affected. Indeed, some research suggests that stigma based on weight is greater than that based on physical handicap.[42] Clearly, a different approach is necessary to address the inequities of weight-related bias.

PROHIBITIONS ON APPEARANCE DISCRIMINATION

Any informed judgment about the law's capacity to cope with appearance discrimination requires a better understanding of how explicit prohibitions play out in practice. To that end, the following analysis offers the first systematic research concerning laws prohibiting such discrimination.

These prohibitions vary in scope and impact. Michigan included height and weight as prohibited forms of discrimination in 1975; Urbana, Illinois, enacted a general prohibition on appearance discrimination in 1979, and the District of Columbia added appearance discrimination to its civil rights law in 1982. The four other American jurisdictions with such bans enacted them in the 1990s and 2000s. Two of the laws (Michigan and San Francisco) cover only height and weight, and one (Santa Cruz) covers only involuntary physical characteristics. The others prohibit appearance discrimination generally but permit reasonable grooming rules. Remedies also differ. One ordinance authorizes fines not to exceed $500 in cases brought only by the city attorney (Urbana). Other laws allow victims to recover reasonable compensatory damages and attorneys' fees (Santa Cruz, Madison), and two permit fines between $10,000 and $50,000 (Michigan and the District of Columbia). Enforcement activity varies from no complaints over fifteen years (Santa Cruz), to an average of thirty a year (Michigan), but many of these complaints involve other grounds in addition to appearance. No jurisdiction has experienced the flood of frivolous litigation and business backlash that critics have predicted.

Local Ordinances: Santa Cruz, Urbana, San Francisco, the District of Columbia, Howard County, and Madison

The most well-publicized prohibition on appearance-related bias is a 1992 ordinance in Santa Cruz, California. As initially proposed, the ordinance banned discrimination based on a variety of factors, including height, weight, and appearance.[43] After an onslaught of protests and negative publicity, the Santa Cruz City Council replaced "appearance" with "physical characteristic," defined as any condition "which is from birth, accident, or disease, or from any natural physical development, or any other event outside the control of that person." Excluded from coverage were characteristics that would "present a danger to the health, welfare or safety of any individual." Courts may grant "appropriate" remedies including compensatory damages, attorneys' fees, and injunctive relief.[44]

As amended, the ordinance permits employers to discriminate on the basis of voluntary aspects of appearance, a fact omitted by many of the law's critics. One of their favorite examples of what the law would protect was a case involving a psychiatric aide with purple hair, five earrings, and a nose ring; it was a tongue piercing that finally cost him his job. Yet the aide did not even work in Santa Cruz, and if he had, his termination would not have been unlawful because the objectionable piercing was not outside his control.[45] Related concerns about a flood of frivolous litigation have proven equally unfounded. Fifteen years after passage of the ordinance, it had prompted not a single recorded complaint based on height, weight, or physical characteristic and no discernible backlash.[46]

Santa Cruz's experience is not unique. Urbana, Illinois, also has had no reported cases on personal appearance in the thirty years since enactment of its ordinance.[47] Part of the reason may be the extremely limited remedies noted above. Without the possibility of significant fines, private claims, or attorneys' fees, victims may have too little incentive to file complaints.[48]

San Francisco has a wider range of remedies, but similarly limited enforcement activity. In 2000, the city added a prohibition against height and weight discrimination to its human rights law.[49] That law provides criminal as well as civil penalties for housing discrimination. For other types of violations, the ordinance authorizes the court to award triple damages, fines between $200 and $400, attorneys' fees, legal costs, and punitive damages.[50] In the first eight years under the amended prohibition, the city's Human Rights Commission received only two complaints of height and weight discrimination.[51] One involved the 240-pound aerobics instructor described in chapter 5.[52] That case attracted sympathetic coverage and public protests, which helped prompt revision of the employer's policy. The other case, a weight discrimination complaint against the San Francisco Ballet School, also generated significant favorable publicity.[53] Krissy Keefer, a San Francisco dancer, claimed that the school had denied admission to her eight-year-old daughter Fredrika, on the basis of height and weight, and had applied its appearance standards "more specifically and unfairly to female applicants." Such bias, the complaint

alleged, contributed to "serious and severe health problems...
including eating disorders such as anorexia nervosa and bulimia."[54]
The school responded that it had denied Fredrika's admission based
on published criteria that did not include height, weight, or gender,
although they did define the ideal candidate as a "healthy child with
a well-proportioned, slender body."[55] The case was settled on confidential terms. However, an interview with Keefer and correspondence from the San Francisco Human Rights Commission confirmed
that the school agreed to remove language involving body type from
its promotional literature, and to conduct a symposium for parents
and staff regarding the dangers of eating disorders. In commenting
on the case, Keefer felt that it had raised public awareness about the
issue but felt hamstrung by the lack of funds to hire a lawyer and
pursue her concerns more aggressively.[56]

The District of Columbia, which passed the nation's first local
Human Rights Act banning discrimination based on "personal
appearance," has also reported relatively little enforcement activity
despite relatively broad remedial provisions.[57] The District's Human
Rights Commission has authority to reinstate employees and to
award back pay, compensatory damages, and reasonable attorneys'
fees. In addition, fines for violations range from a maximum of
$10,000 for first-time offenders up to a maximum of $50,000 for
repeat offenders, payable to the city's General Fund.[58] A comprehensive survey of the first twenty-five years since passage of the act
reveals only eleven complaints.[59] Of those actions, three resulted in
judgments of discrimination against the defendant.[60] A fourth case
survived a motion to dismiss, but its ultimate outcome is unclear.[61]

One reason for the limited enforcement is the act's exception
for any "requirement of cleanliness, uniforms, or prescribed standards, when uniformly applied...for a reasonable business
purpose."[62] Judges and juries have broadly interpreted that exception. For example, the D.C. Court of Appeals determined that the

fire department could regulate facial hair as long as the regulation was uniformly applied, despite findings by the Department of Equal Opportunity that the regulation did not foster morale and had no rational safety justification.[63] In another case, the jury found, and an appellate court agreed, that a janitorial service could apply a requirement of "neat hair" to prohibit a male employee from wearing a pony tail. A client's desire that janitors "look sharp at all times" was thought to be a sufficient business reason for the regulation.[64]

Although the volume of complaints imposes no great burden on business, some cases clearly border on the frivolous. Yet these typically include allegations of discrimination based on additional factors besides appearance and so could have been brought even without the Act. A representative example involved a woman of color who wore African-styled apparel, dreadlocks, and cornrows. These provoked complimentary comments or questions by managers with no supervisory authority over her, such as: "Your earrings are interesting," or "What kind of hair style is this?" After a decade, her position was eliminated, along with the jobs of two white women, and the court found no evidence that her termination reflected bias based on race or appearance.[65]

Of the cases that found discrimination, only one involved appearance alone.[66] The others also included claims of bias based on multiple bases, including sex and disability.[67] One leading case finding discrimination, *Atlantic Richfield Co. v. D.C. Commission on Human Rights*, involved evidence that a supervisor had repeatedly criticized the complainant for low-cut blouses and disheveled hair, and had compared her behavior to that of a prostitute. In finding discrimination, the commission noted that the employee's appearance was similar to that of her coworkers and that Atlantic Richfield did not have a "uniformly prescribed standard of dress [supported by a] reasonable business purpose."[68]

Howard County, Maryland, has had a similar experience. Its civil rights code includes "personal appearance" as one of the prohibited forms of discrimination and defines the term to encompass the "outward appearance of a person with regard to hair style, facial hair, physical characteristics or manner of dress. It does not relate to a requirement of cleanliness, uniforms or prescribed attire, when uniformly applied." Remedies include civil penalties of reasonable attorneys' fees and up to $5,000 for employment claims and $1,000 for other claims.[69] The Office of Human Rights (OHR) refused to release copies of personal appearance complaints for review because the county code requires the investigation to be "conducted without publicity" and the information to be held confidential.[70] According to the OHR administrator, any outside review "would be contrary to the public interest" because it "would have the effect of chilling frank and full disclosure to OHR investigators and discouraging settlement discussion as a result."[71]

However, OHR did release general information on the sixteen physical appearance complaints filed between 2003 and 2007 (an average of four a year). Only one was based on appearance alone; the other characteristics were: physical or mental handicap (six), race (four), sex (four), religion (two), age (two), marital status (two), source of income (two), political opinion (two), and occupation (one). Of the total complaints, two were dismissed, seven resulted in findings of no reasonable cause, three resulted in findings of reasonable cause, and four resulted in settlements. Only one reached a public hearing, and its disposition was still pending at the time of the report. Of the settlements, four included monetary remedies ranging between $787.50 and $5,000, and three included policy changes.[72]

Of all the cities or counties with appearance ordinances, Madison, Wisconsin, has experienced the greatest number of complaints. Its prohibition on discrimination based on "physical appearance" in employment, credit, housing, and public accommodations exempts any "requirement of cleanliness, uniforms, or prescribed attire, if and when such requirement is uniformly applied... for a reasonable business purpose." Remedies include compensatory damages, injunctive relief, and reasonable attorneys' fees and costs.[73] The city's Equal Opportunity Commission reported thirty-six complaints between 2003 and 2007, an average of nine a year. Of these, the commission supplied fifteen complaints that raised colorable claims. None of these cases resulted in a commission finding of discrimination. Forty percent (six of fifteen) resulted in a finding of no probable cause; another 40 percent (six of fifteen) resulted in a settlement. Of the remaining cases, one complaint was withdrawn, one was pending, and the third was being handled by another agency.

One striking feature of these cases is that only one involved an exclusive claim of appearance discrimination. All of the others, including some that appeared frivolous on their face, alleged at least one additional basis for complaint, such as race, sex, age, or sexual orientation. From the limited information available from the files, claims concerning appearance occasionally seemed trivial, particularly in relation to the objective reasons given for rejecting or terminating an employee. A typical example involved a complainant who alleged discrimination based on age and appearance due to his gray hair and facial sores; the employer provided evidence that the dismissal was based on his failure to meet a sales quota.[74] Yet all but one of these seemingly meritless cases could have been brought even without the appearance prohibition. In that single exception, the employer had little apparent difficulty in establishing that its termination of the complainant was due to his marijuana use, not his dreadlocks.[75]

So too, the commission and its investigative staff generally appeared deferential to employers' concerns. For example, it upheld a grooming code of Pet World Warehouse Outlet that prohibited all employees from having visible tattoos or male workers from having visible piercings or wearing earrings. The company's desire to ensure customers a "pleasant shopping experience" was held to be a "reasonable business purpose."[76] Similarly, Wal-Mart's rule that "clothes must fit well and not be too tight" was reasonably applied when a supervisor asked a pregnant employee to wear a jacket or a larger shirt because of the "inappropriate" appearance of her stomach or breasts.[77] Also permissible were bans on facial jewelry by Sam's Club in order to promote a "conservative, no frills" image and requirements of "appropriate accessories" and "stylish shoes" by the American Association of Retired Persons.[78] In the 20 percent of cases (three of fifteen) where the commission's investigator found probable cause to believe discrimination had occurred, the file included uncontested evidence of racial as well as appearance bias, and of grooming requirements selectively applied.[79] All of these cases settled without a formal commission decision.

Michigan

In 1977, Michigan became the first and still only state to prohibit appearance discrimination in employment by adding height and weight to the characteristics protected by its Civil Rights Act. The act invests the Human Rights Commission with broad remedial powers, including the authority to order reinstatement, monetary damages, attorneys' fees, fines ranging from $10,000 to $50,000, and other "appropriate" relief. Alternatively, an individual may bring a civil action and, if successful, can receive injunctive or monetary remedies as well as attorneys' fees.[80]

Not surprisingly, given its state-wide reach, this prohibition has resulted in the greatest enforcement activity. Still, the overall burdens on businesses appear modest at best. In a roughly two-year period between 2005 and 2007, the Department of Civil Rights received sixty-one complaints, forty-eight involving weight, six involving height, and seven involving both. None resulted in a final judgment of discrimination. About two-fifths (43 percent) were dismissed for insufficient evidence; about a quarter (26 percent) remained open; about a fifth (21 percent) settled; 6 percent were withdrawn to pursue action in court; and the remaining 3 percent were withdrawn or dismissed for lack of jurisdiction. Rarely do cases ever reach the courts. Between 1985 and 2007, only eighteen lawsuits alleged height or weight discrimination, fewer than one a year. Only one resulted in a final judgment of discrimination, and that judgment was short-lived; on appeal, the court granted the defendant a new trial on the plaintiff's weight-discrimination claim. Three reversed summary judgments for the defendants, and the ultimate results of those cases are unclear.

A number of factors may account for the lack of litigation and complainants' low success rates. One is that those subject to the law are sufficiently aware of its reach that they avoid discriminating on the basis of height or weight, or at least expressing those factors as a reason for their actions. Another explanation is the difficulty of proving that bias is responsible for substantial damages except in egregious cases, and those may well settle without formal action. In cases where height or weight may be one, but not the only, basis for allegedly unfair treatment, courts tend to side with defendants. A typical case involved an African American man weighing about 300 pounds who unsuccessfully applied for a firefighter position. Although he passed the physical agility test, a psychologist found that he was only "marginally suitable," due to his immaturity, interpersonal difficulties, and problems responding to stress. His excessive weight, according to the psychologist, was a "physical manifestation of an inability to deal with stress." The trial granted summary judgment for the defendant, and the appellate court affirmed on the ground that objective reasons supported the plaintiff's rejection.[81] In a similar case, although a jury found that a physician's obesity was a determining cause for her loss of hospital privileges, the judge granted a new trial; in his view, the "clear preponderance of the evidence" demonstrated that the physician would have been terminated even if her weight had not been a factor.[82] Such judicial rulings may discourage potential plaintiffs and attorneys from pursuing claims in the absence of unequivocal facts, which are hard to come by in discrimination cases.

Yet the cases in which the plaintiffs at least got an opportunity for trial illustrate the kind of inequitable treatment that justifies a ban on appearance discrimination. One case involved Libby Knowlton, a waitress who was told to take early maternity leave when she was six or seven months pregnant despite a doctor's letter indicating that she was still fit for work. Although the restaurant's stated reason was concern for the safety of the mother and her unborn child, three witnesses testified that the manager wanted Knowlton gone because of her appearance. According to one employee's testimony, the manager believed Knowlton was "getting too fat to work on the floor. She didn't look good for business."[83] In another case that was allowed to go to trial, a 5-foot-6-inch tall applicant for a firefighter's position was rejected for failure to meet a 5-foot-8 height requirement. In support of its requirement, the department offered testimony by one witness of unspecified credentials. He concluded that the 5-foot-8 cutoff was based on "safety concerns" and the need for "efficient teamwork," which was impeded by "disparities in height under conditions of emergency." Yet as the court noted, these conclusions were based on personal "observation and experience," not "study or research," and failed to explain why the department had a minimum, but not a maximum, height requirement.[84]

Australia

A comprehensive search revealed only one other nation with an explicit prohibition on discrimination based on appearance. The

1995 Equal Opportunity Act of Australia's state of Victoria prohibits discrimination in employment, education, and other contexts based on characteristics including "physical features." These include height, weight, size, shape, facial features, hair, and birthmarks. The act has a number of exceptions, including discrimination that is reasonably necessary for the protection of health, safety, or property, or for purposes of dramatic, artistic, entertainment, photographic, or modeling work. All complaints are subject to conciliation by the Victorian Equal Opportunity and Human Rights Commission. Those that cannot be resolved are referred to the Victoria Civil and Administrative Tribunal (VCAT) first for mediation, and if that is unsuccessful, then for a hearing and decision on the merits. The tribunal has broad remedial authority to redress and prevent violations. Parties may appeal tribunal decisions to the courts, but not file with them directly to bypass the administrative process.[85]

In the most recent publication available, the commission reported a yearly total of 122 inquiries and 56 complaints of discrimination based on physical features, largely in the employment context.[86] Relatively few of these complaints resulted in a reported tribunal decision. A comprehensive database search over the period since the law's passage identified only ten rulings on appearance discrimination claims.[87] In addition, the tribunal published five decisions concerning appearance-related exemptions from antidiscrimination rules. Several factors may account for the infrequency of complaints and decisions. One is the difficulty of finding legal representation. Very little legal aid or pro bono assistance is available for discrimination claims. Parties who manage to find help and file a complaint are subject to conciliation and mediation processes that are likely to resolve meritorious grievances. The tribunal's frequent practice of awarding costs against a losing party may also deter unsuccessful parties from going forward. Judicial skepticism concerning the merits may have the same effect. Over the last decade, not one of the discrimination cases that have gone before the Australian High Court has been successful, and in the last three discrimination cases before the intermediate appellate court, complainants who had been successful in the administrative tribunal had their judgments overturned.[88]

As is generally true in American jurisdictions, most (60 percent) of the individual complaints of appearance discrimination before the tribunal involved additional factors such as race, sex, religion, or disability. The vast majority (90 percent) were unsuccessful. The only case in which a claimant prevailed involved derogatory comments based on weight. There, a personal care assistant received $2,500 in Australian dollars (roughly $2,000 in U.S. currency) for the "hurt, humiliation, and loss of dignity" resulting from statements made by her manager to her supervisor suggesting that she was "unsightly" and should be fired.[89] Complainants in other cases involving weight, size, tattoos, height, or facial features failed to establish detrimental treatment based on these characteristics. Most of these claims seemed close to frivolous. A majority involved self-represented litigants who seemed intent on exposing ostensible bias even though they could not link it to any demonstrable injury.[90]

By contrast, the petitions for exemptions from the act generally seemed reasonable, and all but one were granted, at least in part. When safety was at issue, such as where individuals might be too heavy for a stable's horses, a favorable decision was always forthcoming.[91] However, where a recruitment business sought to use photographs of interviewees during the selection process to prompt recollections of the applicant, the tribunal denied the exemption. In the judge's view, viewing the photographs "might make it easier for a person to base decisions on physical characteristics."[92] And in a decision involving a dating service, the tribunal allowed only a partial exemption. The service could ask applicants about physical attributes, but not deny them services on that basis.[93]

A COMPARATIVE APPROACH: EUROPEAN RESPONSES
TO APPEARANCE DISCRIMINATION

It is difficult to draw definitive lessons from other countries' approach to appearance discrimination because almost no research and few decisions are published on the issue.[94] The most analogous comparisons are with Europe, where antidiscrimination and privacy laws have some application to appearance claims. European Union law protects against bias based on race, ethnicity, sex, sexual orientation, gender, age, religion, and disability, but not appearance. However, there are some reported challenges to grooming codes as a violation of privacy or gender equality.

Courts have generally interpreted European sex discrimination law as applied to appearance along similar lines as American courts. Sex-specific grooming codes are permissible as long as their overall effect is comparable for men and women and the regulations have a reasonable business justification. So, for example, English courts have held that an employers' interest in projecting a "conventional" image and promoting customer relations is a sufficient justification for requiring short hair for a male supermarket clerk and skirts for female bookstore staff.[95]

The extent of deference to employer concerns is apparent from one British case involving a male administrative assistant whose job involved clerical, mail, and related secretarial duties, but no public contact. The employer required all workers to maintain a "professional and business-like" appearance. Men had to wear a coat and tie and women had to "dress appropriately and to a similar standard," by avoiding "obviously inappropriate" clothing such as "shorts; cropped tops; trainers; and baseball caps." An employment tribunal held for the complainant on the ground that requiring men to wear clothing of a particular kind imposed a "higher level of smartness" than that applicable to women. An appellate court reversed and remanded for more specific findings about whether a coat and tie was the only way in which men could achieve the "smartness" demanded of both sexes.[96] Missing from the court's analysis was any discussion of the business justification for requiring a clerical worker with no public interaction to conform to such a standard.

By contrast, continental Europe, particularly France and Germany, tend to be somewhat more protective of employee interests in privacy and dignity.[97] German law respects a general right of "free development of...personality," which includes rights to express oneself in appearance and dress, subject to employers' demonstration of a countervailing business necessity.[98] Under that standard, a labor court found no reason why a truck driver could not wear shorts in summer.[99] Appearance standards are often set through negotiations between management and elected worker councils, a process subject to bargaining requirements of good faith and fair dealing.[100] So too, French labor law provides that "no one can limit the rights of the individual...unless the limitations are justified by the task to be performed or are in proportion to the goal towards which they are aimed."[101] In assessing such limitations, a French labor court protected the right of an employee of a telemarketing firm to wear a headscarf, despite the objections of her employer.[102] Female workers who are in contact with customers also cannot be required to wear provocative clothing that could subject them to sexual harassment.[103]

Yet the scope that European courts and legal officials allow for individual grooming decisions is not without significant limits. Teachers as well as students have sometimes been prohibited from wearing veils on the ground that they may undermine gender equality or the secular status and security interests of the state.[104] In one widely publicized case, a Parisian swimming pool banned a woman who wanted to swim in a "Burkini"—a Burqa-like version of a bathing suit. In defending the ban, a local official implausibly insisted that it had "nothing to do with Islam; that type of suit does not exist in the Koran."[105] So too, the European Commission of Human Rights upheld the London Education Authority's right to bar a male transvestite from wearing dresses to work. In the commission's view, such a restriction on the employee's right to respect for his private life under Article 8(1) of the European Convention on Human Rights was offset by the authority's interest in "enhancing the employer's public image and facilitating its external contacts."[106]

In general, however, as compared with American law, European privacy standards accord somewhat greater respect for individual self-expression. At least in France and Germany, an employer is more limited in its right to require that workers convey its image rather than their own.[107]

THE CONTRIBUTIONS AND LIMITATIONS OF LEGAL PROHIBITIONS ON APPEARANCE DISCRIMINATION

This analysis of appearance-related prohibitions holds a number of lessons about the capacities of law to reduce social prejudice. First, the limited enforcement activity under explicit prohibitions suggests that their impact is less significant than either critics have warned or supporters have hoped. In some jurisdictions, the same tolerant attitudes that led to passage of the laws may help account for their circumscribed role; employers may be less likely to discriminate or to articulate their biases openly. The existence of legal prohibitions may also discourage discrimination and encourage informal resolution of cases where it occurs. Other explanations for the limited enforcement involve the narrow scope of existing legal prohibitions, the difficulties of proof, the deference given to defendants' interests, and the frequent lack of substantial damages. Appearance laws in Michigan and San Francisco cover only height and weight. Santa Cruz and Victoria include only involuntary physical characteristics, and decision makers in Madison and the District of Columbia are reluctant to second-guess justifications for employment terminations and restrictive grooming policies. Inadequate remedies may also be a problem. Given all these limitations, successful claims are infrequent. However unsuccessful claims are not particularly burdensome, and typically do not involve appearance alone. Most could have been brought under other civil rights laws.

Yet the low incidence of legal victories is not unique to appearance-related law; it is common in other areas of discrimination. Relatively few victims of bias file complaints, and only a tiny percentage successfully litigate their claims.[108] Moreover, despite the infrequency of enforcement, appearance protections, like civil rights law generally, have made substantial contributions. Victims of discrimination have achieved some significant judgments or settlements. Their complaints have also forced changes in policies that reinforce sex stereotypes and gender inequalities.[109]

In some cases, like those involving the San Francisco aerobics instructor and ballet school, complaints have raised public awareness of the costs of discrimination and the importance of focusing on health and fitness, rather than just body image. For decades, critics have noted the physical risks that accompany life as an underweight ballerina. *Dancing on My Grave* was the title of one representative memoir.[110] But it will clearly take greater efforts, in which law can play a role, to challenge the cult of thinness that restricts opportunities for many talented dancers and encourages eating disorders and related diseases for others. In this and other contexts, the adverse publicity or legal costs of potential complaints can encourage desirable policy reforms.

CONSUMER PROTECTION: PROHIBITIONS ON FALSE AND
FRAUDULENT MARKETING PRACTICES

One final area in which law could do more to address appearance-related concerns involves fraudulent beauty and weight-loss advertising claims. As previous chapters have noted, these claims both encourage preoccupation with attractiveness and delude purchasers about what will secure it. Traditionally, resource constraints have prevented the Federal Trade Commission (FTC) and state consumer protection agencies from keeping up with the barrage of false or misleading advertisements involving such products. As one FTC official explained, "[G]eneral appearance-enhancement claims...are not high on our prosecution list."[111] However, where marketers also emphasize health benefits, the commission has begun to take a closer look.

In recent years, an increasing volume of bogus promises and the medical risks of ineffectual dieting have prompted at least some initiatives. One involves the FTC's Red Flag campaign, which urges media to adopt standards that screen out fraudulent weight loss claims and notifies outlets that have run such advertisements. The agency's "Big Fat Lie" initiative also targets companies that make false statements in national marketing campaigns, such as the Hanmeilin "Cellulite Cream with Chinese herbs," which promised up to ninety-five pounds of weight loss while eliminating fat and cellulite with "No Willpower Required."[112]

Many of these products are targeted to populations of limited education and English language skills. To assist consumers, the FTC has also launched a campaign on "Weighing the Evidence in Diet Ads," which includes warnings about specific product claims. The agency has a teaser website that mimics common diet sites. If consumers try to purchase a pill promising "no sweat, no starvation," they receive information about typical weight-loss ripoffs.[113]

Yet despite such efforts, federal and state enforcement agencies have nowhere close to the resources necessary to protect consumers.[114] Electronic marketing deluges Americans with promises to enlarge breasts, reduce thighs, and reverse the aging process with simple pills, patches, and potions. Especially worrisome are the ads for "cosmeceuticals," cosmetic products that include chemicals and druglike ingredients that aren't regulated by the Federal Food and Drug Administration. As chapter 2 noted, some have undisclosed medical risks, and many carry pseudoscientific names and pedigrees. Consider StriVectin wrinkle cream, marketed as "Better than Botox?" selling at $135 a tube, and endorsed by Dr. Daniel B. Mowrey. This "doctor" holds no medical degree; he is a psychologist who works for the manufacturer.[115]

Although consumer-protection law in theory provides remedies for fraudulent claims, in practice it is highly ineffective.[116] Seldom do purchasers have sufficient damages to make challenges worthwhile. "Wrinkle-reducing creams are expensive," notes one expert, "but to litigate against companies is even more expensive."[117] For most appearance products, consumers' only realistic protection is common sense. According to a compliance officer at the Food and Drug Administration, people "need to realize that wrinkles just don't disappear as claimed."[118] But human capacities for wishful thinking should not be underestimated. The substantial market "cosmeceutical" skin care products, about $6.4 billion annually, suggests the gap between what consumers "need" to understand and what they actually do.

DIRECTIONS FOR REFORM

Appearance discrimination is deeply rooted and widely practiced, and there are obvious limits to how much the law can affect it. But the same has been true for other forms of discrimination and consumer fraud, and the last half century leaves no doubt that legal prohibitions can help reduce, remedy, and raise awareness of injustice.

The gaps in existing legal frameworks suggest several directions for reform, discussed more fully in chapter 7. One obvious strategy is to enact or amend civil rights laws to ban discrimination based on appearance. In the absence of such legislative action, courts and enforcement agencies could interpret existing statutes to provide more protection from appearance-related bias. Sex discrimination law could be read to strike down dress, grooming, and weight restrictions that enforce traditional stereotypes. Constitutional and statutory provisions could be more broadly and consistently extended to protect expression of religious values and cultural identity. Disability statutes could be interpreted to ban discrimination based on weight regardless of whether it involves extreme obesity with demonstrable physiological causes.

Finally, more regulation and enforcement could target fraudulent claims and unsafe products involving appearance. Government agencies need more authority to regulate cosmetics, as well as additional resources and stiffer sanctions to combat misleading claims. Consumers should have more financial incentives to hold manufacturers accountable; triple damage awards and attorneys' fees might deter companies that now peddle ineffectual products to vulnerable purchasers.

Fraud and prejudice regarding appearance will be hard to change. But the law can do more to make us conscious of their costs, and to challenge their most unjust consequences.

CHAPTER SEVEN

Strategies for Change

"I'm looking for something less empowering."

Carolita Johnson, *New Yorker*, June 13 and 20, 2005, 81. Reprinted with permission.

SHORTLY AFTER THE turn of the twentieth century, the author of a leading self-help book, *Physical Beauty: How to Keep It*, made clear the importance of her subject:

> By no other plan [than beauty] can woman win love worth having nor keep the love she has won. On no other basis can she win and keep the admiration of the world at large.... If this plan of life be immoral, then so much the worse for morality, for mere morals cannot stand against it.[1]

Over the past century, much has changed, but much has remained the same. As chapter 2 noted, about three-quarters of surveyed women consider appearance important to how they feel about themselves, and half are unhappy with their bodies.[2] Even those who attach relatively little importance to how they look bump up against constant reminders of its cultural significance.

No one advocating change in attitudes toward appearance should be naive about all that stands in the way. The importance of attractiveness is deeply rooted, and the economic stakes in its pursuit are enormous. But the costs of appearance discrimination are also considerable, and we have by no means reached the limit of what can be done to address them.

DEFINING THE GOAL

Our difficulties in making progress on issues of appearance are partly attributable to the lack of consensus on what the goal should be. In an ideal society, how much importance would attractiveness assume? How much diversity in body types and self-expression in grooming practices would we embrace? What further complicates these questions are our mixed experiences with appearance in this society. The presentation of self can be a source of pleasure, self-expression, and identity, but also a source of stigma and shame, and an excessive drain on time and resources.

Yet we need not have a fully developed or widely shared vision of the ideal world to agree on some of what should change in this one. The research summarized in preceding chapters suggests three principal objectives for reform. One should be to promote more attainable, healthy, and inclusive ideals of attractiveness. Our aspirational standards should reflect greater variation across age, weight, race, and ethnicity, and our workplace grooming requirements should reflect greater tolerance for diversity and self-expression. A second goal should be to reduce discrimination and stigma based on appearance, and to combat the double standards and sexualized grooming codes that impose disproportionate costs on women. A third objective should be to encourage lifestyles that place more emphasis on health, rather than simply appearance, and to create a social environment that supports them.

Laws affecting appearance can further that agenda in several respects. One is to promote equal opportunity, and to challenge the biases based on appearance that stand in the way. Another role for law is to foster respect for individual liberty, and to demand reasonable justifications for grooming rules that limit expression of core values. An employer's interest in maintaining a particular image deserves recognition, but it needs to be balanced against employees' expressive interests. Law should also ensure adequate consumer protection from unsafe products or fraudulent practices regarding appearance. And finally, law can play a part in promoting more healthy lifestyles and media images. A nation committed to individual liberty and equal opportunity should more actively foster those values where matters of appearance are at stake.

INDIVIDUALS

Progress starts with individuals. The focus, however, should not be simply on their personal choices. Rather, it should also center on the tolerance they show for others and their support for changes in social attitudes and policies toward appearance. One way to contribute is, of course, through leading by example. Resisting cultural pressures for cosmetic surgery or killer shoes makes it safer for others to do so as well. But there are many way other ways to promote this agenda that do not involve one's own appearance.

For example, parents can do more to raise children with positive body images, healthy diets, and active lifestyles. Although recent data suggest that child obesity rates have leveled off at about 16 percent in the last five years, the number of children with unhealthy eating and inadequate fitness behaviors raises serious concerns.[3] Seventy percent of obese children become obese adults, and many develop associated health problems.[4] The extent to which these problems reflect excessive weight, rather than poor diets and sedentary lifestyles remains unclear. What is clear is the need for greater involvement of parents in promoting healthy life styles, both in the behavior they reinforce in their own families and in the policies that they support for their schools and communities. As subsequent discussion notes, limiting access to junk food is part of the answer, but that strategy alone is unlikely to be effective. Deprivation can make forbidden items more attractive, and children may not develop the capacity to self-regulate if rules are too rigid and enforcement is too easily evaded.[5] Schools, families, and policy makers need to work together on coordinated programs that promote healthy diets and enjoyable physical activity without adding to the weight stigma that fuels disordered eating behaviors. A useful model is the "Feed Me Better" campaign, launched by celebrated London chef Jamie Oliver, to improve meals in British schools. After attracting some

270,000 signatures and international media coverage, the effort led to a major increase in funding for healthy options, stricter nutrition guidelines, and improved academic performance in participating schools.[6] Oliver's efforts to jumpstart similar initiatives in the United States deserve greater support and evaluation.[7]

Consumers, for their part, can become more informed about the serious risks or low probabilities of success of many appearance-related purchases and procedures. They can consult government and nonprofit sources and demand adequate factual support for claims about product effectiveness and providers' qualifications.[8] They can also educate themselves about the addictive properties of what social critic Michael Pollan labels "edible foodlike substances."[9] These processed and fast-food products, typically high in sugar, fat, and carbohydrates, can create cravings, encourage overeating, and sabotage health.[10] Individuals with unsuccessful experiences in yo-yo dieting may do better with recently developed approaches that stress "health at every size," rather than simply weight reduction. Some carefully designed research suggests that participants in such programs, which focus on fitness, nutrition, and positive body images, are more likely than those in traditional diet programs to experience sustained improvements in physical and psychological health.[11]

Finally, individuals can engage in all the standard tactics of political activism that pressure businesses, the government, and the media to take issues concerning appearance seriously. People can write letters, op-eds, and blogs. They can support organizations such as the National Association to Advance Fat Acceptance, the Council on Size and Weight Discrimination, or the International Size Acceptance Organization. They can join initiatives including the one that sends a year's cosmetic budget to a women's rights organization instead.[12] They can boycott products, stage protests, and organize lobbying campaigns. As earlier chapters noted, such efforts were responsible for some of the local ordinances prohibiting appearance discrimination. Santa Cruz citizens used an unsuccessful lawsuit with sympathetic facts to enlist support for a law that would help prevent such injustices in the future.[13] San Francisco activists capitalized on an offensive advertisement by a fitness center in order to stage protests, launch hearings, and marshal support for an antidiscrimination ordinance. Their testimony before the San Francisco Human Rights Commission raised awareness of the extent of weight discrimination by employers and health professionals, as well as the lack of appropriately sized public facilities and medical equipment.[14]

On the relatively rare occasions when a critical mass of individuals has registered concern, their complaints have produced results.[15] Marketers have pulled ads, employers have changed policies, and local governments have passed legislations. Activists have also enlisted others in their protests and reduced their own risks of unhealthy behavior. For example, the Body Project recruits female students to design their own plan of activism on appearance issues. Those who do so have a 60 percent lower incidence of eating disorders than others in their age group.[16] One of the fastest-growing Facebook sites provides women with a similar online community that challenges conventional understandings of attractiveness.[17]

Yet not all activism is equally effective, and some can be counterproductive. A European campaign to combat eating disorders by using an emaciated model turned out to have precisely the opposite result. The key target audience, anorexic adolescents, wanted to emulate her body size.[18] In New York, activists gained attention but not necessarily adherents, by placing "feed me" stickers on billboard images of underweight models. Systematic evaluation of various political and media strategies should be a higher priority.

Businesses that contribute to appearance-related problems should also assume more responsibility for solutions. One cluster of strategies should seek to promote more diverse, healthy, and realistic images of attractiveness. Fashion, advertising, publishing, and broadcast industries could develop codes to address the issue, as proposed by the European Parliament.[19] It should not take more tragedies like the deaths of two South American models from anorexia to nudge the relevant organizations into action. In 2006, after Madrid passed the first law banning underweight models, the trade organization that oversees Milan's runways then followed suit.[20] London's Fashion Week now requires a doctor's certificate for models indicating that their health is not at risk, and the Spanish clothing industry has an agreement with the government to use normal-size mannequins.[21] United States businesses need to do their part, including those outside the fashion world. A promising example is the "American Girl" line of dolls. The director of the Center on Media and Child Health at Boston Children's Hospital points out that these dolls "have the advantage of focusing on history and on who the characters *are*, not on how sexy they look...and [they are] proportioned fairly normally in comparison to many other dolls out there."[22]

The media can play a similarly constructive role, not only by reinforcing more diverse and healthy cultural ideals, but also by providing greater coverage of appearance discrimination and more responsible treatment of weight-related issues. All too often, press coverage of the "obesity epidemic" misdescribes the problem and misreads the solution. Systematic studies find that most news articles exaggerate the incidence and risks of obesity and understate the role of environmental and biological causes.[23] In the United States, epidemiological research shows that although the heaviest individuals have gained significant amounts of weight over the last several decades, the main rise in rates of obesity and overweight results from only modest gains by people just below the cutoffs.[24] For these individuals, the primary health risks may relate more to poor diets and inactive lifestyles than body size alone. Sensationalized descriptions of the current trend as the "terror within" or "ticking time bomb" may contribute to what social scientists characterize as a "moral panic," which not only exaggerates risk but also exacerbates stigma.[25] A more responsible approach would stress the complex causes of obesity and the rationale for focusing on healthy eating and fitness behaviors rather than simply weight reduction. Such an approach, together with profiles of victims of weight discrimination, could help pave the way toward more sensible policies and public attitudes.

Employers could also do more to discourage bias based on appearance. As a threshold matter, they could give employees a greater role in developing policies on dress, grooming, and other appearance-related issues. Involving workers could help raise awareness of the injustice of discrimination and the values of self-expression. Employees play such a role in other nations, and survey research indicates that almost two-thirds of American employees would like to have more influence over decisions that affect their workplace conduct.[26] Including appearance as a prohibited form of bias in official antidiscrimination policies and training programs could also raise awareness about stereotypes, stigma, and the price of prejudice.

So too, employers can do more to support workers in making healthy choices that affect appearance. A growing number of businesses are providing wellness programs that include information, counseling, and access to healthy food and fitness facilities. The few studies available suggest that these programs generally save money by reducing insurance costs and absenteeism, and by improving productivity and retention.[27] However, the methodologies of these studies generally do not meet accepted social science research standards. Nor does the information available reveal the long-term impact of strategies that most concern appearance, such as those affecting weight and eating disorders.[28] Better evaluation is necessary to identify the most cost-effective workplace initiatives.

Finally, the food and cosmetics industries could do more to promote health and reduce costs associated with appearance. At a minimum, they should supply more complete and accurate product information. For example, except in the relatively small number of jurisdictions that require fast-food restaurants to post nutrition and calorie content, customers may find it impossible to discover this information. When former Food and Drug Commissioner David Kessler asked Chile employees what was in the menu items he ordered, typical responses were: "We can't tell you that," or "I'm not sure I'm allowed to say."[29] Even more troubling is what marketers do in fact say about certain food and cosmetic purchases. Many health-related claims are, as one industry expert put it, "an exercise in creative writing."[30] Kessler offers as an example Live Bright brain health bars. They include DHA, a fatty acid that the manufacturer claims can sustain brain health. Whatever the truth to that assertion, the rest of the ingredients—sugars and fats—are anything but healthy.[31] Pollan makes a similar point about Frito-Lay chips, which the manufacturer labels "heart healthy" because they are fried in polyunsaturated fat.[32] Rather than mask the content of junk food, sellers would do far better to improve the taste of nutritional alternatives. As one report on market trends noted: "Healthy indulgence is a vast opportunity that is undeveloped by the food and drinks industry."[33] A more socially responsible business community would help consumers make nutritional choices, not delude them about imprudent alternatives.

LAW AND POLICY

Law can also do more to address appearance-related issues. One obvious priority should be to target risky or misleading cosmetic and weight-loss practices. As chapter 6 indicated, sanctions for deceptive claims should be strengthened, and enforcement and public education resources should be increased. Individuals need to become more aware of the serious risks, low probabilities of success, and dubious health-related claims of many appearance-related purchases.[34]

A second priority would be to expand prohibitions on discrimination based on appearance. The most straightforward strategy would be to enact or amend federal, state, or local antidiscrimination rights statutes covering employment, housing, public accommodations, and related contexts. "Appearance" should include not only physical characteristics, but also grooming and dress that reflect core values and that are not inconsistent with reasonable business needs. As with disability and religion, organizations should have to make reasonable accommodations for personal appearance that do not impose undue hardship. A fair and inexpensive dispute-resolution process should be available to resolve controversies, such as a human rights commission or mediation system, coupled with rights of judicial appeal. Parties should have access to compliance guidelines and to staff assistance that can help them assess and present their cases. Attorneys' fees and compensatory damages should be awarded to complainants who establish that appearance bias was the determining factor in the decisions at issue.

In the absence of such specific prohibitions on appearance discrimination, courts, legislatures, and administrative agencies should broaden protections under existing discrimination and disability law. When evaluating sex-specific regulations under Title VII and constitutional provisions, courts should take a realistic view of what constitutes a disproportionate burden on one sex and should disallow rules that reinforce gender stereotypes. Requirements such as makeup, high heels, and provocative uniforms for women and prohibitions on earrings for men should be subject to challenge. It should not require expert witnesses for courts to notice that daily requirements of styled hair, manicures, and makeup for female bartenders impose a greater burden than trimmed fingernails for their male colleagues. Customer preferences for attractive or sexy employees should not constitute a justification for discrimination unless those attributes are a business necessity, as in occupations involving modeling, acting, or sexual entertainment.

So too, disability law should be extended to cover weight discrimination without a showing of extreme obesity that results from physiological disorders and that impairs or is perceived to impair major life activities. Indeed, weight-related bias is even more arbitrary when directed against moderately overweight individuals who have no difficulty with major life functions. It should be enough for these individuals to show that they are qualified for a position and that any necessary accommodations would cause no undue hardship to the organization.

A final cluster of strategies should focus on preventing unhealthy lifestyles that underlie many weight-related problems and their associated costs. A central challenge lies in crafting an environment that encourages sensible eating and fitness behaviors without demonizing those who fall short. Given the difficulties of changing weight-related patterns once they are entrenched, it makes sense to develop more initiatives aimed at children. The World Health Organization's Global Strategy on Diet, Physical Activity, and Health offers sensible recommendations; schools should provide adequate health information, nutritious food, and a daily physical activity program, and should restrict the availability of foods high in sugar, salt, and fat.[35]

In the United States, efforts along these lines have bumped up against strong countervailing financial interests. Many cash-strapped schools have made profitable arrangements with fast-food and vending companies in order to support valuable educational programs. These companies have also become more adept at marketing to youth and making offers that are hard to refuse, such as product discounts and scholarships for students who meet high academic achievement standards.[36] Yet as one surveyed student put it, " 'How can we stay healthy when you're throwing all of this [junk food] in front of us?"[37] Many schools have also lacked resources for adequate physical education and after-school sports programs, and have often failed to respond to the teasing, bullying, and excessive competitiveness that discourage participation by overweight, sedentary children who need it most.[38] To address these concerns, more legislatures and administrators should follow the lead of those requiring better nutrition, health curricula, and physical education programs, as well as bans on junk food and soft drinks.[39] Other promising proposals include restrictions on children's advertisements and educational initiatives that enhance critical media-viewing skills and discourage appearance-related biases.[40]

Large majorities of Americans support improvements in school nutrition and fitness programs, and experts generally agree about the harms of marketing unhealthy products to children.[41] Yet the United States has yet to follow the example of 62 other nations which regulate food marketing to children, and most schools have yet to implement prohibitions on the sale of such foods or to require daily physical education.[42] Additional funding will be necessary to support fitness and curricular reforms, and to replace the revenues now available from franchises with fast-food vendors. Educational decision makers also need to educate themselves about the effects of other recent initiatives, such as body mass index report cards that inform parents of their child's weight and any associated risks.[43] Do such disclosures lead to changes in diet and fitness? Do they exacerbate stigma? In short, schools need more pressure, resources, and policy evaluation in order to promote healthy lifestyles and to prevent practices that disadvantage children based on appearance.

Local communities can join these efforts through zoning laws and financial incentives that increase recreational opportunities and reduce "nutritional deserts" in low-income communities.[44] A promising example is the Somerville, Massachusetts, "Shape Up" program designed by Tufts researchers. It has achieved modest success in reducing weight gain among at-risk children through measures such as replacing unhealthy school food, adding bicycle lanes and exercise opportunities, and encouraging restaurants to offer more healthy choices.[45]

Another cluster of strategies should center on fiscal and regulatory policies that affect the food industry. The World Health Organization put the point directly in its recommendations on global diet: national governments "need to take healthy nutrition into account in their agricultural policies."[46] Obvious though this point seems, it has had little influence on United States decision making. Massive agricultural subsidies for products such as corn, wheat, and soy have encouraged overconsumption of inexpensive processed products high in fat and carbohydrates.[47] From a health standpoint, such reliance on cheap food turns out to be very expensive. Modern societies generally operate with a Gresham's law of food; bad drives out good, and health costs escalate accordingly.[48] If we want Americans to make more healthy choices, our agricultural subsidies and government-supported school lunch, food stamp, and related programs should push in that direction.

Other public policies can do the same. One possibility is labeling laws. A growing number of states and localities require fast-food restaurants to post nutrition content, and Congress is considering a federal requirement as part of health care reform. Recent research suggests that most consumers want and need such information, and that some modify their menu choices as a result.[49] Fast food accounts for about three quarters of restaurant purchases, and without labels, the average American, and even trained nutritionists, substantially underestimate the calories of many restaurant items.[50] When New York put its menu disclosure requirement into effect, one study revealed that about a third of consumers who saw the information reported that it had affected their choices, and that the calories consumed by those consumers dropped by modest amounts.[51] However, other research has found no such effects. In one survey of low- income minority communities, about a quarter of fast-food customers who saw labels said the information influenced their food choices, but their total calories did not decline.[52] Much more research is needed to assess the long-term health impact of such requirements and the additional public education or related strategies that might make them more effective. Product warnings in some contexts can arouse cravings rather than increase self-control, and past nutritional labeling efforts have not reduced obesity rates, so continued evaluation of recent initiatives is essential.[53]

The same is true of tax policies that seek to discourage risky choices. A few states have considered or enacted taxes on cosmetic surgery, junk food, and soft drinks.[54] What little information is available suggests that these policy initiatives have often failed to meet health objectives. For example, in four states that have taxed soft drinks, the result has not been a significant decrease in consumption. Some economists estimate that extremely large increases in prices would be necessary to achieve even a 10 percent reduction in sales.[55] By contrast other evidence suggests that modest taxes could affect consumption, and more data are necessary to determine whether the taxes that are politically plausible would significantly reduce purchases, and, if so, whether individuals would substitute more nutritious alternatives.[56] More experimentation and evaluation is also necessary with strategies that seek not only to discourage risky choices, but also to make healthy choices more attractive, convenient, and affordable.

So too, we need further information about what might improve the effectiveness of other legal strategies. Although we know that most appearance-discrimination laws have not resulted in significant enforcement, we should learn more about why. Are their remedies insufficient? Do victims of bias lack proof or the information and legal assistance necessary to file complaints? Is the stigma of doing so too substantial? More research about what works, or fails to work, in practice is necessary to craft effective policy initiatives.

Yet while continued innovation and evaluation of legal strategies is essential, we can also do without some recently proposed measures that trivialize the issues. A case in point involves 2009 West Virginia legislation that would have banned the sale of "Barbie dolls and other similar dolls that promote or influence girls to place an undue importance on physical beauty to the detriment of their intellectual and emotional development."[57] Jeff Eldridge, the bill's sole sponsor, told media that he didn't expect it to pass but wanted to draw attention to the issue. "I just hate the image that we give to our kids that if you're beautiful…you don't have to be smart. I'd like to send a message to not only our children but parents and educators that let's push education over the importance of beauty." It is unlikely that his proposed legislation was the right vehicle for that message. The response of one West Virginian was typical: "With everything that is wrong in this world and lawmakers are focused on Barbie? These IDIOTS make me want to move to Canada. Please focus on real issues."[58]

The same could be said of some state legislative proposals concerning obesity, such as the 2008 Mississippi effort to prohibit certain fast-food restaurants from serving a person deemed obese under state Department of Health criteria; a Texas "Safe Cupcake" amendment to preserve parents' right to provide the dessert at school functions; a 2006 Massachusetts proposal to ban marshmallow fluff from school lunch programs; and a counterproposal to make Fluffernutter the state's official sandwich.[59] Such symbolic gestures divert attention from serious efforts to grapple with serious issues.

Several years before starting on this book, I delivered a series of lectures on gender inequality sponsored by the Phi Beta Kappa (PBK) Association. As part of the series, I also attended one university's annual PBK banquet, which honored students graduating with the highest academic records. While recipients of the award paraded across a stage, the combination of their drab graduation robes and flamboyant footwear caught my attention. Almost none of these high-achieving women were wearing sensible shoes. And some, including a 6-foot-3-inch forward on the women's basketball team, were teetering precariously on stiletto heels. Following my lecture the next day, I quizzed some of the students about their footwear choices. Many had stories to tell. On evenings and mornings after major campus social events, the local hospital emergency room was overrun with women suffering shoe-related injuries. Spike heels, dancing, and alcohol were a lethal combination. Yet none of the women with whom I spoke seemed to consider this a problem, much less their problem. It made me wish my lecture had been about shoes, not wage gaps.

That is not a statement about the relative importance of the issue. On the reform agenda of women's rights advocates, appearance does not deserve top billing. But in terms of public recognition of a problem, it remains a major challenge. The kind of attention people once gave to the state of their souls, they now give to the state of their bodies.[60] And too often, the result is far from constructive. Beauty may be only skin deep, but the costs associated with its pursuit go much deeper. The financial, physical, and psychological price of appearance demands closer attention and collective action. We will never eliminate all the injustices, but we can surely do better. That will require treating appearance not only as an aesthetic issue, but as a legal and political one as well.

Notes

. . .

CHAPTER 1

1. Charles Darwin, *The Descent of Man and Selection in Relation to Sex* (New York: D. Appleton and Co., 1888), 586.

2. See discussion in chapter 2.

3. See Gordon L. Patzer, *The Physical Attractiveness Phenomena* (New York: Plenum, 1985), 5 (discussing popular misconceptions).

4. Alison Schneider, "Frumpy or Chic? Tweed or Kente? Sometimes Clothes Make the Professor," *Chronicle of Higher Education*, January 23, 1998, A12–14; Valerie Steele, "The 'F' Word," *Lingua Franca*, April 1991, 16.

5. See discussion in chapter 2.

6. Terri Agins, "Women Fall Head Over Heels for Shoe Makers' Arch Designs," *Wall Street Journal*, October 14, 2008, A1, A16 (quoting Claudia Chen).

7. Belinda Luscombe, "Heeling Power," *Time*, October 13, 2008, 63–64.

8. Patricia Marks, "Sole Sisters," *New Yorker*, September 1, 2008, 84, 89.

9. Lorraine Kreahling, "In the Relentless Pursuit of Fashion, the Feet Pay the Price," *New York Times*, August 31, 2004, D5; Gardiner Harris, "If Shoe Won't Fit, Fix the Foot? Popular Surgery Raises Concern," *New York Times*, December 7, 2003, 1, 24.

10. Nancy Friday, *The Power of Beauty* (New York: HarperCollins, 1997), 465. See also Kreahling, "In the Relentless Pursuit of Fashion," D5.

11. Deborah L. Rhode, "Step, Wince, Step," *New York Times*, October 18, 2000, A31.

12. See studies described in chapter 2.

13. Princeton Survey Research Associates, *Possibilities and Perils: How Gender Issues Unite and Divide Women* (Princeton, N.J.: Princeton Survey Research Associates, 2001), 66; Courtney Martin, "One Big Fat Lie," http:?//www.worldproutassembly.org/archives/2006/03one_big_fat_lie. html; See generally Courtney E. Martin, *Perfect Girls, Starving Daughters: The Frightening New Normalcy of Hating Your Body* (New York: Simon and Schuster, Free Press, 2007).

14. See the studies described in chapter 2; Gina Kolata, "Longing to Lose, at a Cost," *New York Times*, January 4, 2005, 6; Christina C. Wee et al., "Understanding Patients' Value of Weight Loss and Expectations for Bariatric Surgery," *Obesity Surgery* 16 (2006): 496, 499.

15. See the studies described in chapter 2.

16. See Wendy Chapkis, *Beauty Secrets: Women and the Politics of Appearance* (Boston: South End Press, 1986), 93.

17. See the studies described in chapter 2; James Gorman, "Plastic Surgery Gets a New Look," *New York Times*, April 27, 2004, F1.

18. See the research reviewed in chapter 3.

19. Thorstein Veblan, *The Theory of the Leisure Class* (New York: Dover, 1994).

20. See the discussion in chapter 2.

21. See the advertisements discussed in chapters 3 and 6.

22. See studies cited in chapter 3.

23. Naomi Wolf, *The Beauty Myth: How Images of Beauty Are Used against Women* (New York: Perennial, 2002), 113 (quoting Raymond Marks).

24. See the advertisements discussed in chapter 4.

25. Susan Brownmiller, *Femininity* (New York: Simon and Schuster, 1983), 83.

26. *Jesperson v. Harrah's Operating Company*, 444 F. 3d 1104 (9th Cir. 2006), affirming 392 F.3d 1076 (9th Cir. 2005).

27. *Jesperson v. Harrah's Operating Company*, 444 F. 3d 1104, 1117–1118 (9th Cir. 2006) (Kozinski, J., dissenting).

28. Ibid., 116 (Pregerson, J., dissenting).

29. See surveys discussed in chapter 5.

30. See requirements discussed in chapter 5.

31. Deborah L. Rhode, "P.C. or Discrimination?" *National Law Journal*, January 22, 1996, A 19 (quoting Mike McNeil).

32. For a case refusing to accept customer preferences for female stewardesses in hot pants as a business necessity under federal civil rights law, see *Wilson v. Southwest Airlines*, 517 F. Supp. 292 (N.D. Texas 1981).

33. Richard Ford, *The Race Card: How Bluffing about Bias Makes Race Relations Worse* (New York: Farrar, Straus and Giroux, 2007), 176.

34. Bob Elko, "Court OKs Sex Based Grooming Standards," *San Francisco Chronicle*, April 15, 2006, B1.

35. Telephone Interview with Jennifer Pizer, LAMBDA Legal Defense Fund, September 10, 2008.

36. See the discussion in chapter 6.

37. See the discussion in chapter 6 and *Eatman v. United Parcel Service*, 194 F. Supp. 2d 256 (S.D.N.Y. 2002) (cornrows); *Rodgers v. American Airlines*, 527 F. Supp. 229 (S.D.N.Y. 1981) (cornrows); *Birdi v. UAL Corp.*, 2002 WL 471999 (N.D. Ill.) (Sikhs who wanted to wear turbans could be discharged for failure to accept alternative positions); *EEOC v. Sambo's of Georgia, Inc.*, 530 F. Supp. 86, 89–90 (N.D. Ga. 1981) (Sikh's beard not protected given employer's image concerns).

38. Steven Greenhouse, "Overweight, but Ready to Fight: Obese People Are Taking Their Bias Claims to Court," *New York Times*, August 4, 2003, B1.

39. Joseph Farah, "Job Bias Takes a Walk in Purple Zone: Some Cities May Prohibit Discrimination in Hiring on the Basis of Appearance," *Los Angeles Times*, February 7, 1993, 5.

40. *Knowlton v. Levi's of Knochville, Inc.*, 1997 WL 33345022 (Mich. App. 1992).

41. See the discussion in chapter 6.

42. Cases that cannot be resolved through conciliation by an Equal Opportunity and Human Rights Commission proceed to a hearing before an administrative tribunal, which averages only about one decision a year. See chapter 6.

43. Madison Equal Opportunity Commission, EOC Case No. 20042029, Luis James Burns, January 30, 2004, *Sam's Club, Inc. v. Madison Equal Opportunities Commission*, 668 N.W. 2d 562 (Wis. Ct., App. 2003).

44. Letter from C. Robert Sturm, Law Firm of Littler Mendelson, to the San Francisco Commission on Human Rights, October 26, 2001, 6. The case was mediated to a successful resolution and the complaint dismissed.

45. Elizabeth Fernandez, "Teacher Says Fat, Fitness Can Mix," *San Francisco Chronicle*, February 24, 2002 (quoting Portnick).

46. Terry Poulton, *No Fat Chicks: How Big Business Profits by Making Women Hate Their Bodies—and How to Fight Back* (Secaucus, NJ: Carol, 1997), 195; Abby Ellin, "New Breed of Trainers Are Proving Fit Is Fat," *New York Times*, September 1, 2005, B8. For discussion of the role of fitness, see chapter 2.

47. See the advertisements for Femina Siluette Patch and Hanmeilin Cellulite Cream, discussed in chapter 6 and included on the FTC website, http://www.ftc.gov.

48. "Widespread Ignorance of Regulation and Labeling of Vitamins, Minerals and Food Supplements," *Health Care News*, Harris Interactive (December 23, 2002), 1.

49. Sam Wood, "Borgata Babes Settle Discrimination Suit," *Philly Com*, July 31, 2008; Jennifer Friedlin, "Gaining Weight Cost Me My Job," *Marie Claire*, October 1, 2005.

50. Friedlin, "Gaining Weight Cost Me My Job"; "High Stakes Weight Discrimination," *Good Morning America*, ABC News Transcripts, May 3, 2005.

51. Suzette Parmley, "At Borgata Casino, Its Fit the Mold—Or Else," *Philadelphia Inquirer*, May 22, 2005, B1.

CHAPTER 2

1. Employment Law Alliance, "National Poll Shows Public Opinion Sharply Divided in Regulating Appearance—From Weight to Tattoos—in the Workplace," March 22, 2005, http://www.employmentlawalliance.com/en/node/1321.

2. Gordon L. Patzer, *The Physical Attractiveness Phenomena* (New York: Plenum, 1985), 10–13. For the extent of bias, see the discussion later in this chapter and in chapter 5.

3. See Denis Donoghue, Speaking of Beauty (New Haven: Yale University Press, 2003), 38–41.

4. April Fallon, "Culture in the Mirror: Sociocultural Determinants of Body Image," in Thomas F. Cash and Thomas Pruzinsky, eds., *Body Images: Development, Deviance, and Change* (New York: Guilford Press, 1990), 80, 82.

5. Patzer, *Physical Attractiveness Phenomena*, 16–17.

6. See, e.g., Linda A. Jackson, *Physical Appearance and Gender: Sociobiological and Sociocultural Perspectives* (New York: SUNY Press, 1992), 4; Patzer, *Physical Attractiveness Phenomena*, 17; Vicki Ritts, Miles Patterson, and Mark E. Tubbs, "Expectations, Impressions, and Judgments of Physically Attractive Students: A Review," *Review of Education Research* 62 (1992): 413, 414.

7. See sources cited in note 6 in this chapter.

8. Mark V. Roehling, "Weight Based Discrimination in Employment: Psychological and Legal Aspects," *Personnel Psychology* 52 (1999): 969. As Roehling explains, researchers do not always distinguish between obesity and overweight.

9. Centers for Disease Control and Prevention, "Prevalence of Overweight and Obesity among Adults: United States (2006), 2003–2004," http://www.cdc.gov/nchs/data/hestat/overweight/overwght_adult_03.htm BMI is calculated by dividing weight by the square of height in inches and then multiplying the result by 703. The CDC defines overweight as having a BMI between 25 and 29.9 and a BMI of above 30 as obese; Centers for Disease Control and Prevention, "About BMI for Adults" (2008), http://www.cdc.gov/nccdphp/dnpa/healthyweight/assessing/bmi/adult_BMI/

about_adult_BMI.htm#Interpreted. See also American Obesity Association, "Fact Sheets: What Is Obesity?" http://obesity1.tempdomainname. com/subs/fastfacts/obesity_what2.shtml (defining obesity and BMI). For clinical definitions, see sources cited in Jane Byeff Korn, "Fat," *Boston Law Review* 77 (1997): 25.

10. National Association to Advance Fat Acceptance, "Constitution for the National Association to Advance Fat Acceptance, Inc." (2008), 2, www. naafaonline.com/dev2/about/byLaws/Constitution-VER08.pdf; Sondra Solovay, *Tipping the Scales of Justice: Fighting Weight-Based Discrimination* (New York: Prometheus Books, 2000), 29 n.4.

11. Bonnie Berry, *Beauty Bias* (New York: Westport, CT: Praeger, 2007), 9. For an overview of the debate, see Marilyn Wann, "Fat Studies: An Invitation to a Revolution," in Esther Rothblum and Sondra Solovay, eds., *The Fat Studies Reader* (New York: New York University Press, 2009).

12. Fallon, "Culture in the Mirror," 80, 81; Nancy Etcoff, *Survival of the Prettiest: The Science of Beauty* (New York: Doubleday, 1999), 32 (describing research of Julian Langlois).

13. Kathleen Le Besco, *Revolting Bodies? The Struggle to Redefine Fat Identity* (Amherst: University of Massachusetts Press, 2004), 59.

14. For parents, see Steve Jeffes, *Appearance Is Everything: The Hidden Truth Regarding Your Appearance and Appearance Discrimination* (Pittsburgh, PA: Sterling House Books, 1998), 91; Patzer, *Physical Attractiveness Phenomena*, 9. For teachers, see Gerald R. Adams, "Racial Membership and Physical Attractiveness Effects on Preschool Teachers' Expectations," *Child Study Journal* 8 (1978): 29. For the positive effect of physical attractiveness and grooming on high school grades, see Michael T. French, "Effects of Physical Attractiveness, Personality, and Grooming on Academic Performance in High School," *Labour Economics* 84 (August 2009): 373–82.

15. Patzer, *Physical Attractiveness Phenomena*, 9; Solovay, *Tipping the Scales of Justice*, 33–35; Karen K. Dion and Ellen Berscheid, "Physical Attractiveness and Peer Perception among Children," *Sociometry* 37 (1974): 1.

16. See Janet D. Latner and Marlene B. Schwartz, "Weight Bias in a Child's World," in Kelly D. Brownell, Rebecca M. Puhl, Marlene B. Schwartz,

and Leslie Rudd, eds., *Weight Bias: Nature, Consequences, and Remedies* (New York: Guilford Press, 2005), 54, 57–62; Dianne Neumark-Sztainer and Marla Eisenberg, "Weight Bias in a Teen's World," in Brownell et al., "Weight Bias," 68, 69–71.

17. Amy Slater and Marika Tiggemann, "A Test of Objectification Theory in Adolescent Girls," *Sex Roles: A Journal of Research* 46 (2002): 343; American Psychological Association, *Report of the APA Task Force on the Sexualization of Girls* (Washington, DC: American Psychological Association, 2007), 18, 22–23.

18. Karen Dion, Ellen Berscheid, and Elaine Walster, "What Is Beautiful Is Good," *Journal of Personality and Social Psychology* 24 (1972): 285; see Ellen Berscheid, "An Overview of the Psychological Effects of Physical Attractiveness," in G. William Lucker et al., eds., *Psychological Aspects of Facial Form* (Ann Arbor, MI: Center for Human Growth and Development, 1981), 1, 9–10; Thomas F. Cash, "The Psychology of Physical Appearance: Aesthetics, Attributes, and Images," in Cash and Pruzinsky, *Body Images*, 51, 53.

19. Etcoff, *Survival of the Prettiest*, 85; Patzer, *Physical Attractiveness Phenomena*, 93, 119; Cash, "The Psychology of Physical Appearance," 51, 55 (describing the relationship between attractiveness and intimacy levels).

20. Berry, *Beauty Bias*, 33 (reviewing studies); Arthur M. Vener, Lawrence R. Krupka, and Roy J. Gerard, "Overweight/Obese Patients: An Overview," *Practitioner* 226 (1982): 1102, 1103 (documenting students' preferences).

21. Stephen S. Hall, *Size Matters: How Height Affects the Health, Happiness and Success of Boys, and the Men They Become* (Boston: Houghton Mifflin, 2006); Berry, *Beauty Bias*, 60; Natalie Angier, "Short Men, Short Shrift: Are Drugs the Answer?" *New York Times*, June 22, 2006, section 4, 12.

22. Cedric Herring, "Skin Deep: Race and Complexion in the 'Color Blind' Era," in Cedric Herring, Verna Keith, and Hayward Derrick Horton, eds., *Skin Deep: How Race and Complexion Matter in the "Color Blind" Era* (Chicago: University of Chicago Press, 2004), 1, 7–8; Margaret Hunter, "Light, Bright, and Almost White," in Herring, Keith, and Horton, *Skin Deep*, 22, 30; Korie Edwards, Katrina M. Carter-Tellison, Cedric Herring, "For Richer, For Poorer, Whether Dark or Light: Skin Tone, Marital Status, and Spouse's Earnings," in Herring, Keith, and Horton, *Skin Deep*, 65, 73–78.

23. David B. Gray and Richard D. Ashmore, "Biasing Influence of Defendants' Characteristics on Simulated Sentencing," *Psychology Report* 38 (1976): 727; Ronald Mazzella and Alan Feingold, "The Effects of Physical Attractiveness, Race, Socioeconomic Status, and Gender of Defendants and Victims on Judgments of Mock Jurors: A Meta-Analysis," *Journal of Applied Social Psychology* 24 (1994): 1315; Cookie Stephan and Judy Corder Tully, "The Influence of Physical Attractiveness of a Plaintiff on the Decisions of Simulated Jurors," *Journal of Social Psychology* 101 (1977): 149.

24. Jeffes, *Appearance Is Everything*, 56–57; Cash, "The Psychology of Physical Appearance," in Cash and Pruzinsky, *Body Images*, 53, 57; Judith H. Langlois et al., "Maxims or Myths of Beauty? A Meta-Analytic and Theoretical Review," *Psychological Bulletin* 126 (2000): 390, 404–5.

25. David Landy and Harold Sigall, "Beauty Is Talent: Task Evaluation as a Function of the Performer's Physical Attractiveness," *Journal of Personality and Social Psychology* 29 (1974): 299.

26. M. Y. Qureshi and Janet P. Kay, "Physical Attractiveness, Age, and Sex as Determinants of Reactions to Résumés," *Social Behavior and Personality* 14 (1986): 103.

27. Solovay, *Tipping the Scales of Justice*, 101–5; Roehling, "Weight-Based Discrimination," 983; Janna Fikkan and Esther Rothblum, "Weight Bias in Employment," in Brownell et al., *Weight Bias*, 15, 16–18; Janet D. Latner, Albert J. Stunkard, and G. Terence Wilson, "Stigmatized Students: Age, Sex, and Ethnicity Effects in the Stigmatization of Obesity," *Obesity Research* 13 (2005): 1226 (finding that stigmatization of obese people was greater than stigmatization of those with physical disabilities).

28. Daniel S. Hamermesh and Amy Parker, "Beauty in the Classroom: Instructors' Pulchritude and Putative Pedagogical Productivity," *Economic Education Review* 24 (2005): 369; Vicki Ritts, Miles L. Patterson, and Mark E. Tubbs, "Expectations, Impressions, and Judgments of Physically Attractive Students: A Review," *Review of Education Research* 62 (1992): 413; French, "Effects of Physical Attractiveness."

29. Jeffes, *Appearance Is Everything*, 87.

30. Daniel S. Hamermesh and Jeff E. Biddle, "Beauty and the Labor Market," *American Economic Review* 84 (1994): 1174; Megumi Hosoda, Eugene F. Stone-Romero, and Gwen Coats, "The Effects of Physical Attractiveness on Job-Related Outcomes: A Meta-Analysis of Experimental

Studies," *Personnel Psychology* 56 (2003): 431; Markus M. Mobius and Tanya S. Rosenblat, "Why Beauty Matters," *American Economic Review* 96 (2006): 222, 233–34; Stephanie Armour, "Your Appearance, Good or Bad, Can Affect Size of Your Paycheck," *USA Today*, July 20, 2005, 1B.

31. Jeff E. Biddle and Daniel S. Hamermesh, "Beauty, Productivity, and Discrimination: Lawyers' Looks and Lucre," *Journal of Labor Economics* 16 (1998): 172. Even on tasks such as completing a computer maze, where appearance is demonstrably irrelevant, attractive individuals are erroneously predicted to perform better. Mobius and Rosenblat, "Why Beauty Matters," 229, 234.

32. See research discussed in Robert B. Cialdini, *Influence: The Psychology of Persuasion* (New York: Harper Collins, 2007 ed.), 171.

33. Margaret Morganroth Gullette, *Aged by Culture* (Chicago: University of Chicago Press, 2004); Nicole Buonocore Porter, "Sex Plus Age Discrimination: Protecting Older Women Workers," *Denver University Law Review* 81 (2003): 79, 91.

34. Solovay, *Tipping the Scales of Justice*, 103 (describing survey by the National Association to Advance Fat Acceptance).

35. Berry, *Beauty Bias*, 43 (reviewing studies finding heavy women fare worst, earning up to 24 percent less); J. Eric Oliver, *Fat Politics: The Real Story Behind America's Obesity Epidemic* (New York: Oxford University Press, 2006), 80 (discussing studies finding a wage penalty for white women); Solovay, *Tipping the Scales of Justice*, 106 (citing research finding an income penalty for overweight male MBAs); Charles L. Baum II and William F. Ford, "The Wage Effects of Obesity: A Longitudinal Study," *Health Economics* 13 (2004): 885, 896–98 (finding wage penalty for both sexes that cannot be explained by socioeconomic status and other variables); John H. Cawley, "The Labor Market Impact of Obesity," in Zoltan J. Acs and Alan Lyles, eds., *Obesity, Business and Public Policy* (Northampton, MA: Edward Elgar, 2007), 76 (summarizing research finding wage penalties for obese white women and women of color, and for overweight white women); Kate Sablosky, "Probative 'Weight': Rethinking Evidentiary Standards in Title VII Sex Discrimination Cases," *New York University Review of Law and Social Change* 30 (2006): 325, 334–35 (citing studies finding higher poverty rates and income penalties ranging from 6 percent to 24 percent among obese women, irrespective of socioeconomic status

and test scores); Eric Nagourney, "Vital Signs: Patterns When Obesity Comes with a Price Tag," *New York Times*, November 28, 2000, F9 (finding a net worth differential of $136,000 for obese women ages 57–67 as compared to nonobese women); David Lempert, "Women's Increasing Wage Penalties from Being Overweight and Obese" (U.S. Bureau of Labor Statistics, Working Paper No. 414, 2007), available at http://www.bls.gov/osmr/pdf/ec070130.pdf (finding a significant and continual increase in the wage penalty for overweight and obese white women over the course of twenty years).

36. Sablosky, "Probative 'Weight,'" 334–35.

37. Patzer, *Physical Attractiveness Phenomena*, 164–65; Sidney Katz, "The Importance of Being Beautiful," in James M. Henslin, ed., *Down to Earth Sociology: Introductory Readings* (New York: Prentice-Hall, 1997), 312.

38. Herring, "Skin Deep," 9.

39. See Marilyn Gardner, "Is 'White'" the Only Color of Success, *Christian Science Monitor*, October 31, 2005, 13 (discussing research by Sylvia Ann Hewlett and Cornell West).

40. Nancy Friday, *The Power of Beauty: Men, Women and Sex Appeal since Feminism* (New York: HarperCollins, 1996), 368.

41. Shaun Dreisbach, "How Women Feel Now," *Glamour*, April, 2009, 254.

42. Nancy Etcoff, "Foreword," "The Real Truth about Beauty: A Global Report: Findings of the Global Study on Women, Beauty and Well-Being" (2004), available at http://www.campaignforrealbeauty.com/uploadedfiles/dove_white_paper_ final.pdf.

43. "It's Official! Bad Hair Can Ruin Your Day," *Yale Alumni Magazine*, available at www.yalealumnimagazine.com/issues/00_03/landv.html (citing research by Marianne La France).

44. Rebecca Puhl and Chelsea Heuer, "The Stigma of Obesity: A Review and Update," *Obesity* 17 (2009): 941; Susan Bordo, "Reading the Slender Body," in Mary Jacobus, Evelyn Fox Keller, and Sally Shuttleworth, eds., *Body Politics: Women and the Discourse of Science* (London: Routledge, 1990), 94–95. Gina Kolata, *Rethinking Thin: The New Science of Weight Loss—and the Myths and Realities of Dieting* (New York: Farrar, Straus and Giroux: 2007), 93.

45. Kolata, *Rethinking Thin*, 69; Rebecca M. Puhl, "Coping with Weight Stigma," in Brownell et al., *Weight Bias*, 275, 280. See also Solovay, *Tipping the Scales of Justice*, 41, 59–62.

46. Kolata, *Rethinking Thin*, 69 (citing Colleen Rand study).

47. Marlene B. Schwartz, "Weight Bias among Health Professionals Specializing in Obesity," *Obesity Research* 11 (2003): 1033; Rebecca Puhl and Kelly D. Brownell, "Bias, Discrimination and Obesity," *Obesity Research* 9 (2001): 788.

48. For a summary of the evidence and a finding of poorer satisfaction, see Kylie Ball, David Crawford, and Justin Kenardy, "Longitudinal Relationships among Overweight, Life Satisfaction, and Aspirations in Young Women," *Obesity Research* 12 (June 2004): 1019, 1020–27. For research suggesting no differences in mental health, see Kolata, *Rethinking Thin*, 93.

49. Peter Muennig et al., "I Think Therefore I Am: Perceived Ideal Weight as a Determinant of Health," *American Journal of Public Health* 98 (2008): 501, 504 (finding that the difference between actual and desired body weight was a stronger predictor of health problems than individuals' body mass index); Jennifer Crocker and Julia A. Garcia, "Self-Esteem and the Stigma of Obesity," in Brownell et al., *Weight Bias*, 165, 166–68 (discussing role of blame).

50. Rita Freedman, *Beauty Bound* (Lexington, MA. D. C. Heath, 1986), 36.

51. Hunter, "Light, Bright, and Almost White," 30, Maxine F. Thompson and Verna M. Keith, "Copper Brown and Blue Black: Colorism and Self-Evaluation," in Herring, Keith, and Horton, *Skin Deep*, 50–54; Berry, *Beauty Bias*, 68.

52. For appearance, see Etcoff, *Survival of the Prettiest*, 85–87 Richard Layard, *Happiness: Lessons from a New Science* (New York: Penguin Press, 2005), 62. For consumption generally, see Robert E. Lane, "Does Money Buy Happiness?" *Public Interest* 113 (1993): 56, 61, 63; Robert Frank, *Luxury Fever* (New York, Free Press, 1999). David G. Myers, *The Pursuit of Happiness: What Makes a Person Happy—and Why* (New York: HarperCollins, 1992), 31–46.

53. Martin E. P. Seligman, *Authentic Happiness: Using the New Positive Psychology to Realize Your Potential for Lasting Fulfillment* (New York: Simon

and Schuster, 2002), 49; Ed Diener, Richard E. Lucas, and Christie Napa Scollon, "Beyond the Hedonic Treadmill: Revising the Adaptation Theory of Well Being," *American Psychologist* 61 (2006): 305. For application of this concept to appearance, see Alex Kuczynski, *Beauty Junkies: In Search of the Thinnest Thighs, Perkiest Breasts, Smoothest Faces, Whitest Teeth, and Skinniest, Most Perfect Toes in America* (New York: Broadway Publishers, 2008).

54. See Myers, *Pursuit of Happiness*, 31–46; David G. Myers and Ed Diener, "Who Is Happy?" *Psychological Science* 6 (1995): 10. For the role of dissatisfaction with body image in contributing to psychological problems, see Muennig et al., "I Think Therefore I Am," and the discussion later in this chapter.

55. Seligman, *Authentic Happiness*, xiii; Kennon M. Sheldon and Sonja Lyubomirsky, "Achieving Sustainable Gains in Happiness: Change Your Actions, Not Your Circumstances," *Journal of Happiness Studies* 7 (2006): 55, 82–83; Myers, *Pursuit of Happiness*, 31–46; Myers and Diener, "Who Is Happy?" 10. For evidence on the contribution of volunteer activity to well-being, see studies reviewed in Allan Luks with Peggy Payne, *The Healing Power of Doing Good: The Health and Spiritual Benefits of Helping Others*, 2nd ed. (San Jose, CA: iUniverse.com, 2001), xi–xii, 17–18, 45–54, 60; Deborah L. Rhode, *Pro Bono in Principle and in Practice: Public Service and the Professions* (2005), 58–59.

56. Fallon, "Culture in the Mirror," 81.

57. Berry, *Beauty Bias*, 43; Sablosky, "Probative 'Weight,'" 333–35; Solovay, *Tipping the Scales of Justice*, 105; Brownell et al., *Weight Bias*, 16; Fikkan and Rothblum, "Weight Bias in Employment," 16; For racial comparisons, see Latner, Stunkard, and Wilson, "Stigmatized Students," 1226, 1229.

58. Steven L. Gortmaker, Aviva Must, James M. Perrin, Arthur Sobol, and William H. Dietz, "Social and Economic Consequences of Overweight in Adolescence and Young Adulthood," *New England Journal of Medicine* 329 (1993): 1018. See also Berry, *Beauty Bias*, 33.

59. Freedman, *Beauty Bound*, 10, 12.

60. Patzer, *Physical Attractiveness Phenomena*, 91, 93; Langlois et al., "Maxims or Myths?"

61. Susan Sontag, "The Double Standard of Aging," *Saturday Review*, September, 1972, 29–30.

62. Caryl Rivers, "Mockery of Katherine Harris Shows Double Standard," Women's eNews, http://www.womensenews.org, November 29, 2000; Katherine Woodward, "Introduction," in Katherine Woodward, ed., *Figuring Age: Women, Bodies, Generations* (Bloomington: University of Indiana Press, 1999), ix, xiii–xiv (quoting Carolyn Heilbrun).

63. Sontag, "Double Standard of Aging," 36, 35.

64. Berry, *Beauty Bias*, 49; Peter Glick et al., "Evaluations of Sexy Women in Low- and High-Status Jobs," *Psychology of Women Quarterly* 29 (2005): 389; Hosoda, Stone-Romero, and Coats, "The Effects of Physical Attractiveness on Job-Related Outcomes," 451–53.

65. Patzer, *Physical Attractiveness Phenomena*, 91–93.

66. Susan Brownmiller, *Femininity* (New York: Simon and Schuster, 1984), 98. See also Michael Kimmel, "The Flight from the Feminine: Masculinity as Homophobia," in Stephen J. Whitehead and Frank J. Barrett, eds., *The Masculinities Reader* (Malden, MA: Blackwell, 2001), 266–67.

67. Angelika Taschen, "Beauty and Beauty Surgery," in Angelika Taschen, ed., *The Astonishing History of Aesthetic Surgery* (London: Taschen Publishers, 2005), 9.

68. One recent study of some 3300 adults found that for men, unlike women, there was no relationship between footwear and foot pain, in part because fewer than 2 percent of men reported frequently wearing shoes that lacked adequate support and structure. Alyssa B. Dufour et al. "Foot Pain: Is Current or Past Shoewear a Factor?," *Arthritis and Rheumatism* 61 (October, 2009): 1352.

69. See Shari L. Dworkin and Faye Linda Wachs, *Body Panic: Gender, Health and the Selling of Fitness* (New York: New York University Press, 2009), 8–9; Harrison G. Pope Jr., Katharine A. Phillips, and Roberto Olivardia, *The Adonis Complex: The Secret Crisis of Male Body Obsession* (New York: Free Press, 2000).

70. Kuczynski, Beauty Junkies, 91 (noting over 250 percent increase in men's cosmetic procedures, up to over a million by 2004): "Skin Care: Male Vanity Spurs Development of Skin Care: Department Store Sales of Men's Products Jumped 13 percent Last Year," MSNBC, July 19, 2005, available at http://www.msnbc.msn.com/id/8631299 (noting that sales of skin care

products for men were increasing faster than for women); Berry, *Beauty Bias*, 69 (noting escalating male expenditures).

71. Dawn Atkins, "Body Image," in George E. Haggerty, ed., *Gay Histories and Culture* (London: Taylor and Francis, 2000): 201; Michael D. Siever, "Sexual Orientation and Gender as Factors in Socioculturally Acquired Body Dissatisfaction and Eating Disorders," *Journal of Consulting and Clinical Psychology* 62 (1994): 252.

72. "How We Spend Time," *Time*, October 30, 2006, 53. For men's increasing concern, see note 65 earlier this chapter.

73. Deborah L. Rhode, *Speaking of Sex* (Cambridge, MA: Harvard University Press, 1998), 76.

74. American Society for Aesthetic Plastic Surgery, "Statistics on Cosmetic Surgery," 2007, http://www.surgery.org/sites/default/files/2007stats .pdf.

75. Kuczynski, *Beauty Junkies*, 7-8.

76. For diets, see Gina Kolata, "Health and Money Issues Arise over Who Pays for Weight Loss," *New York Times*, September 30, 2004, A1; National Eating Disorders Association, "Statistics: Eating Disorders and Their Precursors" (2006), http://www.sc.edu/healthycarolina/pdf/ facstaffstu/eatingdisorders/EatingDisorderStatistics.pdf. For fitness, see Sharlene Hesse-Biber, *Am I Thin Enough Yet? The Cult of Thinness and the Commercialization of Identity* (New York: Oxford University Press, 1997), 47.

77. For diets, see Kolata, *Rethinking Thin*; Traci Mann et al., "Medicare's Search for Effective Obesity Treatments," *American Psychologist* 62 (2007): 220, 230; Francine Grodstein, Ross Levine, Troy Spencer, Graham A. Colditz, M. J. Stampfer, "Three Year Follow Up of Participants in a Commercial Weight Loss Program: Can You Keep It Off?" *Archives of Internal Medicine* 156 (1996): 1302. For cosmetics such as antiaging and cellulite treatments, see Berry, *Beauty Bias*, 81; Natasha Singer, "The Cosmetics Restriction Diet," *New York Times*, January 4, 2007, G1.

78. Kuczynski, *Beauty Junkies*, 231.

79. "How We Spend Time," 52, 53.

80. Nora Ephron, *I Feel Bad about My Neck* (New York: Alfred A. Knopf, 2006), 48, 33.

81. "Double Take: Will You Be Much Longer, Dear?" *Globe and Mail*, July 27, 2007, 42.

82. See Sandra Lee Bartky, *Femininity and Domination: Studies in the Phenomenology of Oppression* (New York: Routledge, 1990), 42; Lynn S. Chancer, *Reconcilable Differences: Confronting Beauty, Pornography, and the Future of Feminism* (Berkeley: University of California Press, 1998); Kathy Davis, *Reshaping the Female Body: The Dilemma of Cosmetic Surgery* (New York: Rutledge, 1995), 85.

83. See *FTC v. AVS Marketing, Inc.*, No. 04-C-6915 (N.D. Ill. June 13, 2005), available at http://www.ftc.gov/os/caselist/0423042/0423042.shtm (Himalayan Diet Breakthrough); *FTC v. CHK Trading Corp.*, No. 04-CV-8686 (S.D.N.Y. June 8, 2005), available at http://www.ftc.gov/os/caselist/0423003/0423003.shtm (Hanmeilin Cellulite Cream); *FTC v. Iworx*, No. 2:04-CV-00241-GZS (D. Me. May 24, 2005), available at http://www.ftc.gov/os/caselist/0423151/0423151.shtm (gel•ä•thin and LipoLean); *FTC v. Femina, Inc.*, No. 04–61467 (S.D. Fla. May 17, 2005), available at http://www.ftc.gov/os/caselist/0423114/0423114.shtm (Siluette Patch, Fat Seltzer Reduce, and Xena RX).

84. Pallavi Gogoi, "An Ugly Truth about Cosmetics," *Business Week Online*, November 30, 2004, http://www.businessweek.com/bwdaily/dnflash/nov2004/nf20041130_2214_db042.htm

85. "Widespread Ignorance of Regulation and Labeling of Vitamins, Minerals and Food Supplements," *Health Care News* 2 (2002): 1.

86. Wendy Chapkis, *Beauty Secrets: Women and the Politics of Appearance* (Boston: Southend Press, 1986), 93; Singer, "The Cosmetics Restriction Diet," G1; Wolf, *Beauty Myth*, 113.

87. Roseann B. Termini and Leah Tressler, "American Beauty: An Analytical View of the Past and Current Effectiveness of Cosmetic Safety Regulations and Future Direction," *Food and Drug Law Journal* 63 (2008): 257, 271; Natasha Singer, "The Cosmetics Restriction Diet," G1 (discussing the *Consumer Reports* study).

88. Etcoff, *Survival of the Prettiest*, 95.

89. For health care, see Michelle Roberts, "Agency for Healthcare Research and Quality, Racial and Ethnic Differences in Health Insurance Coverage and Usual Source of Health Care," 2002 (2006), http://www

.meps.ahrq.gov/mepsweb/data_files/publications/cb14/cb14.shtml. For the increase in cosmetic surgery, see Davis, *Reshaping the Female Body*, 21; Kuczynski, *Beauty Junkies*, 10.

90. Howard S. Levy, *Chinese Footbinding: The History of a Curious Exotic Custom* (New York: Walton Rawls, 1966); Susan Greenhalgh, "Bound Feet, Hobbled Lives: Women in Old China," *Frontiers: Journal of Women's Studies* 2 (1977): 7–21; C. Fred Blake, "Footbinding in Neo-Confucian China and the Appropriation of Female Labor," *Signs* 19 (1994): 676–712.

91. Harold Korda, *Extreme Beauty: The Body Transformed* (New York: Metropolitan Museum, 2002), 140; Teri Agins, "Women Fall Head over Heels For Shoe Makers' Arch Designs," *Wall Street Journal*, October 14, 2008, A1, A16 (quoting the curator of the Bata Shoe Museum in Toronto).

92. Fallon, "Culture in the Mirror," 104.

93. Christopher Powell, "New Study Shows Female Genital Mutilation Exposes Women and Babies to Significant Risk at Childbirth" (June 2, 2006), available at http://www.who.int/mediacentre/news/releases/2006/pr30/en/index.html; Fallon, "Culture in the Mirror," 103. For the international community's condemnation of the practice, see Inter-African Committee on Traditional Practices Homepage, http://www.iac-ciaf.com; World Health Organization, "Eliminating Female Genital Mutilation: An Interagency Statement OHCHR, UNAIDS, UNDP, UNECA, UNESCO, UNFPA, UNHCR, UNICEF, UNIFEM, WHO" (2008), http://www.who.int/reproductive-health/publications/fgm/fgm_statement_2008.pdf.

94. UNFPA, "State of the World Population: Women and Migration" (2006); William Saletan, "When Cutting Isn't Cruel," *Washington Post*, Aug. 20, 2006; U.S. State Department, "Prevalence of the Practice of Female Genital Mutilation" (Washington, DC: U.S. Department of State, 2001).

95. Fallon, "Culture in the Mirror," 102; Barbara Ehrenreich and Deirdre English, *For Her Own Good: Two Centuries of Expert Advice to Women* (New York: Random House, 1978), 120; Elayne A. Saltzberg and Joan C. Chrisler, "Beauty Is the Beast: Psychological Effects of the Pursuit of the Perfect Female Body," in Estelle Disch, ed., *Reconstructing Gender: A Multicultural Anthology* (Mountain View, CA: Mayfield Publishing, 1997), 136.

96. Teresa Riordan, *Inventing Beauty* (New York: Broadway Books, 2004), 192.

97. For the weight of skirts, see Ehrenreich and English, *For Her Own Good*, 120. For the number and risks of petticoats, see Riordan, *Inventing Beauty*, 228–29.

98. Freedman, *Beauty Bound*, 89. See Ehrenreich and English, *For Her Own Good*, 120.

99. Hesse-Biber, *Am I Thin Enough Yet?* 24.

100. Sander L. Gilman, *Creating Beauty to Cure the Soul: Race and Psychology in the Shaping of Aesthetic Surgery* (Durham, NC: Duke University Press, 1998), 25 (quoting Ovid).

101. Sally Pointer, *The Artifice of Beauty* (Phoenix Mill, Gloustershire, U.K.: Sutton Publishing 2005), 40 (quoting Clement of Alexandria).

102. Pointer, *Artifice of Beauty*, 141 (quoting Butterick's "Beauty: Its Attainment and Preservation").

103. Fallon, "Culture in the Mirror," 98; John Liggett, *The Human Face* (New York: Stein and Day, 1974), 68–69, 88; Riordan, *Inventing Beauty*, 150.

104. Mitchell Clute, "European Union Regs Make Cosmetic Ingredients Safer," *National Foods Merchandiser*, March 2005, 20.

105. See Federal Food, Drug, and Cosmetic Act §§ 601–603, 21 U.S.C. §§ 361–363 (2006). For an overview, see Termini and Tressler, "American Beauty," 257.

106. Russell Mokhiber, "Toxic Beauty," *Multinational Monitor*, September/October 2007, 48.

107. Abby Ellin, "A Simple Smooch or a Toxic Smack?" *New York Times*, May 28, 2009, 3; Sarah E. Schaffer, "Reading Our Lips: The History of Lipstick Regulation in Western Seats of Power," *Food and Drug Journal* 62 (2007): 165, 223–30.

108. Imani Perry, "Buying White Beauty," *Cardozo Journal of Law and Gender* 12 (2006): 579, 593; Marc Lacy, "Fighting 'Light Skin' as a Standard of Beauty," *New York Times*, June 15, 2002, A4 (noting prevalence of high-risk lighteners in Africa); Catherine Reedy, "Ads Pressure Hong Kong Women to Lighten Up," Women's eNews, http://www.womensenews.org, February 12, 2009 (reporting a survey of 2,500 women in Hong Kong, Korea, Malaysia, the Philippines, and Taiwan which found that 38 percent had used skin-whitening chemicals, including those linked to cancer).

109. Humane Society of the United States, "Dark Side of Beauty: BOTOX Kills Animals," May 5, 2008, http://www.hsus.org/animals_in_ research/animal_testing/the_beauty_myth_ botox_kills_animals; see also Termini and Tressler, "American Beauty," 270–71 (discussing inhumane treatment). For the European Union ban, see Directive 2003/15/EC of the European Parliament and of the Council of 27, February 2003, *Official Journal of the European Union*, Nov. 3, 2003, available at http://eur-lex. europa.eu/LexUriServ/LexUriServ.do?uri=OJ:L:2003:066:0026:0035:EN: PDF. [Directive 2003–15 available at: http://eur-lex.europa.eu/LexUriServ/ LexUriServ.do?uri=OJ:L:2003:066:0026:0035:EN:PDF] For discussion, see the statement on cosmetics and animal tests on the European Commission website, http://ec.europa.eu/health/ph_risk/committees/04_sccp/ docs/sccp_s_08.pdf.

110. American Society for Aesthetic Plastic Surgery, "2006 Cosmetic Surgery National Data Bank Statistics" 3 (2007), available at http://www. surgery.org/media/news-releases/115-million-cosmetic-procedures-in-2006.

111. See, e.g., Darlene Ghavimi, "Cosmetic Surgery in the Doctor's Office: Is State Regulation Improving Patient Safety?" *Widener Law Review* 12 (2005): 249, 250–51.

112. Margaret Morganroth Gullette, "Plastic Surgery (Thankfully) Is Under the Knife," Women's eNews, http://www.womensenews.org, November 26, 2008; Anemona Hartocollis and Christina Davidson, "Warning of a Cheap, Fast, and Sometimes Deadly Way to Get Beautiful," *New York Times*, April 17, 2009, A20.

113. Ghavimi, "Cosmetic Surgery in the Doctor's Office," 255.

114. Elizabeth Haiken, *Venus Envy: A History of Cosmetic Surgery* (Baltimore, MD: Johns Hopkins University Press, 1997) 295; Tanya Darisi, Sarah Thorne, and Carolyn Iacobelli, "Influences on Decision-Making for Undergoing Plastic Surgery: A Mental Models and Quantitative Assessment," *Plastic and Reconstructive Surgery* 116 (2005): 907, 913.

115. See Rajesh Balkrishnan et al., "No Smoking Gun: Findings from a National Survey of Office-Based Cosmetic Surgery Adverse Event Reporting," *Dermatologic Surgery* 29 (2003): 1093, 1098 (discussing inadequacy of data concerning office-based cosmetic surgery). For findings that patients believe that risks are minimal if they pick the right doctor, see

Darisi, Thorne, and Iacobelli, "Influences on Decision-Making," 912–13. For the actual risks posed by practicing surgeons, see Kuczynski, *Beauty Junkies*, 94–95; Saltzberg and Chrisler, "Beauty Is the Beast," 306, 308. For ethical standards, see Theresamarie Mantese, Christine Pfeiffer, and Jacquelyn McClinton, "Cosmetic Surgery and Informed Consent: Legal and Ethical Considerations," *Michigan Business Journal* 85 (2006): 26, 28.

116. See, e.g., *Lynn G. v. Hugo*, 752 N.E.2d 250 (N.Y. 2001) (involving plastic surgeon's failure to ascertain a patient's possible body dysmorphic disorder before performing elective cosmetic surgeries).

117. Virginia L. Blum, *Flesh Wounds: The Culture of Cosmetic Surgery* (Berkeley: University of California Press, 2005), 21.

118. Eugina Kau, "The Medicalization of Racial Features," in Rose Weitz, *The Politics of Women's Bodies* (Oxford University Press, 1998), 167.

119. Timothy Egan, "Body-Conscious Boys Adopt Athletes' Taste for Steroids," *New York Times*, November 22, 2002, A1; Gina Kolata, "With No Answers on Risks, Steroid Users Still Say Yes," *New York Times*, December 2, 2002, A1.

120. See Jo Anne Grunbaum et al., "Youth Risk Behavior Surveillance—United States, 2003," *Morbidity and Mortality Weekly Report*, May 21, 2004, 25, available at http://www.cdc.gov/mmwr/PDF/ss/ss5302.pdf (adolescent girls); press release, Calorie Control Council, "New Survey Reveals Dieting a Constant Concern," August 9, 2007, available at http://www.caloriecontrol.org/pressrelease/majority-of-americans-think-about-dieting-year-round-number-of-dieting-attempts-on-the- (adults).

121. Eating Disorders Coalition, "Eating Disorder Statistics: 9 Million Americans, Thousands Dying Each Year" (2007), http://www.eatingdisorderscoalition.org/documents/Statistics.pdf; see also Rebecca Pollack Seid, *Never Too Thin* (New York: Prentice Hall, 1989), 21. Joan Jacobs Brumberg, "Introduction," in Lauren Greenfield, ed., *Thin* (San Francisco: Chronicle Books, 2006), x; Seid, *Never Too Thin*, 45; Arline Kaplan, "Why Girls Starve Themselves: New Research in Anorexia Nervosa," *Psychiatric Times*, January 2008, 25 (discussing Sir Richard Morgan's *Phthisiologia, or a Treatise on Consumption*, 1687).

122. Brumberg, "Introduction"; Seid, *Never Too Thin*, 45.

123. Eating Disorders Coalition, "Eating Disorder Statistics," and Lisa Lilenfeld, "Congressional Briefing on Eating Disorders Research," http://

www.eatingdisorderscoalition.org/documents /Statistics_000.pdf; National Institute of Mental Health, *Eating Disorders* (Bethesda, MD: National Institute of Mental Health, 2001), 1–5; Kaplan, "Why Girls Starve Themselves," 2.

124. Steven Grinspoon et al., "Prevalence and Predictive Factors for Regional Osteopenia in Women with Anorexia Nervosa," *Annals of Internal Medicine* 133 (2000): 790, 793.

125. Joel Yager et al., *Practice Guideline for the Treatment of Patients with Eating Disorders*, 3rd ed. (Arlington, VA: American Psychiatric Association, 2006), 32–33.

126. See University of Virginia Health System, "Binge Eating Disorder," http://www.healthsystem.virginia.edu/UVAHealth/adult_mentalhealth/edbinge.cfm; see also P. H. Robinson, "Recognition and Treatment of Eating Disorders in Primary and Secondary Care," *Alimentary Pharmacology and Therapeutics* 14 (2000): 367, 369–71.

127. For the need for psychiatric treatment, see Yager et al., *Practice Guideline*, 74–87.

128. Latner, Stunkard, and Wilson, "Stigmatized Students," 1226; Cash and Pruzinsky, *Body Images*, 170, 181–82; Rebecca M. Puhl and Kelly D. Brownell, "Confronting and Coping with Weight Stigma: An Investigation of Overweight and Obese Adults" *Obesity* 14 (2006): 1802, 1812. For shame and anxiety linked to decisions to have cosmetic surgery, see Debra L. Gimlin, *Body Work* (Berkeley: University of California Press, 2002), 93–94.

129. For conflicting studies and research finding negative effects from overweight or obesity, see Kylie Ball, David Crawford, and Justin Kenardy, "Longitudinal Relationships among Overweight, Life Satisfaction, and Aspirations in Young Women," *Obesity Research* 12 (2004): 1019, 1020; Robert E. Roberts, "Are the Fat More Jolly?" *American Behavioral Medicine* 24 (2002): 169. For a finding of no negative effect, see Michael Friedman and Kelly D. Brownell, "Psychological Correlates of Obesity: Moving to the Next Research Generation," *Psychological Bulletin* 117 (1995): 3.

130. For shame and anxiety, see Gimlin, *Body Work*, 102; Darisi, Thorne, and Iacobelli, "Influences on Decision-Making," 912; "Yes I Had Plastic Surgery," *US*, October 2007: 58, 59. See discussion in note 130.

131. Eating Disorders Coalition, "Facts about Eating Disorders: What the Research Shows" (updated May 20, 2009); David Herzog, "Eating Disorders: Truth and Consequences," in Greenfield, *Thin*, 85.

132. Lee Lorenz, cartoon, *New Yorker*, April 10, 2006, 60.

133. See Cynthia S. Pomerleau and Candace L. Kurth, "Willingness of Female Smokers to Tolerate Postcessation Weight Gain," *Journal of Substance Abuse* 8 (1998–99): 371, 374; press release, Kara Gavin, University of Michigan Department of Psychiatry, "Is Fear of Gaining Weight Keeping Many Women from Trying to Quit Smoking? U-M Research Suggests So" (November 5, 2007), available at http://www.psych.med.umich.edu/newsroom/smoking.asp.

134. See Margo Maine, *Body Wars: Making Peace with Women's Bodies* (Carlsbad, CA: Gurze Books, 2000), 47; Oliver, *Fat Politics*, 54–55; Stephen J. Dubner and Steven D. Levitt, "The Stomach-Surgery Conundrum," *New York Times*, November 18, 2007, § 6 (magazine), 26.

135. Dubner and Levitt, "The Stomach-Surgery Conundrum," 28.

136. Paul Campos, *The Obesity Myth: Why America's Obsession with Weight Is Hazardous to Your Health* (New York: Gotham Books, 2004), 32–33; Glenn A. Gaesser, *Big Fat Lies: The Truth about Your Weight and Your Health* (New York: Gurze, 2002), 35, 155–56.

137. Kathleen Kingsbury, "Fit at Any Size," *Time*, June 23, 2008, 106.

138. Gaesser, *Big Fat Lies*, 157–59; Maine, *Body Wars*, 48–50; Oliver, *Fat Politics*, 113–15; Jerome P. Kassirer and Marcia Angell, "Losing Weight—An Ill-Fated New Year's Resolution," *New England Journal of Medicine* 338 (1998): 52.

139. See Campos, *The Obesity Myth*; Laura Fraser, *Losing It: America's Obsession with Weight and the Industry That Feeds on It* (New York: Dutton Adult, 1997), 176; Tara Parker-Pope, "Better to Be Fat and Fit Than Skinny and Unfit," *New York Times*, August 19, 2008, F5.

140. For studies see Katherine M. Flegal, Barry I. Graubard, David F. Williamson, and Mitchell H. Gail, "Cause Specific Excess Deaths Associated with Underwieght, Overweight, and Obesity," *Journal of American Medical Association* 298 (November 7, 2008): 2028; Heather M. Orpana, "BMI and Mortality: Results From a National Longitudinal Study of Canadian Adults," *Obesity* (2009): 1; Campos, *The Obesity Myth*, 140–41; Oliver,

Fat Politics, 25; Gina Kolata, "Chubby Gets a Second Look," *New York Times*, November 11, 2007, D4.

141. See studies discussed in Patricia R. Owen and Erika Laurel-Seller, "Weight Shape and Ideals: Thin Is Dangerously In," *Journal of Applied Psychology* 30 (2000): 979, 980.

142. American Obesity Association, "Obesity in the U.S. Fact Sheet," available at http://obesity1.tempdomainname.com/subs/fastfacts/obesity_US.shtml. For discussion of the importance of focusing on nutrition and fitness, rather than simply weight reduction, see Linda Bacon, *Health at Every Size: The Surprising Truth about Your Weight* (Dallas: BenBella Books, 2008), 125–26, and chapter 7 of this book.

143. See, e.g., Rogan Kersh and James A. Morone, "Obesity, Courts, and the New Politics of Public Health," *Journal of Health Politics, Policy, and Law* 30 (2005): 839, 843–44; see also Weight-Control Info. Network, National Institute of Diabetes and Digestive and Kidney Diseases, "Statistics Related to Overweight and Obesity" (2007), http://www.win.niddk.nih.gov/statistics/.

144. See, e.g., Solovay, *Tipping the Scales of Justice*, 35; Janet D. Latner and Albert J. Stunkard, "Getting Worse: The Stigmatization of Obese Children," *Obesity Research* 11 (2003): 452, 452; Latner, Stunkard, and Wilson, "Stigmatized Students," 1226–27; Carey Goldberg, "Fat People Say an Intolerant World Condemns Them on First Sight," *New York Times*, November 5, 2000, 36.

145. Maine, *Body Wars*, 119; Jeffrey Zaslow, "Girls and Dieting, Then and Now," *Wall Street Journal*, September 2, 2009, B7.

146. Tatiana Andreyeva, Rebecca M. Puhl, and Kelly D. Brownell, "Changes in Perceived Weight Discrimination among Americans, 1995–1996 through 2004–2006," *Obesity* 16 (2008): 1129, 1131–32.

147. See Latner, Stunkard, and Wilson, "Stigmatized Students," 1226. For general research on stigma, see Esther D. Rothblum, "The Stigma of Women's Weight: Social and Economic Realities," *Feminism and Psychology* 2 (1992): 61.

148. Bacon, *Health at Every Size*, 126.

149. See the studies discussed in Carr and Freidman, "Is Obesity Stigmatizing?" *Journal of Health and Social Behavior* 46 (September 2005): 244,

255; Lucy Wang, "Weight Discrimination: One Size Fits All Remedy?" *Yale Law Journal* 117 (2008): 1900.

150. Oliver, *Fat Politics*, 102.

151. Michael Fumento, *The Fat of the Land: The Obesity Epidemic and How Overweight Americans Can Help Themselves* (New York: Viking Press, 1997); Greg Critser, *Fat Land: How Americans Became the Fattest People in the World* (London: Penguin, 2003).

152. See Kolata, *Rethinking Thin*, 116–25; National Institutes of Health et al., *The Practical Guide: Identification, Evaluation, and Treatment of Overweight and Obesity in Adults* (Bethesda, MD. National Institutes of Health. National Heart, Lung, 2000), 5; Michael Gard and Jon Wright, *The Obesity Epidemic: Science, Morality, Ideology* (London: Routledge, 2005), 107–25; Laura Blue, "The Myth of Moderate Exercise," *Time*, July 28, 2008, http://www.time.com/time/health/article/0,8599,1827342,00.html.

153. See Kassirer and Angell, "Losing Weight," 53; see also Gaesser, *Big Fat Lies*, 33; Kolata, *Rethinking Thin*, 117–25; Oliver, *Fat Politics*, 107–8.

154. See Kelly D. Brownell and Katherine Battle Horgen, *Food Fight: The Inside Story of the Food Industry, America's Obesity Crisis, and What We Can Do About It* (Chicago: Contemporary Books, 2004), 7–10; Elizabeth A. Baker et al., "The Role of Race and Poverty in Access to Foods That Enable Individuals to Adhere to Dietary Guidelines," *Preventing Chronic Disease* 3 (2006): 1, available at http://www.cdc.gov/pcd/issues/2006/jul/05_0217.htm; Marsha Katz and Helen Lavan, "Legality of Employer Control of Obesity," *Journal of Workplace Rights* 13 (2008): 59, 61.

155. Michael Lasalandra, "Doctors Say Losing Weight Is Emphasized Too Heavily," *Boston Herald*, June 1, 1998, 20 (quoting Michael Fumento).

156. See Puhl and Brownell, "Confronting and Coping with Weight Stigma," 1808; see also Kolata, *Rethinking Thin*.

157. Paul Ernsberger, "Does Social Class Explain the Connection between Weight and Health?" in Sondra Solovy and Esther Rothblum, eds., *The Fat Studies Reader* (New York: New York University Press, 2009).

158. Baker et al., "The Role of Race and Poverty," 7–8.

159. See generally Jeffrey Kluger, "How America's Children Packed on the Pounds," *Time*, June 23, 2008, 66, 69 (discussing decline in physical education classes due to budget constraints). For an overview of the factors contributing to obesity among lower-income minority communities, see Lenneal J. Henderson, "Obesity, Poverty, and Diversity: Theoretical and Strategic Challenges," in Zolton J. Acs and Alan Lyles, eds., *Obesity, Business, and Public Policy* (Cheltenham, UK: Elgar Books, 2007), 57, 59–68.

160. For the role of fast food in response to stress see David A. Kessler, *The End of Overeating* (New York: Rodale Press, 2009), 80, 151–153.

161. See Oliver, *Fat Politics*, 75.

162. Centers for Disease Control and Prevention, *Differences in the Prevalence of Obesity among Black, White and Latino Adults—United States, 2006–2008* (Atlanta, GA: Centers for Disease Control and Prevention, 2009), available at http://www.cdc.gov/mmwr/preview/mmwrhtml/ mm5827a2.htm.

163. See Jordan D. Bello, "Attractiveness as Hiring Criteria: Savvy Business Practice or Racial Discrimination?" *Journal of Gender, Race and Justice* 8 (2004): 483, 498; Ashleigh Shelby Rosette and Tracy L. Dumas, "The Hair Dilemma: Conform to Mainstream Expectations or Emphasize Racial Identity?" *Duke Journal of Gender Law and Policy* 14 (2007): 407, 411; Maxine Leeds Craig, *"Ain't I a Beauty Queen?" Black Women, Beauty, and the Politics of Race* (New York: Oxford University Press, 2002), 6; Charisse Jones and Kumea Shorter-Gooden, *Shifting: The Double Lives of Black Women in America* (New York: Harper Perennial, 2004), 177; Tracey Owens Patton, "Hey Girl, Am I More than My Hair? African American Women and Their Struggles with Beauty, Body Image and Hair," *National Women's Studies Association Journal* 18 (2006): 24, 25; Perry, "Buying White Beauty," 579; Saltzberg and Chrisler, "Beauty Is the Beast," 307, 311.

164. See Carl Elliott, *Better than Well: American Medicine Meets the American Dream* (New York: Norton, 2003), 190.

165. Elliott, *American Medicine Meets the American Dream*, 190; Haiken, *Venus Envy*, 184.

166. Ellen Goodman, "Stacked Against Us," *Boston Globe*, April 17, 2005, C11.

167. Kau, "Medicalization of Racial Features," 168–73; Sander L. Gilman, "Ethnicity and Aesthetic Surgery," in Taschen, *Aesthetic Surgery*, 122.

168. Taschen, "Beauty and Beauty Surgery," 14.

169. American Society for Aesthetic Plastic Surgery, "Statistics," 3.

170. Robin Givhan, "Once Again, White Is the New White," *Washington Post*, September 30, 2007, M1.

171. Solovay, *Tipping the Scales of Justice*, 105; Fikkan and Rothblum, "Weight Bias in Employment," 16; Sablosky, "Probative 'Weight,'" 333–35. For racial comparisons, see Latner, Stunkard, and Wilson, "Stigmatized Students," 1229.

172. Fallon, "Culture in the Mirror," 81.

173. Oscar Wilde, *The Picture of Dorian Gray* (New York: Oxford University Press, 1998), 18.

CHAPTER 3

1. David. M. Buss, "Sex Differences in Human Mate Selection Criteria: An Evolutionary Perspective," in Charles Crawford, Martin Smith, and Dennis Krebs, *Sociobiology and Psychology: Ideas, Issues, and Applications* (Hillsdale, NJ: Erlbaum, 1987), 335–51; David M. Buss and Michael Barnes, "Preferences in Human Mate Selection," *Journal of Personality and Social Psychology* 50 (1986): 559–70; Don Symons, *The Evolution of Human Sexuality* (New York: Oxford University Press, 1981).

2. Judith Langlois et al., "Maxims or Myths of Beauty: A Meta-Analytic and Theoretical Review," *Psychological Bulletin* 126 (2000): 390, 407–8.

3. Nancy Etcoff, *Survival of the Prettiest* (New York: Doubleday, 1999), 145, 162, 186; Symons, *Evolution of Human Sexuality*, 195–96; Karl Grammer and Randy Thornhill, "Human (Homeo Sapiens) Facial Attractiveness and Sexual Selection: The Role of Symmetry and Averageness," *Journal Comparative Psychology* 105 (1994): 233, 240–41.

4. Etcoff, *Survival of the Prettiest*, 192; B. M. Zaadstra et al., "Fat and Female Fecundity: Prospective Study of Effect of Body Fat Distribution on Conception Rates," *British Medical Journal* 306 (1993): 484; Devendra Singh, "Adaptive Significance of Female Physical Attractiveness: Role of Waist to Hip Ratio," *Journal of Personality and Social Psychology* 65 (1993): 293.

5. David M. Buss, "Sex Differences in Human Mate Preferences: Evolutionary Hypotheses Tested in 37 Cultures," *Behavioral and Brain Science* 12 (1989): 1; Linda A. Jackson, *Physical Appearance and Gender* (Buffalo: State University of New York, 1992); Judith A. Howard, Philip Blumstein, and Pepper Schwartz, "Social Evolutionary Theories? Some Observations on Preferences in Human Mate Selection," *Journal of Personality and Social Psychology* 52 (1987): 194. Some recent research offers a more nuanced account, in which women have evolved to seek provider-related characteristics such as intelligence and fidelity in long-term mates, but to prefer appearance-related characteristics suggesting health in short-term sexual partners. Elizabeth G. Pillsworth and Martie G. Haselton, "Women's Sexual Strategies: The Evolution of Long-Term Bonds and Extrapair Sex," *Annual Review of Sex Research* 17 (2006): 59, 72–82.

6. Gordon L. Patzer, *The Physical Attractiveness Phenomena* (New York: Plenum, 1985), 227; Etcoff, *Survival of the Prettiest*, 138; April Fallon, "Culture in the Mirror: Sociocultural Determinants of Body Image," in Thomas F. Cash and Thomas Pruzinsky, eds., *Body Images: Development, Deviance, and Change* (New York: Guilford Press, 1990): 80, 82.

7. Jackson, *Physical Appearance and Gender*, 207–8; Buss, "Sex Differences in Human Mate Selection Criteria."

8. Etcoff, *Survival of the Prettiest*, 220; Jeffrey Sobal and Albert J. Stunkard, "Socioeconomic Status and Obesity: A Review of the Literature," *Psychological Bulletin* 105 (1989): 260.

9. Etcoff, *Survival of the Prettiest*, 203. See the discussion in chapter 2.

10. "To Those That Have, Shall Be Given," Economist.com, December 19, 2007 (describing research of Daniel Hamermesh).

11. Martin Daly and Margo Wilson, *Sex, Evolution and Behavior*, 2nd ed. (Boston: Willard Grant, 1983); John Tooby and Leda Cosmides, "On the Universality of Human Nature and the Uniqueness of the Individual: The Role of Genetics and Adaptation," *Journal of Personality* 58 (1990): 17, 19–20.

12. Stephen Mithen, *The Prehistory of the Mind: The Cognitive Origins of Art, Religion, and Science* (London: Thames and Hudson, 1996); Richard Corson, *Fashions in Makeup: From Ancient to Modern Times* (London: Peter Owen, 1972).

NOTES TO PAGES 48-50

13. Malcolm Barnard, *Fashion as Communication* (New York: Routledge, 1996); Ruth Rubenstein, *Dress Codes: Meanings and Messages in American Culture* (Boulder, CO: Westview Press, 2001), 103–4; Kate Soper, "Dress Needs: Reflections on the Clothed Body," in Joanne Entwistle and Elizabeth Wilson, eds., *Body Dressing: Dress, Body, Culture* (New York: Berg Publishers, 2001); Entwistle and Wilson, "Introduction," in Entwistle and Wilson, *Body Dressing*, 4.

14. Jackson, *Physical Appearance and Gender*, 37–38; Buss and Barnes, "Preferences in Human Mate Selection," 559, 567.

15. Etcoff, *Survival of the Prettiest*, 203.

16. Thorstein Veblen, *A Theory of the Leisure Class* (Mineola: NY: Dover, 1994).

17. Jill Fields, *An Intimate Affair: Women, Lingerie, and Sexuality* (Berkeley: University of California Press, 2007), 54. For further discussion, see chapter 6.

18. Kathy Peiss, *Hope in a Jar: The Making of America's Beauty Culture* (New York: Henry Holt, 1998), 4–5; "Pots of Promise—The Beauty Business," *Economist*, May 24, 2004, 69–71.

19. Peiss, *Hope in a Jar*, 95 (quoting Rubenstein).

20. Kathy Davis, *Reshaping the Female Body: The Dilemma of Cosmetic Surgery* (New York: Routledge, 1995), 40.

21. Peter N. Stearns, *Fat History: Bodies and Beauty in the Modern West* (New York: New York University Press, 1997), 25, 47.

22. Linda Bacon, *Health at Every Size: The Surprising Truth about Your Weight* (Dallas: BenBella Books, 2008), 149. See also Rebecca Pollack Seid, *Never Too Thin* (Upper Saddle River, NJ: Prentice Hall, 1989), 115–17.

23. Stephanie Saul, "OBESITY INC.: Caveat Dieter," *New York Times*, September 22, 2005, G1.

24. Susie Orbach, *Bodies* (New York: Picador, 2009), 120.

25. Surgeons are among top earners, and cosmetic surgeons are among the top of that specialty. Leonor Vivance, "A Cut Above: Local Plastic Surgeons Cut Through 'Nip/Tuck' Stereotypes," *Chicago Tribune*, October 31, 2007, 8 (noting that plastic surgeons with at least three years experience averaged $412,000 compared with $291,000 for a general surgeon with

similar experience); Joan Kron, "Knife Fight," *Allure*, September 1998, 175 (describing $10 million annual income for Hollywood surgeon).

26. Elizabeth Haiken, *Venus Envy: A History of Cosmetic Surgery* (Baltimore, MD: Johns Hopkins Press, 2004), 1. For discussion of "deformities," see 122–27.

27. American Society for Aesthetic Plastic Surgery, "Quick Facts," http://www.surgery.org; Jennifer Cognard Black, "Extreme Makeover, Feminist Edition," *Ms.*, Summer 2007, 47, 48.

28. "Say It with Liposuction," *Harpers Magazine*, August 1990, 31.

29. Natacha Yazbeck, "Lebanon Plumps for Nip, Tuck, and Tour This Summer," Agence France Presse (AFP), July 15, 2009, available at http://www.google.com/hostednews/afp/article/ALeqM5gCC4DZW9TFOU7P-1TUB7s8bE6qOrg.

30. Amy Chozick, "For the Body-Conscious, It's Now the Ankle that Rankles…Chubby Lower Legs, Latest Styles Don't Mix As Women Wage Costly Fight against 'Cankles,'" *Wall Street Journal*, July 23, 2009, A1.

31. Alison Field et al, "Exposure to the Mass Media and Weight Concerns among Girls," *Pediatrics* 103 (1999): 36.

32. Harpers Index, July 2009; Michael F. Jacobsen and Laurie Ann Mazur, *Marketing Madness* (Boulder, CO: Westview Press, 1995), 210; Field et. al, "Exposure to the Mass Media"; Susan Kreimer, "Teens Getting Breast Implants for Graduation," Women's eNews, http://www.womensenews.org, June 17, 2004. For even higher estimates of the number of fourth grade girls on diets, see chapter 2.

33. American Psychological Association, *Report of the APA Task Force on the Sexualization of Girls* (Washington, DC: American Psychological Association, 2007), 15; Peggy Orenstein, "What's Wrong with Cinderella?" *New York Times Magazine*, December 24, 2006, 35; Celia Rivenbank, *Stop Dressing Your Six-Year-Old Like a Skank* (New York: St. Martin's, 2006), 28; Maria Puente, "From the Sandbox to the Spa," *USA Today*, August 1, 2006 available at http://www.usatoday.com/life/lifestyle/2006–08–01-kids-spa_x.htm.

34. Shari L Dworkin and Faye Linda Wachs, *Body Panic: Gender, Health, and the Selling of Fitness* (New York: New York University Press, 2009), 5; Margo Maine, *Body Wars: Making Peace with Women's Bodies* (Carlsbad, CA: Gurze Books, 2000), 210 (suggesting similar proportions).

35. Rita Rudner, "Married without Children," HBO TV Special, June 24, 1995.

36. American Psychological Association, *Report*, 21.

37. Colin McDowell, *Men of Fashion: Peacock Males and Perfect Gentlemen* (London: Thames and Hudson, 1997).

38. Theresa Riordan, *Inventing Beauty* (New York: Broadway Books, 2004), 35.

39. "Men's Grooming: Worth the Hype," *Global Cosmetic Industry Magazine*, December 10, 2007, available at http://www.gcimagazine.com/marketstrends/consumers/men/12307996.html.

40. Alex Kuczynski, *Beauty Junkies: Inside Our $15 Billion Obsession with Cosmetic Surgery* (New York: Doubleday, 2006), 91; Jacqueline Stenson, "With Cosmetic Surgery, Men Can Change Everything from Pecs to Private Parts," *Washingtonian*, May 1993, 92.

41. Dworkin and Wachs, *Body Panic*, 5.

42. Haiken, *Venus Envy*, 236 (quoting Mead).

43. Haiken, *Venus Envy*, 4; Davis, *Reshaping the Female Body*, 14–16; Sander Gilman, *Making the Body Beautiful: A Cultural History of Aesthetic Surgery* (Princeton, NJ: Princeton University Press, 1999), 8–12.

44. Angelika Taschen, "Beauty and Beauty Surgery," in Angelika Taschen, ed., *Aesthetic Surgery* (London: Taschen Books, 2008), 8, 9; Virginia L. Blum, *Flesh Wounds: The Culture of Cosmetic Surgery* (Berkeley: University of California Press, 2003), 182.

45. Lois W. Banner, *American Beauty* (New York: Alfred A. Knopf, 1983), 202.

46. Patricia Cohen, "Middle Age, Before It Came Out in a Bottle," *New York Times*, March 8, 2009, E3.

47. Mathew Honan, "World's Lamest Social Networks," *Wired*, September 2007, 52; http://www.wired.com/techbiz/people/magazine/15-09/st_socialnetworks. Beautiful People URL: http://www.beautifulpeople.com/.

48. See, e.g., http://members.fortunecity.com/kikienpointe/id23.htm; http://proanamia.com/welcome.html.

49. Orbach, *Bodies*, 1.

50. Peiss, *Hope in a Jar*, 12. Magazines began taking advertisements at the turn of the century. Naomi Wolf, *The Beauty Myth* (New York: Doubleday, 1991), 62.

51. Riordan, *Inventing Beauty*, 221 (quoting M. C. Phillips).

52. Deborah L. Rhode, *Speaking of Sex* (Cambridge, MA: Harvard University Press, 1997), 77; *More* magazine, February 2004.

53. Estee Lauder, *Estee: A Success Story* (New York: Random House, 1985), 213.

54. Susan D. Powers, *The Ugly-Girl Papers: Hints for the Toilet* (New York: Harpers and Brown, 1874), 85, 95.

55. Articles from the leading women's magazines were from November 2006. The evangelical advice is recounted in Wolf, *The Beauty Myth*, 88, and the older women's skin advice comes from *More*, described in Sheila Gibbons, "Women Need More from *More* Magazine," Women's eNews, http://www.womensenews.org, February 26, 2004.

56. Ellen Goodman, "The Beauty Show Goes On—Warts and All," *Boston Globe*, December 5, 2002, A19.

57. Banner, *American Beauty*, 250–252; Sarah Banet-Weiser, *The Most Beautiful Girl in the World: Beauty Pageants and National Identity* (Berkeley: University of California Press, 1999), 33–34.

58. Banet-Weiser, *The Most Beautiful Girl in the World*, 31.

59. Beverly Stoeltje, "The Snake Charmer Queen: Ritual, Competition, and Signification in American Festival," in Colleen Cohen, Richard Wilk, and Beverly Stoeltje, eds., *Beauty Queens on the Global Stage* (New York: Routledge, 1996), 13.

60. A. R. Rivera, *Live from Atlantic City: The History of the Miss America Pageant, Before, After, and in Spite of Television* (Bowling Green, KY: Bowling Green University Popular Press, 1991), 24.

61. Banet-Weiser, *The Most Beautiful Girl in the World*, 26, 66.

62. Ibid., 46.

63. Rhode, *Speaking of Sex*, 74; Jon Hurdle, "Miss America to Showcase More Skin, Less Talent," Reuters News, September 17, 2004.

64. Banet-Weiser, *The Most Beautiful Girl in the World*, 124, 203.

65. Ibid., 27, 116, 136–37.

66. David Casstevens, "The Princess Diaries," *Fort Worth Star Telegram*, Oct. 8, 2006, G1; Frank Rich, "Let Me Entertain You," *New York Times*, January 18, 1997, A1; Henry A. Giroux, "Nymphet Fantasies: Child Beauty Pageants and the Politics of Innocence," *Social Text* 57 (1998): 31.

67. Brian Baxter, "Skadden Blog's 'Hot Associate' Contest Is Put on Ice," *American Lawyer*, February 12, 2008; David Lat, "Skadden's Hotness Contest, Chilled by the Powers That Be," *Above the Law*, http://www.abovethelaw.com/2008/02/skadden.php. The comments come from Lat, "Skadden's Hotness Contest."

68. Taschen, "Beauty and Beauty Surgery," 12.

69. June Deery, "Trading Faces: The Makeover Show as Prime Time Infomercial," *Feminist Studies* 4 (2004): 211, 212.

70. *Cosmetic Surgery Newsletter*, September 2004.

71. Jessica Bennett, "Tales of a Modern Diva," *Newsweek*, April 6, 2009, 42.

72. Alessandra Stanley, "Plus Size Sideshow," *New York Times*, August 24, 2008, 1, 19.

73. Amanda Hall Gallagher and Lisa Pecot-Hebert, "'You Need a Makeover!' The Social Construction of Female Body Image in *A Makeover Story*, *What Not to Wear*, and *Extreme Makeover*," *Popular Communication* 5 (2007): 57, 70–73; Richard D'Amico, "Medicine and Society: Plastic Surgery Is Real, Not Reality TV," *American Medical Association Journal of Ethics* 9 (2007): 215, 217.

74. Kelly Kubic and Rebecca Chory, "Exposure to Television Makeover Programs and Perceptions of Self," *Communication Research Report* 24 (2007): 283; Suzanne Mazzeo, Sara Trace, Karen Mitchell, and Rachel Walker Gow, "Effects of a Reality TV Cosmetic Surgery Makeover Program on Eating Disordered Attitudes and Behaviors," *Eating Behavior* 8 (2007): 390; Richard Crockett, Thomas Pruzinsky, and John Persing, "The Influence of Plastic Surgery 'Reality TV' on Cosmetic Surgery Patient Expectations and Decisionmaking," *Journal of the American Society of Plastic Surgeons: Plastic and Reconstructive Surgery* 120 (2007): 316.

75. Eve Ensler, *The Good Body* (New York: Villard, 2005), 9.

76. April E. Fallon, "Culture in the Mirror," 71; Laura Hensley Choate, "Toward a Theoretical Model of Women's Body Image Resilience: Practice

and Theory," *Journal of Counseling and Development* 83 (2005): 320–30; http://www.nytimes.com/2008/08/24/arts/television/24stan.html?_ r=1&sq=biggest%20loser&st=cse&scp=1&pagewanted=print.

77. Seid, *Never Too Thin*, 261.

78. Fallon, "Culture in the Mirror," 89–90; Patricia R. Owen and Erika Laurel-Seller, "Weight and Shape Ideals," *Journal Applied Psychology* 30 (2001): 975, 985.

79. Bradley S. Greenberg, Mathew Eastin, Linda Hofshire, Ken Lachlan, and Kelly D. Brownell, "Portrayals of Overweight and Obese Individuals on Commercial Television," *American Journal of Public Health* 93 (2003): 1342, 1343–47.

80. Dworkin and Wachs, *Body Panic*, 36.

81. David Sarwer, "Female College Students and Cosmetic Surgery: An Investigation of Experiences, Attitudes and Body Image," *Plastic and Reconstructive Surgery* 115 (2005): 931.

82. Seid, *Never Too Thin*, 257.

83. Dworkin and Wachs, *Body Panic*, 36, 71, 87.

84. Jeremy Earp and Jackson Katz, *Media Education Foundation Study Guide: Tough Guise: Violence, Media, and the Crisis in Masculinity* 11 (2005); Media Education Foundation, 2009, available at http://www.mediaed.org/ assets/products/211/studyguide_211.pdf; Guy Trebay "The Vanishing Point," *New York Times*, February 7, 2008, G1. See also Harrison G. Pope Jr., Katharine A. Phillips, and Roberto Olivardia, *The Adonis Complex: The Secret Crisis of Male Body Obsession* (New York: Free Press, 2000).

85. Trebay, "The Vanishing Point," G1 (quoting model Stas Svetlichnyy).

86. A. E. Anderson and L. Di Domenico, "Diet vs. Shape Content of Popular Male and Female Magazines: A Dose-Response Relationship to the Incidence of Eating Disorders?" *International Journal of Eating Disorders* 11 (1992): 283; Dworkin and Wachs, *Body Panic*, 76 (comparing articles in health and fitness magazines).

87. *Ladies Home Journal*, January 1955, 75.

88. Catherine G. Valentine, "Female Bodily Perfection and the Divided Self," in Karen Callaghan, ed., *Ideals of Feminine Beauty* (New York: Greenwood Publishing Group, 1994), 118; Patricia van den Berg,

Dianne Neumark-Sztainer, Peter J. Hannan, and Jess Haines, "Is Dieting Advice from Magazines Helpful or Harmful? Five Year Associations with Weight Control Behaviors and Psychological Outcomes in Adolescents," *Pediatrics* 119 (2007): 30; Kimberly K. Vaughan and Gregory T. Fouts, "Changes in Television and Magazine Exposure and Eating Disorder Symptomatology," *Sex Roles* 49 (2003): 313; Lisa M. Groesz, Michael P. Levine, and Sara K. Murnen, "The Effect of Experimental Presentation of Thin Media Images on Body Satisfaction: A Meta-Analytic Review," *International Journal of Eating Disorders* 31 (2002): 1.

89. Ann E. Becker, "Television, Disordered Eating and Young Women in Fiji: Body Image and Negative Identity during Rapid Social Change," *Culture, Medicine, and Psychiatry* 28 (2004): 533, 546.

90. Sharlene Hesse Biber, *Am I Thin Enough? The Cult of Thinness and the Commercialization of Identity* (New York: Oxford University Press, 1998), 100, 107.

91. Rhode, *Speaking of Sex*, 74–75.

92. "From the Women's Desk—Why Does Larry King Think Hillary Clinton's Hair, Legs, Smile and Figure Are News?" *FAIR*, June 14, 1999, available at http://www.fair.org/index.php?page=1781.

93. David Nason, "Are We Ready to See Hillary Age?" *Australian*, December 19, 2007.

94. Martha M. Lauzen and David M. Dozier, "Maintaining the Double Standard: Portrayals of Age and Gender in Popular Films," *Sex Roles* 52 (2005): 437, 443; Sherlynn Teas'La'Nea Howard-Byrd, *Gender and Age Discrimination among Women in the Broadcast News Industry* (Lewistown, NY: Edwin Mellen Press, 2008), 38–39, 94; Doris G. Bazzini, William D. McIntosh, Stephen M. Smith, Sabrina Cook, and Caleigh Harris, "The Aging Woman in Popular Film: Underrepresented, Unattractive, Unfriendly, and Unintelligent," *Sex Roles* 36 (1997): 531, 533, 541.

95. Caryl Rivers, "Mockery of Katherine Harris," WomenEnews.org, November 29, 2000, http://womensenews.org/story/commentary/001129/mockery-katherine-harris-shows-double-standard.

96. Betty Friedan, *The Fountain of Age* (New York: Simon and Schuster, 1993), 46.

97. Ellen Goodman, "The Aging Battle," *Boston Globe*, November 19, 1992, 21.

98. Jan Hoffman, "The Buzz about Palin Started Here," *New York Times*, September 14, 2008, Style, 1; Patrick Healy and Michael Luo, "150,000 Wardrobe for Palin May Alter Tailor-Made Image," *New York Times*, October 23, 2008, A1.

99. Fiona Morgan, "No Way to Treat a Lady: Was the *New York Times* Profile of Condoleezza Rice Sexist or Just Silly?" Salon.com, available at http://www.salon.com/politics/feature/2000/12/18/rice/index.html. For the cartoon, see http://www.cagle.com/politicalcartoons/pccartoons/archives/siers.asp?Action=GetImage, December 7, 2005.

100. Jennifer Goodwin, "Makeup Secrets," *San Diego Union-Tribune*, July 31, 2005, E1.

101. Alessandra Stanley, "Morning to Night: The TV Watch," *New York Times*, April 6, 2006, C4. See also Denise Flaim, "A Classic New Look for Katie," *Newsday*, September 5, 2006, A12 (pondering her wardrobe transition from chartreuse to navy blue).

102. Alessandra Stanley, "Good Evening America," *New York Times*, September 7, 2009, wk. 1.

103. For discrimination against older women and women of color, see Howard-Byrd, *Gender and Age Discrimination*, 37–38, 93–109; Russell K. Robinson, "Casting and Caste-ing: Reconciling Artistic Freedom and Antidiscrimination Norms," *California Law Review* 95 (2007): 1, 22, 26–27.

104. Jennifer L. Pozner, "Media Discrimination Begets Biased Content," *Women's Review of Books*, May 2006.

105. Letty Cottin Pogrebin, "Why Susan Boyle Makes Us Cry," *Huffington Post*, April 16, 2009.

106. Oprah Winfrey. "How Did I Let This Happen Again," *O Magazine*, January 2009, http://www.oprah.com/article/omagazine/200901_omag_oprah_weight.

107. For critical overviews, see Michael Gard and Jan Wright, *The Obesity Epidemic: Science, Morality and Ideology* (New York: Routledge, 2005), 22–25, 135–48; Dworkin and Wachs, *Body Panic*, 64; Abigail Saguey and Kevin R. Riley, "Weighing Both Sides: Morality, Mortality, and Framing Contests over Obesity," *Journal of Health Politics, Policy, and Law*, 30 (2005): 869; Abigail Saguey and Rene Almeling, "Science, the News Media, and the 'Obesity Epidemic,'" *Sociological Forum* 23 (2008): 53.

108. For individuals and technology, see Gregg Critser, *Fat Land: How Americans Became the Fattest People in the World* (London: Penguin Books, 2003); Michael Fumento, *The Fat of the Land: The Obesity Epidemic and How Overweight Americans Can Help Themselves* (New York: Viking, 1997). For the food industry, see Eric Schlosser, *Fast Food Nation: What the All-American Meal Is Doing to the World* (London: Allen Lane, 2001); Marion Nestle, *Food Politics: How the Food Industry Influences Nutrition and Health* (Berkeley: University of California Press, 2002). For feminism and working mothers, see Natalie Boero, "Fat Kids, Working Moms, and the 'Epidemic of Obesity': Race, Class and Mother Blame," in Esther Rothblum and Sandra Solovay, *The Fat Studies Reader* (New York: New York University Press, 2009); Mary Ebersadt, "The Child-Fat Problem," *Policy Review* (February/March 2003): 3, 9–1; Marjie. Lundstrum, "New Wake Up Call: Study Ties Kids' Obesity to Mom's Job," *Sacremento Bee*, November 21, 2002, A3.

109. Janet S. Fink and Linda J. Kensicki, "An Imperceptible Difference: Visual and Textual Constructions of Femininity in *Sports Illustrated* and *Sports Illustrated for Women*," *Mass Communication and Society* 5 (2002): 317.

110. Paul Campos, *The Obesity Myth: Why America's Obsession with Weight Is Hazardous to Your Health* (New York: Gotham Books, 2004), 92.

111. "Court-esans," *New York Times*, June 25, 2006, 52–56.

112. John Harris and Ben Clayton, "Femininity, Masculinity, Physicality, and the English Tabloid Press: The Case of Anna Kournikova," *International Review for the Sociology of Sport* 37 (2002): 397, 398.

113. Denis Donoghue, *Speaking of Beauty* (New Haven, CT: Yale University Press, 2003), 169.

114. Caroline Heldman, "Out of Body Image," *Ms.*, Spring 2008: 52; "Our Rising Ad Dosage: Its Not as Oppressive as Some Think," *Media Matters*, February 15, 2007; American Association of Advertising Agencies, "How Many Advertisements Is a Person Exposed to in a Day?" available at http://www.aaaa.org/eweb/upload/FAQs/adexposures.pdf (discussing estimates, including *Media Matters* figure of 600–625).

115. Stuart Ewen, *Captains of Consciousness: Advertising and the Social Roots of Consumer Culture* (New York: McGraw Hill, 1976); Sut Jhally, *The Codes of Advertising* (London: Frances Pointer, 1987).

116. Steve Jeffes, *Appearance Is Everything: The Hidden Truth Regarding Your Appearance and Appearance Discrimination* (Pittsburgh, PA: Sterling House, 1998), 134.

117. Jacobsen and Mazur, *Marketing Madness*, 75.

118. Sandra Lee Bartky, *Femininity and Domination* (New York: Routledge, 1990), 41.

119. Jennifer Kahn, "Cottage-Cheese Smoothie?" *New York Times*, October 26, 2006, 45.

120. Susan Douglas, *Where the Girls Are: Growing Up Female with the Mass Media* (New York: Times Books, 1994), 260 (describing gold); Kahn, "Cottage-Cheese Smoothie?" 45 (describing product ineffectiveness).

121. Jacobsen and Mazur, *Marketing Madness*, 76.

122. Wendy Chapkis, *Beauty Secrets: Women and the Power of Appearance* (Boston: South End Press, 1988), 8.

123. Peiss, *Hope in a Jar*, 152.

124. Bobbi Brown, *Living Beauty* (New York: Springboard Press, 2007), xv.

125. Germaine Greer, "Shopping as Seduction? Yes I Think I Can Buy That," *London Times*, July 18, 2000.

126. T. Jackson Learns, "American Advertising and the Construction of the Body," in Kathryn Grover, ed., *Fitness in American Culture: Images of Health, Sport, and the Body, 1830–1940* (Amherst: University of Massachusetts Press, 1989): 62.

127. Advertisements quoted in Diane Barthel, *Putting on Appearances: Gender and Advertising* (Philadelphia: Temple University Press, 1988), 88–96, 189, 196.

128. Barthel, *Putting on Appearances*, 144–45.

129. Roger Highfield, "Descriptions of Cosmetic Properties Baffle the Experts: Roger Highfield Asks Top Scientists Whether They Understand the Language Used to Describe Cosmetics," *London Daily Telegraph*, December 6, 2005, 27; Bartky, *Femininity and Domination*, 70 (ad for Biotherm).

130. Peiss, *Hope in a Jar*, 152.

131. Susan Bordo, *Unbearable Weight: Feminism, Western Culture, and the Body* (Berkeley: University of California Press, 2003), 246–47.

CHAPTER 4

1. Dave Barry, "When She Asks How She Looks, Any Answer Could Get Ugly," February 1, 1998.

2. Mary Wollstonecraft, *A Vindication of the Rights of Women*, vol. 5 (1792), in Janet Todd and Marilyn Butler, *The Works of Mary Wollstonecraft* (London: William Pickering and Chatow, 1958), 113.

3. Samuel Johnson, *The Rambler*, ed. W. J. Bate and Albrecht B. Strauss, vol. 2 (New Haven, CT: Yale University Press, 1969), 344–45.

4. Elizabeth Haiken, *Venus Envy: A History of Cosmetic Surgery* (Baltimore, MD: Johns Hopkins University Press, 1997), 163.

5. Virginia Woolf, *A Room of One's Own and Three Guineas*, with an Introduction by Hermione Lee (London: Hogarth Press, 1984), 84

6. Lois Banner, *American Beauty* (New York: Knopf, 1983), 42.

7. Sarah E. Schaffer, "Reading Our Lips: The History of Lipstick Regulation in Western Seats of Power," *Food and Drug Law Journal* 62 (2007): 165, 174. Such prohibitions were modeled on an English statute providing similar relief, as well as subjecting the woman to potential charges for witchcraft. See Schaffer, "Reading Our Lips," 173 and discussion in chapter 6 of this book.

8. Kathy Peiss, *Hope in a Jar: The Making of America's Beauty Culture* (New York: Holt, 1999), 57.

9. Peiss, *Hope in a Jar*, 207 (quoting Nannie Burroughs).

10. Ayana D. Byrd and Lori L. Tharps, *Hair Story: Untangling the Roots of Black Hair in America* (New York: St. Martin's Griffin, 2002), 38; Tracey Owens Patton, "Hey Girl, Am I More Than My Hair? African American Women and Their Struggles with Beauty, Body Image and Hair," *National Women's Studies Association Journal* 18 (2006): 29.

11. Peiss, *Hope in a Jar*, 57.

12. Zelda Fitzgerald, in Mathew Broccoli, ed., *Collected Writings of Zelda Fitzgerald* (New York: MacMillan, 1992), 416.

13. Schaffer, "Reading Our Lips," 176.

14. Susan Brownmiller, *Femininity* (New York: Simon and Schuster, 1984), 88. See Banner, *American Beauty*, 86–87.

15. Banner, *American Beauty*, 98–99, 147–50.

16. Brownmiller, *Femininity*, 23. See also Lynn Chancer, *Reconcilable Differences: Confronting Beauty, Pornography and the Future of Feminism* (Berkeley: University of California Press, 1998), 158.

17. Brownmiller, *Femininity*, 160, 162.

18. Janet Radcliffe Richards, *The Sceptical Feminist: A Philosophical Enquiry* (London: Penguin, 1994), 339.

19. Jody Rohlena, *Sounds Like a New Woman* (New York: Penguin, 1993), 57 (quoting Rush Limbaugh).

20. Anna Quindlin, "And Now, Babe Feminism," *New York Times*, January 19, 1994, A21 (quoting Christina Hoff Sommers).

21. Leslie Heywood and Jennifer Drake, eds., *Third Wave Agenda: Being Feminist, Doing Feminism* (Minneapolis: University of Minnesota Press, 1997); Jennifer Baumgardner and Amy Richards, *Manifesta: Young Women, Feminism and the Future* (New York: Farrar, Straus and Giroux, 2000); Astrid Henry, *Not My Mother's Sister: Generational Conflict and Third Wave Feminism* (Indianapolis: Indiana University Press, 2004).

22. Jannika Bock, *Riot Grrrl: A Feminist Re-Interpretation of the Punk Narrative* (La Vergne, Tennessee: VDM Verlag Dr. Muller, 2008), 24–25; Lauraine Leblanc, *Pretty in Punk: Girls' Gender Resistance in a Boys' Subculture* (New Brunswick, NJ: Rutgers University Press, 1999), 13, 219. See generally Cherie Turner, *The Riot Grrrl Movement: The Feminism of a New Generation* (New York: Rosen Publishing, 2001).

23. Naomi Wolf, *The Beauty Myth: How Images of Beauty Are Used against Women* (New York: Harper, 2002), 53.

24. Susan Bordo, *Unbearable Weight* (Berkeley: University of California Press, 1993).

25. Karen A. Callaghan, *Ideals of Feminine Beauty: Philosophical, Social, and Cultural Dimensions* (New York: Greenwood Press, 1994), vi, ix.

26. Sarah Banet-Weiser, *The Most Beautiful Girl in the World: Beauty Pageants and National Identity* (Berkeley: University of California Press, 1999), 146 (quoting Women against Pornography).

27. Sandra Bartky, *Femininity and Domination: Studies in the Phenomenology of Oppression* (London: Routledge Publishers, 1990), 42.

28. Kathryn Pauley Morgan, "Women and the Knife: Cosmetic Surgery and the Colonization of Women's Bodies," *Hypatia* 6 (1991): 25, reprinted in Rose Weitz, ed., *The Politics of Women's Bodies* (New York: Oxford University Press, 1998), 147, 150.

29. Morgan, "Women and the Knife," 37.

30. Nathaniel Hawthorne, "The Birthmark," in Norman Holmes Pearson, ed., *The Hawthorne Treasure: Complete Novels and Selected Tales of Nathaniel Hawthorne* (New York: Random House, Modern Library, 1999), 285, 286.

31. Hawthorne, "The Birthmark," 296, 297.

32. Kathy Davis, "Remaking the She-Devil: A Critical Look at Feminist Approaches to Beauty," *Hypatia* 6 (1991): 21, 28.

33. Linda Scott, *Fresh Lipstick: Redressing Fashion and Feminism* (New York: Palgrave Macmillan, 2006), 325.

34. Bartky, *Femininity and Domination*.

35. For letting yourself go, see Katha Pollitt, *Learning to Drive* (New York: Random House, 2007), 192–200.

36. Chancer, *Reconcilable Differences*, 110; Rita Freedman, *Beauty Bound* (Lexington, MA: Lexington Books, 1986), 64. For the need to look natural, see Wendy Chapkis, *Beauty Secrets: Women and the Politics of Appearance* (Cambridge, MA: South End Press, 1999), 2; Davis, "Remaking the She-Devil," 25, 27.

37. Ellen Goodman, "The Aging Battle," *Boston Globe*, November 19, 1992, 21 (quoting Greer).

38. Myra Dinnerstein and Rose Weitz, "Jane Fondu, Barbara Bush, and Other Aging Bodies," in Rose Weitz, *The Politics of Women's Bodies*, 196 (quoting Andrea Messina).

39. Dinnerstein and Weitz, "Jane Fonda," 196 (quoting Fonda).

40. Ibid., 197–98 (quoting Bush).

41. Kathy Davis, *Reshaping the Female Body: The Dilemma of Cosmetic Surgery* (New York: Routledge, 1995), 85.

42. Chapkis, *Beauty Secrets*, 2.

43. Eve Ensler, *The Good Body* (New York: Villard, 2005), 5–6.

44. Morgan, "Women and the Knife," 158.

45. Debra L. Gimlin, *Body Work*, (Berkeley: University of California Press, 2002), 142.

46. Banet-Weiser, *The Most Beautiful Girl in the World*, 17.

47. Decca Aitkenhead, "Most British Women Now Expect to Have Cosmetic Surgery in Their Lifetime: How Did the Ultimate Feminist Taboo Just Become Another Lifestyle Choice?" *Guardian* (London), September 14, 2005, 10.

48. Davis, *Reshaping the Female Body*, 126.

49. Gimlin, *Body Work*, 146.

50. Davis, *Reshaping the Female Body*, 71.

51. Ibid., 74.

52. Ibid., 90, 98: Davis, *Reshaping the Female Body*, 74.

53. Karen Lehman, *The Lipstick Proviso: Women, Sex and Power in the Real World* (New York: Doubleday 1997), 80 (quoting Clinton).

54. Thomas Pruzinsky and Milton T. Egerton, "Body Image: Change in Cosmetic Plastic Surgery," in Thomas Cash and Thomas Pruzinsky, eds., *Body Images: Development, Deviance, and Change* (New York: Guilford Press, 1990), 217, 222–23. See also Davis, *Reshaping the Female Body*, 120–40, 156.

55. Davis, *Reshaping the Female Body*, 139–40; Pruzinsky and Egerton, "Body Image," 223–24; Sander L. Gilman, *Creating Beauty to Cure the Soul: Race and Psychology in the Shaping of Aesthetic Surgery* (Durham, NC: Duke University Press, 1998), 144–45.

56. Gimlin, *Body Work*, 97.

57. Davis, *Reshaping the Female Body*, 140, 156, 162.

58. Kirsten Dellinger and Christine L. Williams, "Makeup at Work: Negotiating Appearance Rules in the Workplace," *Gender and Society* 11 (1997): 151, 160, 165.

59. Ibid., 178–79; Gimlin, *Body Work*, 12.

60. Laura T. Coffey, "Do High Heels Empower or Oppress Women," MSNBC, September 23, 2009, available at http://www.msnbc.msn.com/id/32970817/ns/today_fashion_and_beauty/.

61. Jan Breslauer, "Stacked Like Me," *Playboy*, July 1957, 64, 66, 67.

62. Susan Dominus, "The Seductress of Vanity," *New York Times*, May 5, 2002, Section 6, 48 (quoting Pat Wexler).

63. Aitkenhead, "Most British Women Now Expect to Have Cosmetic Surgery," 10.

64. Ann Kreamer, "The Gray Wars," *Time*, September 7, 2007, 72.

65. Ibid., 73.

66. Brownmiller, *Femininity*, 167.

67. Carolyn Heilbrun, "Coming of Age," *New York Woman*, February 1991, 56, 58.

68. Ensler, *The Good Body*, xv.

69. Nora Ephron, *Crazy Salad* (New York: Knopf, 1975), 19.

70. Ellen Goodman, "Stacked Against Us," *Boston Globe*, April 17, 2005, C11.

71. Davis, *Reshaping the Female Body*, 170.

72. Dellinger and Williams, "Makeup at Work," 156.

73. Ibid., 163.

74. Davis, *Reshaping the Female Body*, 162.

75. Ibid.

76. Pollitt, *Learning to Drive*, 202.

77. Gimlin, *Body Works*, 107.

78. Ibid.

79. Michelle Cottle, "Bodywork," *New Republic*, March 5, 2002, 16, 19.

80. Peiss, *Hope in a Jar*, 256.

81. Ibid.

82. Angela Neustatter, "My Eyes, My Decision," *Scotsman*, July 10, 1997, 13

83. Katharine Viner, "The New Plastic Feminism," *Guardian* (London), July 21, 1997, T4 (quoting Neustatter).

84. Viner, "The New Plastic Feminism," T4 (quoting Breslauer).

85. Breslauer, "Stacked Like Me," 66.

86. Ellen Goodman, "Singing Sensation Defies Beauty Culture (Sort of)," *San Jose Mercury*, May 1, 2009, np (quoting Boyle).

87. Goodman, "Singing Sensation," np.

88. Chancer, *Reconcilable Differences*, 171.

89. Brownmiller, *Femininity*, 81, 156.

90. Patricia Williams, "Have Pantsuit, Will Travel," *Nation*, August 27, 2008.

91. Chapkis, *Beauty Secrets*, 131.

92. Lehman, *Lipstick Proviso*, 9.

93. Chapkis, *Beauty Secrets*. See Davis, "Remaking the She-Devil," 27.

94. Bordo, *Unbearable Weight*. See also Davis, "Remaking the She-Devil," 27.

95. Pollitt, *Learning to Drive*, 192.

96. "Women Now Empowered by Everything a Woman Does," *The Onion*, February 19, 2003, available at http://www.theonion.com/content/node/38558.

97. Pollitt, *Learning to Drive*, 204.

98. Nancy Etcoff, *Survival of the Prettiest* (New York: Doubleday, 1999), 243–44.

99. Nancy Friday, *The Power of Beauty* (New York: HarperCollins, 1996), 359.

100. Barbara J. Risman, *Gender Vertigo* (New Haven, CT: Yale University Press, 1998), 157–58, 170. For discussion of the sex and eye color analogy, see Deborah L. Rhode, *Justice and Gender* (Cambridge, MA: Harvard University Press, 1998), 313–15.

101. See research discussed in Cecilia J. Ridgeway and Shelley J. Correll, "Limiting Inequality through Interaction: The End[s] of Gender," *Contemporary Sociology* 29 (2000): 110, 111–13.

102. Chancer, *Reconcilable Differences*, 171.

103. Lisa de Moraes, "Greta, Is That You? Analyst Moves From CNN to Uh, Fox," *Washington Post*, February 3, 2002, C1; Kim Ode, "The Heart Has Reasons: It's Easy to Understand Why Van Susteren Chose the Eye Tuck: It May Even Be Tempting," *Minneapolis Star Tribune*, February 12, 2002, E12.

104. Maureen Dowd, "Facing Up to a Botox Nation," *Times Union*, February 10, 2002, B5.

105. Chancer, *Reconcilable Differences*, 96.

CHAPTER 5

1. A review of Lexis, the main legal search engine; the Europa Case Law Index, the official database for European nations; and several treatises, including Susan Mayne and Susan Malyon, *Employment Law in Europe* (London: Butterworths Tolly, 2001) and Jeff Kenner, *EU Employment Law: From Rome to Amsterdam and Beyond* (Portland, OR: Hart Publishing, 2003), revealed only one case on appearance discrimination. See *Smith v. Safeway*, 1996 Industrial Case Reports 868 (1996) (upholding the dismissal of a male delicatessen worker for unconventionally long hair, where no similar rule applied to women because their long hair was not unconventional). For the results in other cases involving grooming codes, which are not indexed as appearance discrimination, see chapter 6.

2. Sidney Katz, "The Importance of Being Beautiful," in James M. Henslin, ed., *Down to Earth Sociology: Introductory Readings* (New York: Prentice-Hall, 1997), 312; Gordon L. Patzer, *The Physical Attractiveness Phenomena* (New York: Plenum, 1985), 164–65.

3. National Education Association, "Report on Size Discrimination" (1994), available at http://www.lectlaw.com/files/con28.htm; see also Gina Kolata, "For a World of Woes, We Blame Cookie Monsters," *New York Times*, October 29, 2006, E14.

4. Robert Crosnoe, "Gender, Obesity, and Education," *Social Education* 80 (2007): 241, 242–43, 254–57.

5. Gina Kolata, *Rethinking Thin: The New Science of Weight Loss—and the Myths and Realities of Dieting* (New York: Farrar, Straus and Giroux, 2007), 69; Rebecca Puhl, "Coping with Weight Stigma," in Kelly, D, Brownell, Rebecca M. Puhl, Marlene B. Schwartz, and L. Rudd, eds., *Weight Bias, Nature, Consequences, and Remedies* (New York: The Guilford Press, 2005), 275, 280; Sondra Solovay, *Tipping the Scales of Justice: Fighting Weight-Based Discrimination* (Buffalo, NY: Prometheus Books, 2000), 40–41, 58–59.

6. Steven L. Gortmaker et al., "Social and Economic Consequences of Overweight in Adolescence and Young Adulthood," *New England Journal of Medicine* 329 (2003): 1008, 1011; Jane Byeff Korn, "Fat," *Boston Law Review* 77 (1997): 25. For examples of cases involving nicknames, see *Doe v. City of Belleville*, 119 F.3d 563, 566 (7th Cir. 1997), vacated, 523 U.S. 1001

(1998) ("fat boy"); *Butterfield v. New York State*, No. 96Civ.5144(BDP)LMS, 1998 WL 401533, at 6 (S.D.N.Y. July 15, 1998) ("butterball").

7. Rebecca Puhl and Kelly D. Brownell, "Bias, Discrimination, and Obesity," *Obesity Research* 9 (2001): 788, 789–90.

8. Michael Fumento, *The Fat of the Land: Our Health Problem Crisis and How Overweight Americans Can Help Themselves* (New York: Penguin, 1997), 49.

9. Paul Campos, *The Obesity Myth: Why America's Obsession with Weight Is Hazardous to Your Health* (New York: Gotham Books, 2004), 65; see also Solovay, *Tipping the Scales of Justice*, 106 (citing a *New York Times* finding that fewer than 10 percent of top male executives were fat). For employer attitudes, see generally ibid., 99–121.

10. Paul Campos, "Fat Judges Need Not Apply," *Daily Beast*, May 4, 2009, available at http://www.thedailybeast.com/blogs-and-stories/2009–05–04/fat-judges-need-not-apply/pl.

11. K. Anthony Appiah, "Stereotypes and the Shaping of Identity," in Robert C. Post et al., *Prejudicial Appearances: The Logic of American Antidiscrimination Law* (Durham, NC: Duke University Press, 2001), 55, 57.

12. One study found that weight was irrelevant to 90 percent of workplace jobs. Kara Swisher, "Overweight Workers Battle Bias on the Job: Looks Discrimination Called Common, but Hard to Prove," *Washington Post*, January 24, 1994, A1.

13. Michael Walzer, *Spheres of Justice: A Defense of Pluralism and Equality* (New York: Basic Books, 1984).

14. Richard C. Paddock, "California Album: Santa Cruz Grants Anti-Bias Protection to the Ugly," *Los Angeles Times*, May 25, 1992, A3 (quoting City Councilman Neil Coonerty).

15. Martha Groves, "Looks Won't Mean a Lot if Anti-Bias Law Is Approved," *Los Angeles Times*, January 24, 1992, A3 (quoting City Councilman Neil Coonerty).

16. *EEOC v. Texas Bus Lines*, 923 F. Supp. 965, 967–68 (S.D. Tex. 1996).

17. Jack M. Balkin, "The Constitution of Status," *Yale Law Journal* 106 (1997): 2313, 2359–60; Cass R. Sunstein, "The Anticaste Principle," *Michigan Law Review* 92 (1994): 2410, 2428–29.

18. Balkin, "The Constitution of Status," 2359–60; Sunstein, "The Anticaste Principle," 2428–29.

19. Michael Sandel, *The Case against Perfection: Ethics in the Age of Genetic Engineering* (Cambridge, MA: Harvard University Press, 2007), 91.

20. For the bias against minorities who look "too ethnic" see the discussion later in this chapter and in chapter 2.

21. *Hollins v. Atlantic Co.*, 188 F.3d 652, 655–57 (6th Cir. 1999).

22. Peter Glick et al., "Evaluations of Sexy Women in Low- and High-Status Jobs," *Psychology of Women Quarterly* 29 (2005): 389. For findings concerning upper-level positions, see Megumi Hosoda, Eugene F. Stone-Romero, and Gwen Coats, "The Effects of Physical Attractiveness on Job-Related Outcomes: A Meta-Analysis of Experimental Studies," *Personnel Psychology* 56 (2003): 451–53.

23. American Psychological Association, *Report of the APA Task Force on the Sexualization of Girls*, (Washington, DC: American Psychological Association, 2007), 32–33.

24. Kathy Davis, *Reshaping the Female Body: The Dilemma of Cosmetic Surgery* (New York: Routledge, 1995), 42.

25. "How We Spend Time," *Time*, October 30, 2006, 53. For women's disproportionate financial expenditures, see sources cited in Deborah L. Rhode, *Speaking of Sex* (1998), 76. Men's share of the skin care market is, however, growing. Alex Kuczynski, *Beauty Junkies: In Search of the Thinnest Thighs, Perkiest Breasts, Smoothest Faces, Whitest Teeth, and Skinniest, Most Perfect Toes in America* (New York: Broadway Publishers, 2008), 91.

26. American Society for Aesthetic Plastic Surgery, "Cosmetic Surgery National Data Bank Statistics," 2007, 3; http://www.surgery.org/sites/default/files/2007stats.pdf. Daniel DeNoon, "Latest Plastic Surgery Trends and Stats," WebMd Health News, June 5, 2003, http://www.webmd.com (noting that nine out of ten cosmetic surgery patients are women); Frederick M. Grazer and Rudolph H. de Jong, "Fatal Outcomes from Liposuction: Census Survey of Cosmetic Surgeons," unpublished survey, Penn State University School of Medicine and Thomas Jefferson Medical College, June 11, 1999 (noting the health risks women assume); Karen Wells et al., "The Health Status of Women Following Cosmetic Surgery," unpublished study, University of South Florida College of Medicine and

College of Public Health, April 26, 1993, 907, 912 (noting health risks for breast augmentation surgery).

27. Michael Luo and Cathy Horyn, "Three Palin Stylists Cost Campaign More Than $165,000," *New York Times*, December 6, 2008, A9, A11.

28. See *EEOC v. Sage Realty Corp.*, 87 F.R.D. 365 (S.D.N.Y. 1980) (finding legal liability based on employer's requirement of a sexually provocative uniform that exposed employee to harassment); Dianne Avery and Marion Crain, "Branded: Corporate Image, Sexual Stereotyping and the New Face of Capitalism," *Duke Journal of Gender Law and Policy* 14 (2007): 13, 17, 104; Marc Linder, "Smart Women, Stupid Shoes, and Cynical Employers: The Unlawfulness and Adverse Health Consequences of Sexually Discriminatory Workplace Footwear Requirements for Female Employees," *Journal of Corporate Law* 22 (1997): 295, 298. For a recent law firm grooming policy that advised women to wear high heels and provoked considerable objection from the legal community, see Dan Slater, "Firm to Female Lawyers: Wear High Heels, Embrace Your Femininity," *Wall Street Journal* Law Blog, December 23, 2008, http://blogs.wsj.com/law/2008/12/23/firm-to-female-lawyers-wear-high-heels-embracy-your-femininity/.

29. *Alam v. Reno Hilton Corp.*, 819 F. Supp. 905, 913 (D. Nev. 1993) (casino policy); *Craft v. Metromedia*, 572 F. Supp. 868 (W.D. Mo. 1983), rev'd in part, 766 F.2d 1205, 1214–15 (8th Cir. 1985) (television station); Christine Craft, *Too Old, Too Ugly, Not Deferential to Men* (New York: Prime Publishing of St. Martin's, 1986) (television station); Janelle Brown, "Baby, You Can Park My Car," *New York Times*, March 27, 2005, E1 (valet parking service); Amy Roe, "Some Coffee Stands Get Steamier," *Seattle Times*, January 22, 2007, A1 (espresso bar); "Waitresses Dressed as Naughty Nurses Rile RNs," MSNBC.com, December 8, 2006, http://www.msnbc.msn.com/id/16112393/print/1/displaymode/1098/ (naughty nurse waitresses); William M. Welch, "These Baristas Add a Jolt to Coffee Shops," *USA Today*, June 3, 2009, 3A (Vietnamese coffee shops in Los Angeles).

30. Brown, "Baby, You Can Park My Car," E1.

31. Sam Wood, "'Borgata Babes' Settle Discrimination Suit," *Philadelphia Inquirer*, July 31, 2008, 28; Jennifer Friedlin, "Gaining Weight Cost Me My Job," *Marie Claire*, October 1, 2005, 153.

32. John Curran, "Casino Weight Rule Faces New Attacks," *Philadelphia Inquirer*, April 28, 2005; see also Friedlin, "Gaining Weight Cost Me My Job."

33. Dan Gross, "Ex-Servers Sue Borgata," *Philadelphia Daily News*, January 31, 2006, 25; see also Friedlin, "Gaining Weight Cost Me My Job."

34. See Friedlin, "Gaining Weight Cost Me My Job."

35. Ibid.; "Good Morning America: High Stakes Weight Discrimination?" ABC News television broadcast, May 3, 2005.

36. Marilyn Brown, "Gay Teen Sues School over Yearbook Photo," *Tampa Tribune*, June 20, 2002, MI (quoting Karen Doering).

37. Susan Brownmiller, *Feminity* (New York: Simon and Schuster, 1984), 76 (quoting Edith Wharton).

38. Susan Sontag, *"Against Interpretation" and Other Essays* (New York: Farrar, Strauss and Giroux, 1966), 18.

39. For headscarves, see Anita L. Allen, "Undressing Difference: The Hijab in the West," *Berkeley Journal of Gender Law and Justice* 23 (2008): 208, 211–16 (reviewing Joan Wallach Scott, *The Politics of the Veil* [Princeton, NJ: Princeton University Press, 2007]); Gil Grantmore, "Lex and the City," *Georgetown Law Journal* 91 (2002): 913, 917. For leading cases on hair braiding and cornrows, see *Rogers v. American Airlines, Inc.*, 527 F. Supp. 229 (S.D. N.Y. 1981); *McBride v. Lawstaf, Inc.*, No. 1:96-cv-0196-cc, 1996 WL755779 (N.D. Ga. Sept 19, 1996). For other cases, see chapter 6 and Elizabeth M. Adamitis, "Appearance Matters: A Proposal to Prohibit Appearance Discrimination in Employment," *Washington Law Review* 75 (2000): 195, 205.

40. *Smith v. City of Salem*, 378 F.3d. 566, 568, 574 (6th Cir. 2004) (reversing a dismissal of a transsexual's challenge to dress and grooming requirements); *De Santis v. Pac. Tel. and Tel. Co.*, 608 F.2d 327, 33a (9th Cir 1979) (holding that barring men from wearing earrings would be permissible); *Lanigan v. Bartlett and Co. Grain*, 466 F. Supp. 1388, 1392 (W.D. Mo. 1979) (upholding an employer's skirt requirement for all female employees); *Pecenka v. Fareway Stores, Inc.*, 672 N.W.2d 800, 804 (Iowa 2003). See generally Karl E. Klare, "Power/Dressing: Regulation of Employee Appearance," *New England Law Review* 26 (1992): 1395 (discussing the content and meaning of appearance-regulation laws).

41. The leading racial grooming case upheld the prohibitions on cornrows. *Rogers v. Am. Airlines, Inc.*, 527 F. Supp. 229 (S.D.N.Y. 1981). For more recent cases, see *McManus v. MCI Commc'ns Corp.*, 748 A.2d 949, 952 (D.C.

Cir. 2000); *McBride v. Lawstaf, Inc.*, 71 Fair Empl. Prac. Cas. (BNA) 1758, 1759–60 (N.D. Ga. Sept. 19, 1996); Monica C. Bell, "The Braiding Cases, Cultural Deference, and the Inadequate Protection of Black Women Consumers," *Yale Journal of Law and Feminism* 19 (2007): 125, 133 (describing a 2006 Baltimore police department prohibition on hair braiding);. Lewis and Roca, LLP, "Tattoos, Piercings, and Other Looks—Where Can You Draw the Line?" *Arizona Employee Law Letter* 8 (2001): 7. For more successful litigation involving hair length and Native Americans, see Grantmore, "Lex and the City," 914–15. For critiques of prohibitions that have been upheld, see Paulette M. Caldwell, "A Hair Piece: Perspectives on the Intersection of Race and Gender," *Duke Law Journal* (1991): 365, 371–72; Kenji Yoshino, "Covering," *Yale Law Journal* 111 (2002): 769, 890–93.

42. *Rogers*, 527 F. Supp. at 232.

43. Caldwell, "A Hair Piece," 379; Michelle L. Turner, "The Braided Uproar: A Defense of My Sister's Hair and a Contemporary Indictment of *Rogers v. American Airlines*," *Cardozo Women's Law Journal* 7 (2001): 115.

44. *Rogers*, 527 F. Supp. at 231. For other examples, see cases cited in note 41 this chapter.

45. See Ingrid Banks, *Hair Matters: Beauty, Power, and Black Women's Consciousness* (New York: New York University Press, 2000); Ayana D. Byrd and Lori L. Tharps, *Hair Story: Untangling the Roots of Black Hair in America* (New York: St. Martin's Griffin, 2002); Bell, "The Braiding Cases," 128–31; Caldwell, "A Hair Piece," 379, 391–93; Tracey Owens Patton, "Hey Girl, Am I More than My Hair? African American Women and Their Struggles with Beauty, Body Image and Hair," *National Women's Studies Association Journal* 18 (2006): 26–27.

46. Yoshino, "Covering," 896.

47. *Hander v. San Jacinto Junior College*, 519 F. 2d 273, 281–82 (5th Cir. 1975) (Brown, C.J., concurring).

48. *Hosapple v. Woods*, 500 2d 49, 52 (7th Cir. 1974) (Pell, J., concurring). See also cases cited in Gowri Ramachandran, "Freedom of Dress: State and Private Regulation of Clothing, Hairstyle, Jewelry, Makeup, Tattoos, and Piercing," *Maryland Law Review* 66 (2006): 11, 44.

49. Mark McGraw, "Limiting Looks," Human Resource Executive Online, Oct. 2, 2005, available at http://www.hrexecutive.com/HRE/story.jsp?storyId=4269043 (describing policy).

50. See Sarah Kershaw, "Move Over, My Pretty, Ugly Is Here," *New York Times*, October 30, 2008, E1 (noting that " '[m]ost people would want to disclaim membership' " in any group labeled "ugly").

51. Larry Alexander, "What Makes Wrongful Discrimination Wrong? Biases, Preferences, Stereotypes, and Proxies," *University of Pennsylvania Law Review* 141 (1992): 149, 166.

52. Richard Thompson Ford, *The Race Card: How Bluffing about Bias Makes Race Relations Worse* (New York: Farrar, Straus and Giroux, 2008), 159.

53. Tatiana Andreyeva, Rebecca M. Puhl, and Kelly D. Brownell, "Changes in Perceived Weight Discrimination among Americans, 1995–1996 through 2004–2006," *Obesity* 16 (2008): 1129, 1131 (12 percent); Employment Law Alliance, "Nearly One Half of Americans Polled Believe Obese Workers Are Discriminated Against on the Job," November 6, 2003, http://www.employmentlawalliance.com/en/node/1293 (16 percent).

54. Andreyeva, Puhl, and Brownell, "Changes in Perceived Weight Discrimination," 1131 (reporting 14 percent for age and 18.7 percent for sex; *NBC News/Wall Street Journal* Poll, June 2008, available at http://roperweb. ropercenter.uconn.edu/ (reporting 12 percent for sex, 12 percent for race, 9 percent for age, and 3 percent for ethic or religious bias).

55. Employment Law Alliance, "Nearly One-Half of Americans Polled Believe Obese Workers Are Discriminated Against on the Job," November 6, 2003, http://www.employmentlawalliance.com/en/node/1293. The poll did not use the term "often," so its results are not exactly comparable to other surveys using that term, such as the Harris Poll. Humphrey Taylor, "Workplace Discrimination against, and Jokes about, African Americans, Gays, Jews, Muslims and Others," Harris Poll #61, November 13, 2002, http://www.harrisinteractive.com/harris_poll/index.asp?PID=340. When asked how often certain groups experienced discrimination in the workplace, the following percentages reported "often": age (32 percent); sexual orientation (29 percent); people with disabilities (21 percent); women (19 percent); African Americans (18 percent); Muslims (14 percent); Hispanics (12 percent); Jews (5 percent); Asian Americans (5 percent); ibid.

56. Employment Law Alliance, "Nearly One-Half."

57. For example, support for affirmative action is lower when questions are framed in terms of special treatment or preferences than for other strategies that equalize opportunities or take qualifications into account.

See Loan Le and Jack Citrin, "Affirmative Action," in Nathaniel Persily, Jack Citrin, and Patrick J. Egan, eds., *Public Opinion and Constitutional Controversy* (New York:Oxford University Press, 2008), 162, 172–73; Faye J. Crosby, *Affirmative Action Is Dead; Long Live Affirmative Action* (New Haven, CT: Yale University Press, 2004), 73–81.

58. See, e.g., Terry Poulton, *No Fat Chicks: How Big Business Profits by Making Women Hate Their Bodies—and How to Fight Back* (Secaucus, NJ: Carol, 1997), 126–32; Stephanie B. Goldberg, "Obesity: Discrimination Violates Rehab Act," *American Bar Association Journal* 80 (1994): 95; Sharlene A. McEvoy, "Fat Chance: Employment Discrimination against the Overweight," *Labor Law Journal* 43 (1992): 3; Tamar Lewin, "Workplace Bias Tied to Obesity Is Ruled Illegal," *New York Times*, November 24, 1993, A18.

59. Poulton, *No Fat Chicks*, 133.

60. *McDermott v. Xerox Corp.*, 478 N.Y.S.2d 982, 983 (App. Div. 1984).

61. For a leading decision striking down discrimination in the insurance context, see *City of L.A. Department of Water and Power v. Manhart*, 435 U.S. 702 (1978).

62. Natalie Angier, "Why So Many Ridicule the Overweight," *New York Times*, November 22, 1992, 38 (internal quotation marks omitted).

63. Ford, *The Race Card*, 132.

64. See, e.g., Campos, *The Obesity Myth*; Kolata, *Rethinking Thin*.

65. See the discussion in chapter 2.

66. Elizabeth Fernandez, "Exercising Her Right to Work," *San Francisco Chronicle*, May 7, 2002, A1; Abby Ellin, "New Breed of Trainers Are Proving Fat Is Fit," *New York Times*, September 1, 2005, G8.

67. Joshua L. Weinstein, "Nurse Ousted for Obesity Sues School," *St Petersburg (FL) Times*, April 8, 1989, 3B (quoting Steven Snow); *Russell v. Salve Regina Coll.*, 890 F.2d 484, 488 (1st Cir. 1989).

68. "Is It Such a Crime?" *ABC News*, November 15, 1991; Richard C. Dujardin, "Update: Still Fighting for Rights of Overweight," *Providence (RI) Journal-Bulletin*, April 10, 1994, 2B.

69. See Poulton, *No Fat Chicks*, 195; see also Ellin, "New Breed of Trainers" (discussing the growing acceptance of overweight trainers and a fitness class that is "designed for people of all sizes").

70. Fernandez, "Exercizing Her Right to Work"; see also Ellin, "New Breed of Trainers."

71. See Avery and Crain, "Branded," 15–19; Jordan D. Bello, "Attractiveness as Hiring Criteria: Savvy Business Practice or Racial Discrimination?" *Journal of Gender, Race, and Justice* 8 (2005): 483, 494–97 (citing studies showing that employee attractiveness can positively influence consumer perceptions); Brian D. Till and Michael Busler, "Matching Products with Endorsers: Attractiveness versus Expertise," *Journal of Consumer Marketing* 15 (1998): 576; Robert J. Barro, "So You Want to Hire the Beautiful. Well, Why Not?" *Business Week*, March 16, 1998, 18.

72. Gersh Kuntzman, "Casino Gals' Fat Chance—Hotel's Weightress Rule: Gain Pounds, Lose a Job," *New York Post*, February 18, 2005, 3. "Any employee who gains more than seven percent of his or her body weight will be required to lose the weight in a gym that the casino pays for. Failure to do so will result in termination"; ibid.

73. *Yanowitz v. L'Oreal USA, Inc.*, 131 Cal. Rptr. 2d 575, 582, 588 (Ct. App. 2003) (finding the "hot" directive impermissible); Steven Greenhouse, "Going for the Look, but Risking Discrimination," *New York Times*, July 13, 2003, A12 (describing preferences for young and trendy restaurant staff); Steven Greenhouse, "Abercrombie and Fitch Bias Case Is Settled," *New York Times*, November 17, 2004, A16 (noting that Abercrombie and Fitch ultimately settled claims of race discrimination by agreeing to integrate its staff and advertisements); Ford, *The Race Card*, 138–40 (defending preferences for chic staff by hotels and bars).

74. Paddock, "California Album."

75. Ford, *The Race Card*, 143.

76. Barro, "So You Want to Hire the Beautiful," 18.

77. Greenhouse, "Going for the Look," A12 (describing lawsuits against Abercrombie and Fitch, Mondrian Hotel, and a Missouri restaurant that fired a forty-seven-year-old waitress for failure to conform to its trendy image).

78. 42 U.S.C. § 703(6).

79. 29 Code of Federal Regulations, §1604.2(a) (December 2005).

80. *Wilson v. Southwest Airlines Co.*, 517 F. Supp. 292 (S.W. Texas, 1981); *Diaz v. Pan American Airways*, 442 F. 2d 385 (5th Cir.), cert. denied, 404

U.S. 950 (1971). See also *Gerdun v. Continental Airlines*, 692 F. 2ds 602, 609 (9th Cir., 1982) (policy requiring slender appearance by female but not male employees).

81. *Craft v. Metromedia, Inc.*, 572 F. Supp. 868 (W.D. Mo. 1983), aff'd in part, rev'd in part, 766 F.2d 1205 (8th Cir. 1985); see also Craft, *Too Old, Too Ugly*.

82. *Craft*, 572 F. Supp. at 879 (noting that "ratings routinely serve as the basis for personnel changes").

83. *Wilson v. Southwest Airlines Co.*, 517 F. Supp. 292, 295 (N.D. Tex. 1981)(hot pants); Deborah L. Rhode, "P.C. or Discrimination?" *National Law Journal*, January 22, 1996, A19 ("wholesome sexuality").

84. Ford, *The Race Card*, 160.

85. *Jespersen v. Harrah's Operating Co.*, 444 F.3d 1104, 1106–07 (9th Cir. 2006); Paddock, "California Album."

86. *Jespersen*, 444 F.3d at 1106–08.

87. Santa Cruz, Cal., Mun. Code §§ 9.83.010, .020(13) (2008).

88. Ford, *The Race Card*, 160–61. See Thomas C. Grey, "Cover Blindness," in Post, *Prejudicial Appearances*, 85, 86–87; James J. McDonald Jr., "Civil Rights for the Aesthetically-Challenged," *Employee Relations Law Journal* 29 (2003): 118; Robert C. Post, "Prejudicial Appearances: The Logic of American Antidiscrimination Law," in *Prejudicial Appearances*, 1, 1–2.

89. See, e.g., *Francis v. City of Meriden*, 129 F.3d 281, 286 (2d Cir. 1997); *Andrews v. Ohio*, 104 F.3d 803, 809–10 (6th Cir. 1997); *Forrisi v. Bowen*, 794 F.2d 931, 934 (4th Cir. 1986), *Fredregill v. Nationwide Agribusiness Ins. Co.*, 992 F. Supp. 1082, 1091–92 (S.D. Iowa 1997); Elizabeth E. Theran, "Legal Theory on Weight Discrimination," in Kelly D. Brownell, *Weight Bias* (New York: Guilford Press, 2005), 195, 197–98.

90. Ford, *The Race Card*, 176.

91. Poulton, *No Fat Chicks*, 136 (quoting Mario Cuomo; internal quotation marks omitted).

92. Editorial, "The Tyranny of Beauty," *New Republic*, October 12, 1987, 4.

93. Andrew Sullivan, "The Plump Classes Are on a Roll," *Sunday Times* (London), August 29, 1999, 7.

94. The employee examples come from Joseph Farah, "Job Bias Law Takes a Walk in Purple Zone: Some Cities May Prohibit Discrimination in Hiring on the Basis of Appearance," *Los Angeles Times*, February 7, 1992, B7. The warning about fat jokes appears in Peter Byrne, "As a Matter of Fat," *San Francisco Weekly*, January 17, 2001, http://www.sfweekly.com/2001–01–17/news/as-a-matter-of-fat/.

95. Michael Selmi, "The Many Faces of Darlene Jespersen," *Duke Journal of Gender Law and Policy* 14 (2007): 467, 468.

96. *Alam v. Reno Hilton Corp.*, 819 F. Supp. 905, 914 (D. Nev. 1993).

97. McDonald, "Civil Rights for the Aesthetically Challenged," 127.

98. Ford, *The Race Card*, 176 (noting the concern that appearance-discrimination statutes would erode support for other legislation prohibiting "invidious discrimination"); Byrne, "As a Matter of Fat" (discussing untold costs); Margaret Carlson, "And Now, Obesity Rights," *Time*, December 6, 1993, 96 (quoting Fred Siegal regarding litigiousness; internal quotation marks omitted).

99. Klare, "Power/Dressing," 1446.

100. *Hamm v. Weyauwega Milk Prods., Inc.*, 332 F.3d 1058, 1066–67 (7th Cir. 2003) (Posner, J., concurring).

101. *Rappaport v. Katz*, 380 F. Supp. 808, 811–12 (S.D.N.Y. 1974). For similar views, see *Advanced Mobile Home Systems v. UAC*, 663 So. 2d 1382, 1386–87 (Fla. D.C.A. 1995) («to claim that an unexplained refusal of an employee to shave his stubble is of constitutional magnitude would be to trivialize the constitution»).

102. Swisher, "Overweight Workers Battle Bias," A1 (quoting civil rights attorney Laura Einstein; internal quotation marks omitted).

103. Ibid. (quoting Providence, Rhode Island, ACLU Executive Director Steven Brown; internal quotation marks omitted).

104. For general discussion of in-group bias, see Marilynn B. Brewer and Rupert J. Brown, "Intergroup Relations," in Daniel T. Gilbert et al., eds., *The Handbook of Social Psychology*, 4th ed. (Boston: McGraw Hill, 1998), 554; Susan T. Fiske, "Stereotyping, Prejudice, and Discrimination," in ibid., 357.

105. 163 U.S. 537 (1896); see also Cass R. Sunstein, *The Partial Constitution* (Cambridge, MA: Harvard University Press, 1993), 41.

106. The Gallup Org., Gallup Poll #614, May 29–June 3, 1959, at Q.31A, available at http://roperweb.ropercenter.uconn.edu/cgi-bin/hsrun .exe/Roperweb/Catalog40/Catalog40.htx;start=summary_link?archno =USAIPO1959–0614.

107. Harris Interactive, *Time* Magazine/CNN Poll # 2004–05: 2004 Presidential Election/War in Iraq/Abuse of Iraqi Prisoners, May 12–13, 2004, Q.33, available at http://roperweb.ropercenter.uconn.edu/cgi-bin/ hsrun.exe/Roperweb/Catalog40/Catalog40.htx;start=summary_ link?archno=USHARRISINT2004–05 (when asked whether the *Brown* decision had been good or bad for the United States, 11 percent said bad, 82 percent said good, and 7 percent said not sure); see also Michael Murakami, "Desegregation," in Persily, Citrin, and Egan, eds., *Public Opinion and Constitutional Controversy*, 18, 36–38; Deborah L. Rhode and Charles J. Ogletree Jr., "Preface," in Rhode and Ogletree, eds., *Brown at 50: The Unfinished Legacy* (Chicago: Division for Public Education Division, American Bar Association, 2004).

108. David M. Engel and Frank W. Munger, *Rights of Inclusion: Law and Identity in the Life Stories of Americans with Disabilities* Chicago: University of Chicago Press, 2003), 241–45; Michael Stein, "15 Years from Implementation of ADA in the USA: From the Perspective of Employment and Reasonable Accommodation," http://www.dinf.ne.jp/doc/english/rights/050307/stein.html.

109. For example, compare Penn, Schoen, and Berland Assocs., Poll, July 30–Aug. 2, 1998 (finding only 27 percent believed that homosexuals should be allowed to marry) with Abt SRBI, Inc., Poll, Pew Research Center/Pew Forum on Religion and Public Life Poll #2008–08RELIG: August 2008 Religion and Public Life Survey, July 31–Aug. 10, 2008, available at http://people-press.org/reports/pdf/445.pdf (finding that 47 percent believed gay and lesbian couples should be allowed to marry). For changes in attitudes on other issues involving sexual orientation, see Patrick J. Egan, Nathaniel Persily, and Kevin Wallsten, "Gay Rights," in Persily, Citrin, and Egan, Public Opinion and Constitutional Controversy, 234–55.

110. For two classic accounts, see Murray Edelman, *The Symbolic Uses of Politics* (Urbana: University of Illinois Press, 1985), 44–47; Joseph R. Gusfield, "Moral Passage: The Symbolic Process in Public Designations of Deviance," *Social Problems* 15 (1967): 175, 177–78.

111. Civil Rights Act of 1964, 42 U.S.C. §§ 2000e-1 through 2000e-17 (2006); *Meritor Sav. Bank v. Vinson*, 477 U.S. 57, 66–67 (1986).

112. Eliza G. C. Collins and Timothy B. Blodgett, "Sexual Harassment: Some See It…Some Won't," *Harvard Business Review* 59 (1981): 76, 92.

113. Rhode, *Speaking of Sex*, 98.

114. *Katz v. Dole*, 709 F.2d 251, 256 (4th Cir. 1983); *Zabkowicz v. West Bend Co.*, 589 F. Supp. 780, 784 (D. Wis. 1984).

115. *Henson v. Dundee*, 682 F.2d 897, 900 n.2 (11th Cir. 1982).

116. U.S. Merit Systems Protection Board, *Sexual Harassment in the Federal Workplace: Trends, Progress, Continuing Challenges* Washington, DC: U.S. G.P.O. Supt. of Docs.(1995) 33 (reporting that only 6 percent of victims filed a formal complaint); see also Joanna L. Grossman, "The Culture of Compliance: The Final Triumph of Form over Substance in Sexual Harassment Law," *Harvard Women's Law Journal* 26 (2003): 3, 23–24 (noting studies finding low rates of sexual harassment complaints); Linda Hamilton Krieger, "Employer Liability for Sexual Harassment—Normative, Descriptive, and Doctrinal Interactions: A Reply to Professors Beiner and Bisom-Rapp," *University of Arkansas Little Rock Law Review* 24 (2001): 169, 182–83 (citing Bonnie S. Dansky and Dean G. Kilpatrick, "Effects of Sexual Harassment," in William O'Donohue, ed., *Sexual Harassment: Theory, Research, and Treatment* (Boston: Allyn and Bacon, 1997): 152, 158 (describing various studies showing that only 5 to 15 percent of employees seek organizational remedies for sexual harassment); Tamar Lewin, "The Thomas Nomination: A Case Study of Sexual Harassment," *New York Times*, October 11, 1991, A18 (noting women's reluctance to file complaints due to fear of reprisals and adverse career repercussions).

117. Rhode, *Speaking of Sex*, 101.

118. See Kolata, *Rethinking Thin*, 203–06 and studies cited in chapter 7.

119. Selmi, "The Many Faces of Darlene Jesperson," 481 n. 63, 488; Elizabeth A. Brown, "Many Women Still Battle 'Grooming' Discrimination," *Christian Science Monitor*, June 10, 1991, 1 (discussing refusal by Continental employee to wear makeup); Bob Egelko, "Court OKs Sex-Based Grooming Standards," *San Francisco Chronicle*, April 15, 2006, B1 (noting Harrah's statement that it no longer enforces the makeup requirement and offered to rehire Jespersen without makeup).

120. Suzette Parmley, "At Borgata Casino, It's Fit the Mold—or Else," *Philadelphia Inquirer,* May 31, 2005.

121. See, e.g., Josh Zimmer, "Students Can Challenge Photo Dress Code," *Saint Petersburg (FL) Times,* May 11, 2004, 3B.

122. Ramachandran, "Freedom of Dress," 11, 86; Amy Mitchell Wilson, "Public School Dress Codes: The Constitutional Debtate," *Brigham Young University Education and Law Journal* (1998):147, 147–48.

123. Telephone interview with Jill Owens, lawyer for the plaintiffs; Meiselman, Denlea, Packman, Carton and Eberz P.C.; February 17, 2009.

CHAPTER 6

1. Andrew Hussey, *Paris: The Secret History* (London: Bloomsbury Publishers, 2006), 70; Catherine Kovesi Killerby, *Sumptuary Law in Italy: 1200–1500* (New York: Oxford University Press, 2002), 23–26. An Elizabethan law provided that "any woman who through the use of false hair,...make-up,...high heeled shoes or other devices, leads a subject of Her Majesty into marriage, shall be punished with the penalties of witchcraft." Sally Pointer, *The Artifice of Beauty: A History and Practical Guide to Perfume and Cosmetics* (Charleston, SC: The History Press, 2005), 96.

2. For early laws, see Karlyne Anspach, *The Why of Fashion* (Ames: Iowa State University Press, 1967), 261; Lynn A. Botelho, "Clothing," in Francis J. Bremer and Tom Webster, eds., *Puritans and Puritanism in Europe and America: A Comprehensive Encyclopedia* (2006), 348.

3. Susan Brownmiller, *Femininity* (New York: Simon and Schuster, 1984), 198; Jill Fields, *An Intimate Affair: Women, Lingerie, and Sexuality* (Berkeley: University of California Press, 2007), 53–55.

4. Marcia Pearce Burgdorf and Robert Burgdorf Jr., "A History of Unequal Treatment: The Qualifications of Handicapped Persons as a 'Suspect Class' under the Equal Protection Clause," *Santa Clara Lawyer* 15 (1975): 855, 863–64 (quoting Chi., Ill. Mun. Code § 36–34 (1966) (repealed 1974) (imposing fines on persons appearing in public who were "diseased, maimed, mutilated or in any way deformed so as to be an unsightly or disgusting object").

5. The state senate defeated the measure following ridicule in various national newspapers. Tara Bahrampour, "A Brief Matter of Style: Va. Senate Panel Bags Bill Outlawing Droopy Pants," *Washington Post*, February 11, 2005, B1.

6. Fields, *An Intimate Affair*, 1 (quoting unnamed legislators in Virginia and Louisiana).

7. Margaret Carlson, "And Now, Obesity Rights," *Time*, December 6, 1993, 96 (quoting Fred Siegal).

8. Peter Byrne, "As a Matter of Fat," available at http://www.sfweekly.com/2001–01–17/news/as-a-matter-of-fat/; Richard Ford, *The Race Card: How Bluffing about Bias Makes Race Relations Worse* (New York: Farrar, Straus and Giroux, 2008), 176.

9. Ford, *The Race Card*, 177, 176.

10. Compare *Booth v. Maryland*, 327 F.3d 377 (4th Cir. 2003) (upholding correction officer's challenge to discipline based on his refusal to change his hair style on religious grounds where Jewish and Sikh officers had been granted a religious exemption from hair regulations) with *Daniels v. City of Arlington*, 246 F.3d 500 (5th Cir. 2001) (finding a compelling state interest to justify a police department's ban on an officer's wearing religious jewelry on his uniform), with *Brenda Nichol v. Arin Intermediate Unit 28*, 268 F. Supp. 2d 536 (W.D. Pa., 2003) (enjoining suspension of teacher for wearing a small cross on her necklace) and *Draper v. Logan County Public Library*, 403 F. Supp. 2d 608 (W.D. Kentucky, 2003) (striking down a library's ban on a volunteer's religious T-shirts). For an overview of the inconsistent application of First Amendment protection to religious dress and grooming, see Neha Singh Gohil and Dawinder S. Sidhu, "The Sikh Turban: Post-911 Challenges to This Article of Faith," *Rutgers Journal of Law and Religion* 19 (2008): 54, 57.

11. 545 F.2d 761, 763 (1st Cir. 1976).

12. *Kelley v. Johnson*, 425 U.S. 238 (1976) (hair length); *United States v. Bd. of Educ.*, 911 F.2d 882 (3d Cir. 1990) (head scarf); *Wislocki-Goin v. Mears*, 831 F. 2d 1374, 1376–77 (7th Cir., 1987) (excessive makeup constituting wrong look); *Rathert v. Village of Peotone*, 903 F.2d 510, 516 (7th Cir. 1990) (off-duty police officer).

13. Herbert L. A. Hart, *The Concept of Law* (New York: Oxford University Press, 1961), 169.

14. Katharine T. Bartlett and Deborah L. Rhode, *Gender and Law: Theory, Doctrine, Commentary*, 4th ed. (New York: Aspen, 2006), 94.

15. *Phillips v. Martin Marietta Corp.*, 400 U.S. 542 (1971).

16. *Willingham v. Macon Telephone Publishing Co.*, 507 F.2d 1084, 1091–92 (5th Cir. 1975).

17. *Frank v. United Airlines, Inc.*, 216 F.3d 845, 853–55 (9th Cir. 2000); *Gerdom v. Continental Airlines, Inc.*, 692 F.2d 602 (9th Cir. 1982); *Carroll v. Talman Federal Savings and Loan Association*, 604 F.2d 1028, 1032–33 (7th Cir. 1979).

18. *Jespersen v. Harrah's Operating Co.*, 444 F.3d 1104, 1107 (9th Cir. 2006) (en banc).

19. *Kleinsorge v. Eyeland Corp.*, No. CIV. A. 99–5025, 2000 WL 124559, 2 (E.D. Pa. Jan. 31, 2000); *Rivera v. Trump Plaza Hotel*, 702 A.2d 1359 (N.J. Superior Court, App. Div. 1997).

20. Karl Klare, "Power Dressing: Regulation of Employee Appearance," *New England Law Review* 26 (1992): 1395, 1419.

21. *Price Waterhouse v. Hopkins*, 490 U.S. 228, 235 (1989).

22. Erica Williamson, "Moving Past Hippies and Harassment: A Historical Approach to Sex, Appearance, and the Workplace," *Duke Law Journal* 56 (2006): 681, 699.

23. *EEOC v. Am. Airlines, Inc.*, No. 02 C 6172 (N.D. Ill. Sept. 3, 2002) (order of resolution); *EEOC v. Fed. Express Corp.*, No. CV100–50 (S.D. Ga. May 24, 2001) (consent decree).

24. *Eatman v. United Parcel Serv.*, 194 F. Supp. 2d 256, 261–67 (S.D.N.Y. 2002); *Rogers v. American Airlines, Inc.*, 527 F. Supp. 229, 231–32 (S.D.N.Y. 1981).

25. *Cloutier v. Costco Wholesale Corp.*, 390 F.3d 126, 134–37 (1st Cir. 2004).

26. *EEOC v. Sambo's of Georgia, Inc.*, 530 F. Supp. 86, 89–90 (N.D. Ga. 1981); *accord Birdi v. UAL Corp.*, No. 99 C 5576, 2002 WL 471999, 1–2 (N.D. Ill. March 26, 2002).

27. 42 U.S.C.A. § 12111(8) (2000); see also 29 U.S.C.A. § 705 (2000).

28. 29 C.F.R. § 1630.1(g) (2008). Amendments passed in 2008 made clear that an individual can satisfy the requirement of being regarded as impaired "whether or not that impairment actually limits or is believed to

limit a major life activity." House Committee on the Judiciary, quoted in 1 Disability Law Compliance Manual § 1:23. The amendments also direct the EEOC to rewrite regulations on substantial limitation to be more consistent with the remedial nature of the statute; PL110–325, 122 Stat3553, (8)(b)(6).

29. Kari Horner, "A Growing Problem: Why the Federal Government Needs to Shoulder the Burden in Protecting Workers from Weight Discrimination," *Catholic University Law Review* 54 (2005): 589, 609–10.

30. Marsha Katz and Helen Lavan, "Legality of Employer Control of Obesity," *Journal Workplace Rights* 13 (2008): 59, 67.

31. 29 C.F.R. pt. 1630 app. § 1630.2(j) (stating that "except in rare circumstances, obesity is not considered a disability").

32. For morbid obesity, not all of which is caused by physiological disorders, see Department of Health and Human Services, National Center for Health Statistics, "Prevalence of Overweight, Obesity, and Extreme Obesity among Adults: United States, Trends 1976–80 through 2005–2006," at tbl.1 (2008), available at http://www.cdc.gov/nchs/data/hestat/overweight/overweight_adult.pdf (finding that 5.9 percent of Americans are extremely obese); Sondra Solovay, *Tipping the Scales of Justice: Fighting Weight-Based Discrimination* (Amherst, NY: Prometheus Books, 2000), 149; Maggie Fox, "Obese Americans Now Outweigh the Merely Overweight," Reuters, January 9, 2009. See Jane Byaff Korn, "Too Fat," Arizona Legal Studies Discussion Paper No. 09–27 (2009), available at http://www.law.arizona.edu/scholarship/facultypubs.cfm?type=als&link=scholar (discussing difficulty of proving that obesity is caused by an underlying physiological disorder); see also 29 C.F.R. § 1630.2(j) (2008) (requiring mental or physiological disorder for qualification); Brief of EEOC Amicus Curiae, *Cook v. Rhode Island Department of Mental Health, Retardation, and Hospitals*, 10 F.3d 17 (1st Cir. 1993).

33. Elizabeth E. Theran, "Legal Theory on Weight Discrimination," in Kelly D. Brownell, Rebecca M. Puhl, Marlene B. Schwartz, and Leslie Rudd, eds., *Weight Bias:Nature, Consequences, and Remedies* (New York: Guilford Press, 2005): 195, 206. See also Korn, "Too Fat."

34. See note 28. For an overview, see Korn, "Too Fat."

35. *Cook v. Rhode Island*, No. Civ. A. 90–0560, 1992 WL 535788, 7 (D.R.I. Sept. 21, 1992), aff'd sub nom. *Cook v. R.I. Dep't. of Mental Health, Retardation and Hospitals*, 10 F.3d 17 (1st Cir. 1993).

NOTES TO PAGES 124–126

36. Terry Poulton, *No Fat Chicks: How Big Business Profits by Making Women Hate Their Bodies—and How to Fight Back* (Secaucus, NJ: Carol, 1997), 126 (quoting Steve Brown, executive director of the Rhode Island ACLU).

37. *Nedder v. Rivier College*, 944 F. Supp. 111, 119 (D.N.H. 1996).

38. *Francis v. City of Meriden*, 129 F.3d 281, 286 (2d Cir. 1997) (relying on EEOC guidelines to find no disability); *Coleman v. Georgia Power Co.*, 81 F. Supp. 2d 1365, 1370 (N.D. Georgia 2000) (no showing of physiological disorder); *Hazeldine v. Beverage Media*, Ltd., 954 F. Supp. 697, 703, 705 (S.D.N.Y. 1997) (no showing that obesity limited life activity or that employer regarded plaintiff as disabled); *Cassista v. Community Foods, Inc.*, 856 P.2d 1143, 1154 (California 1993) (no proof of impairment affecting job or life activities); *Civil Service Commission v. Pennsylvania Human Relations Commission*, 591 A.2d 281, 284 (Pennsylvania 1991) (no proof of impairment or perception of disability).

39. *Hazeldine*, 954 F. Supp. 701.

40. See, e.g., *Spiegel v. Schulmann*, No. 03-CV-5088, 2006 WL 3483922, 14 (E.D.N.Y. November 30, 2006); *Goodman v. L.A. Weight Loss Centers, Inc.*, No. 04-CV-3471, 2005 U.S. Dist. LEXIS 1455, 7 (E.D. Pennsylvania, February 1, 2005); *Fredregill v. Nationwide Agribusiness Ins. Co.*, 992 F. Supp. 1082, 1092 (S.D. Iowa 1997).

41. Solovay, *Tipping the Scales of Justice*, 149–52; Michelle Levander, "A Disabling Prejudice: Voluntarily Obese Deserve Protection, EEOC Says," *San Jose Mercury News* Nov. 13, 1993, 10D (quoting Dawn Atkins of the Santa Cruz Body Image Task Force, noting that "[m]ost of us in fat acceptance don't want it to be seen as disability"); compare Adam R. Pulver, "An Imperfect Fit: Obesity, Public Health, and Disability Antidiscrimination Law," *Columbia Journal of Law and Social Problems* 41 (2008): 365, 373–74.

42. Korn, "Too Fat," 60. For a review of research on weight stigma, see Katz and Lavan, "Legality of Employer Control of Obesity," 60, and chapter 2.

43. Robert Post, "Prejudicial Appearances: The Logic of American Antidiscrimination Law," *California Law Review* 88 (2000): 1, 2.

44. Santa Cruz, Cal., Mun. Code § 9.83.020(13) (2008) (defining *physical characteristic*). The ordinance prohibits discrimination in employment, educa-

tion, housing, and public accommodation "based on age, race, color, creed, religion, national origin, ancestry, disability, marital status, sex, gender, sexual orientation, height, weight or physical characteristic." For exclusions, see ibid., § 9.83.010. Discrimination based on personal appearance generally is prohibited only in housing. Ibid., § 21.01.010. See also Santa Cruz, Cal., Mun. Code §§ 9.83.010, 9.83.020(13) (2008). For remedies, see ibid., § 9.83.120(2)(c) (authorizing a court to "grant such relief as it deems appropriate, including but not limited to, compensatory damages, attorney's fees, equitable relief, and injunctive relief including an injunction ordering the respondent to cease and desist from the unlawful discriminatory practice. Punitive damages are not recoverable in any civil action brought pursuant to this chapter").

45. Ford, *The Race Card*, 10, 137; Linda Hamilton Krieger, "Afterword: Socio-Legal Backlash," *Berkeley Journal of Employment and Labor Law* 21 (2000): 476, 498–99.

46. E-mail from Joe McMullen, Principal Analyst, Human Resources Department, City of Santa Cruz, April 8, 2007.

47. Urbana, Ill., Mun. Code § 12–37 (2007), vailable at http://www.city .urbana.il.us/ (online version notes that the code was adopted in 1979); telephone interview by Sonia Moss with Todd Rent, Human Relations Officer, City of Urbana (April 12, 2007).

48. Urbana, Ill., Mun. Code §§ 12–101–103(c) (2007) provides that "[a]ny person found in violation of any provision of this article by the commission, or in subsequent judicial proceedings in a court of law, shall be fined not more than five hundred dollars ($500.00) for each violation." Only the city attorney has the power to seek injunctive relief.

49. S.F., Cal., Admin. Code § 12A.1 (2008); Carole Cullum, "We Won: A Victory for San Francisco—and a Springboard for Communities Everywhere," *Radiance Online*, http://www.radiancemagazine.com/issues/2000/summer_00/we_won.htm.

50. S.F., Cal., Police Code §§ 3304, 3306, 3308 (2008).

51. Letter from Larry Brinkin, Senior Contract Compliance Officer, S.F. Human Rights Comm'n, to Sonia Moss (April 5, 2007).

52. Complaint of Discrimination, *Portnick v. Jazzercise, Inc.* (S.F. Human Rights Comm'n, September 25, 2001).

53. Complaint of Discrimination, *Krissy Keefer v. S.F. Ballet Ass'n/S.F. Ballet School* (S.F. Human Rights Comm'n, November 13, 2000). For coverage,

see Joan Acocella, "A Ballerina Body," *New Yorker*, March 5, 2001, 38; Beverly Beyette, "Pride and Prejudice at the Barre," *Los Angeles Times*, December 26, 2000, E1; Jennifer Dunning, "Dance Notes: Measuring Up for Ballet Class," *New York Times*, January 13, 2001, B23; Edward Epstein, "Girl Fights for a Chance to Dance," *San Francisco Chronicle*, December 7, 2000, A1.

54. Keefer Complaint, 3.

55. Letter from Emily E. Flynn, Pillsbury, Madison and Sutro, LLP, to Larry Brinkin, Senior Contract Compliance Officer, S.F. Human Rights Comm'n, December 6, 2000.

56. Telephone interview with Krissy Keefer, March 4, 2008.

57. D.C. Code Ann. § 2–1401.01 (LexisNexis 2008).

58. Ibid., § 2–1403.13. If plaintiffs file a grievance with the commission, they may not, however, pursue legal action in the courts. Ibid., § 2–1403.16.

59. For a listing, see Deborah L. Rhode, "The Injustice of Appearance," *Stanford Law Review* 61 (2009):1033, 1084, n. 320.

60. *Natural Motion by Sandra v. D.C. Comm'n on Human Rights*, 687 A.2d 215; *Kennedy v. District of Columbia*, 654 A.2d 847; *Atlantic Richfield v. D.C. Comm'n on Human Rights*, 515 A.2d 1095.

61. *Underwood v. Archer Management Services, Inc.*, 857 F. Supp. 97 (finding that plaintiff stated a claim of personal appearance discrimination under the DCHRA where plaintiff alleged she was terminated by defendant employer because she was "a transsexual and retain[ed] some masculine traits").

62. D.C. Code Ann. § 2–1401.02(22) (LexisNexis 2008). Personal appearance includes "the outward appearance of any person... with regard to bodily condition or characteristics, manner or style of dress, and manner or style of personal grooming, including, but not limited to, hair style and beards."

63. *Kennedy v. District of Columbia*, 654 A.2d at 855–57 (ruling that regulation was permissible but that substantial evidence supported the finding that the regulation was discriminatory as applied).

64. *Turcios v. U.S. Services Industries*, 680 A.2d 1023, 1024–25 (D.C. 1996).

65. *McManus v. MCI Commc'ns Corp.*, 748 A.2d 949, 952–54 (D.C. 2000).

66. *Atlantic Richfield Co. v. D.C. Comm'n on Human Rights*, 515 A.2d 1095, 1097 (D.C. 1986).

67. *Natural Motion by Sandra, Inc. v. D.C. Comm'n on Human Rights*, 687 A.2d 215 (D.C. 1997) (disability and appearance based on AIDS-related disease). In *Underwood v. Archer Management Services, Inc.*, 857 F. Supp. 96 (D.D.C. 1994), which involved sex, sexual orientation, and personal appearance claims by a transvestite, the court permitted the appearance claim to go forward.

68. 515 A.2d. 1095, 1100 (D.C. 1986).

69. County of Howard, Md., Code §§ 12.200(II), 12.201(XIV) (1992).

70. Ibid., § 12.214(I).

71. Letter from C. Vernon Gray, Adm'r, Howard County Office of Human Rights, to Sonia H. Moss, Robert Crown Law Library, Stanford Law School, September 19, 2008.

72. C. Vernon Gray, Report on Howard County MD Office of Human Rights, "Personal Appearance" Cases Filed Between January 1, 2003 and December 31, 2007 (September 19, 2008) (unpublished report).

73. Madison, Wis., Code of Ordinances §§ 39.03(1), 39.03(2)(bb) (2007); § 39.03(10)(b)(7) (granting the Equal Opportunities Commission the power to adopt necessary rules and regulations); Equal Opportunities Comm'n, Madison, Wis., Rules of the Equal Opportunities Comm'n § 10 (2008), available at http://www.cityofmadison.com/dcr/documents/Rules.pdf.

74. EOC Case No. 20032013, Karl Wayne Dersch (May 12, 2003),

75. EOC Case No. 20032178, Christopher Brickman (March 3, 2004).

76. EOC Case No. 20042029, Luis James Burns (May 5, 2004).

77. EOC Case No. 20062058, Heather Ehlert (November 2, 2006).

78. EOC Case No. 20062112, Jill Watskcy (March 27, 2007); *Sam's Club, Inc. v. Madison Equal Opportunities Comm'n*, No. 02–2024, 2003 WL 21707207 (Wis. Ct. App., July 24, 2003).

79. EOC Case No. 20042095, Camara Stovall (May 17, 2004) (race and Afro hair style); EOC Case No. 20062029, Deirdra Nash (April 20, 2006) (race and lip ring); EOC Case No. 20033219, Gregory B. Banks II (October 14, 2003) (race and bandana head covering).

80. Elliott-Larsen Civil Rights Act, Mich. Comp. Laws Ann. § 37.2202(1)(a) (West 2008) (effective March 31, 1977). For the commission's remedial authority, see §37.2605(2). For individual causes of action,

see § 37.2801(1). Unlike the District of Columbia, Michigan permits either remedy and does not foreclose someone who has filed with the commission from subsequently suing in court.

81. *Howard v. City of Southfield*, No. 95–1014, 1996 WL 518062, 1, 8 (6th Cir. Sept. 11, 1996).

82. *Ross v. Beaumont Hosp.*, 687 F. Supp. 1115, 1125 (E.D. Mich. 1988).

83. *Knowlton v. Levi's of Kochville, Inc.*, No. 190677, 1997 WL 33345022,1, 2 (Mich. Ct. App., June 3, 1997).

84. *Micu v. City of Warren*, 382 N.W.2d 823, 823, 825, 827–28 (Mich. Ct. App., 1985).

85. Equal Opportunity Act, 1995 (Vict., Austl.) §§ 4(1), 6(f), available at http://www.austlii.edu.au/au/legis/vic/consol_act/eoa1995250/index. html#205; see also Victorian Equal Opportunity and Human Rts. Comm'n, "Your Right to a Fair Go: Discrimination—Physical Features 1" (2007), available at http://www.humanrightscommission.vic.gov.au/pdf/attributes/ physical%20features.pdf. For exceptions, see §§ 17(3)-(4), 80(1). For conciliation requirements, see § 112(1). For remedies, see § 159(1); see also Carol Andrades, "What Price Dignity? Remedies in Australian Anti-Discrimination Law," Parliament of Australia, Research Paper No. 13 1997–98, 1998, available at http://www.aph.gov.au/library/Pubs/rp/1997–98/98rp13.htm.

86. See Victorian Equal Opportunity and Human Rts. Comm'n, Annual Report 2006/2007, (2007), 35–36, available at http://www.human-rightscommission.vic.gov.au/pdf/veohrcannualreport2007.pdf.

87. Search engines have limited coverage of Australian case law. Lexis-Nexis does not carry decisions from the Victorian Civil and Administrative Tribunal. Westlaw carries only some VCAT decisions, without their full texts. A search of all case law under the Equal Opportunity Act under the Australian Legal Information Institute search engine revealed ten cases involving appearance-discrimination claims, excluding cases of disability discrimination or sex harassment in which appearance was mentioned.

88. E-mail correspondence from Beth Gaze, Associate Professor, Melbourne Law School, to Deborah Rhode, October 9, 2008.

89. *Hill v. Canterbury Road Lodge Pty. Ltd.* (2004) VCAT 1365, ¶¶ 45, 77.

90. See, e.g., *Prolisko v. Arthur Knight Management Party Ltd.* (2005) VCAT 1868, ¶ 19 (no showing that complainant was the subject of derogatory statements about weight since she was "skinniest" staff member); *Kenyon v. Austl. Coop. Foods* (2001) VCAT 1981 (pro se litigant made no showing that unfavorable treatment was related to his tattoos); *Ruddell v. State of Victoria Dep't of Human Servs.* (2001) VCAT 1510 (no showing that child protection worker's size or loud voice adversely affected employer's treatment of him); *Judd v. Department of Transportation and Reg'l Services* (2000) VCAT 2495 (pro se litigant made no showing that tourist bus services provided unsatisfactory seating for persons of his height); *Jamieson v. Benalla Golf Club Inc.* (2000) VCAT 1849 (finding that complainant's tattoo was not the reason he was not hired, but rather that the position was deemed unnecessary); *Hanson v. Perera* (2000) VCAT 1285 (pro se litigant made no showing of detrimental impact from surgeon's comment about patient's gross overweight); *Mondio v. Toyota Motor Corp. Austl.* (1999) VCAT 653 (pro se litigant made no showing that abuse by coworkers related to physical features such as his nose).

91. See, e.g., In re Riding for the Disabled Ass'n of Victoria (2000) VCAT 1085; In re Council of Adult Educ. (2000) VCAT 411.

92. In re N2N People Pty. Ltd. (2001) VCAT 1507, ¶ 28.

93. In re People Matching Pty. Ltd. (1997) VCAT 55.

94. The Lexis and Europa Case Law indexes include no cases or statutes on appearance discrimination, and the most accessible treatises on employment law do not address the issue. Leigh-Anne Buxton, ed., *Employment Law in Europe*, 2nd ed. (West Sussex: Tottel Pub., 2008); Jeff Kenner, *EU Employment Law: From Rome to Amsterdam and Beyond* (Portland, OR: Hart Publishing, 2003); Susan Mayne and Susan Malyon, *Employment Law in Europe* (London: Butterworths Tolly, 2001); Alan C. Neal, *European Labour Law and Social Policy* (The Hague: Kluwer Law International, 1999). For European references I am indebted to Annabelle Lever of University College London, and her paper, "What's Wrong with That Beard? Privacy and Equality in the Workplace: The Struggle Over Dress and Grooming Codes," September 2004 (unpublished paper for the Priority in Practice Workshop, School of Public Policy, University College, London).

95. *Smith v. Safeway* (1996) I.C.R. 868 (U.K.) (hair); *Schmidt v. Austicks Bookshops* (1978) I.C.R. 85 (U.K.) (skirts).

96. *Dep't for Work and Pensions v. Thompson* (2004), I.R.L.R. 348 (Employment Appeal Tribunal) (U.K.).

97. James Q. Whitman, "The Two Western Cultures of Privacy: Dignity versus Liberty," *Yale Law Journal* 113 (2004): 1151, 1155–56; see also Matthew W. Finkin, "Menschenbild: The Conception of the Employee as a Person in Western Law," *Comparative Labor Law and Policy Journal* 23 (2002): 577, 578–80.

98. Grundgesetz für die Bundesrepublik Deutschland (GG) (Basic Law), May 23, 1949, art. 2(1); see also Matthew W. Finkin, "Employee Privacy, American Values, and the Law," *Chicago-Kent Law Review* 72 (1996): 221, 258; Finkin, "Menschenbild," 580, 582; Manfred Weiss and Barbara Geck, "Worker Privacy in Germany," *Comparative Labor Law Journal* 17 (1995): 75, 78–79.

99. Finkin, "Menschenbild," 583.

100. Ibid., 581. But see Michael Ford, "Two Conceptions of Worker Privacy," *Industrial Law Journal* 31 (2002): 135, 146.

101. Labor Code art. L.120–2, Law No. 92–1446 of December 31, 1992, *Journal Officiel de la République Française* (J.O.) (*Official Gazette of France*), January 1, 1993, 19; see also Jean-Emmanuel Ray and Jacques Rojot, "Worker Privacy in France," *Comparative Labor Law Journal* 17 (1995): 61, 64; Matthew W. Finkin, "Life Away from Work," *Louisiana Law Review* 66 (2006): 945, 947.

102. Paul Michaud, "Court Allows French Muslim Woman to Wear Headscarf at Work," *Arab News*, December 19, 2002, available http://www.aljazeerah.info/News%20archives/2002%20News%20archives/Dec%20 2002%20News/Dec%2019,%202002%20News.htm (discussing Dallila Tahri's lawsuit against Téléperformance France and the court's decision that Tahri must be reinstated, reimbursed for lost salary, and allowed to wear her headscarf at work).

103. Ray and Rojot, "Worker Privacy in France," 66.

104. See, e.g., *Sahin v. Turkey*, 44 European Human Rights Rep. 5 (2007); *Dahlab v. Switzerland*, App. No. 42393/98, 2001-V Eur. Ct. H.R. 1, available at http://cmiskp.echr.coe.int/tkp197/view.asp?action=html&doc

umentId=670930&portal=hbkm&source=externalbydocnumber&table=
F69A27FD8FB86142BF01C1166DEA398649.

105. "Paris Pool Bans Woman in 'Burqini' Swim Suit," AFP, August 12, 2009, available at http://www.google.com/hostednews/afp/article/ALeqM5g-8SIBOp1Y256l.

106. *Kara v. United Kingdom*, App. No. 36528/97, *European Human Rights Law Review* (London: European Commission on Human Rights, 1999), 232, 233.

107. Anita Bernstein, "Foreword: What We Talk About When We Talk About Workplace Privacy," *Louisiana Law Review* 66 (2006): 923, 928–31; Lawrence E. Rothstein, "Privacy or Dignity? Electronic Monitoring in the Workplace," *New York Law School Journal of International and Comparative Law* 19 (2000): 379, 399.

108. Bartlett and Rhode, *Gender and Law*, 420 (citing surveys finding that only 5 percent to 15 percent of sex harassment victims make any complaint, and far fewer bring lawsuits); Laura Beth Nielsen et al., *Contesting Workplace Discrimination in Court: Characteristics and Outcomes of Federal Employment Discrimination Litigation, 1987–2003* (Chicago: American Bar Association, 2008), 29, 41 (finding that only 5.5 percent of federal employment discrimination claims survived to trial, of which only a quarter were successful). For other studies showing low success rates, see Derrick Bell, "Racial Equality: Progressives' Passion for the Unattainable," *Virginia Law Review* 94 (2008): 495, 514; Kevin M. Clermont and Stewart J. Schwab, "How Employment Discrimination Plaintiffs Fare in Federal Court," *Journal of Empirical Legal Studies* 1 (2004): 429, 445.

109. The San Francisco Ballet School changed its recruitment materials and added training on weight disorders. Jazzercise dropped its weight requirement. Even when claims are unsuccessful, as in the Title VII suit against Harrah's Casino, they can often force policy changes, such as elimination of the makeup requirement. See discussion in chapters 1 and 5.

110. Gelsey Kirkland with Greg Lawrence, *Dancing on My Grave* (New York: Berkley, 1986); see also Suzanne Gordon, *Off Balance: The Real World of Ballet* (New York: McGraw-Hill, 1984), chap. 6; Lewis Segal, "The Shape of Things to Come," *Los Angeles Times*, April 1, 2001, 9.

111. Pallavi Gogoi, "An Ugly Truth about Cosmetics," *Business Week* online, November 30, 2004, http://www.businessweek.com (quoting Heather Hippsley).

112. CHK Trading Co. Inc. (Hanmeilin Cellulite Cream); copies are available from the FTC website, http://www.ftc.gov.

113. http://www.wemarket4u.net/fatfoe/.

114. Jodie Sopher, "Weight Loss Advertising Too Good to Be True: Are Manufacturers or the Media to Blame?" *Cardozo Arts and Entertainment Law Journal* 22 (2005): 933; Roseann B. Termini and Leah Tressler, "American Beauty: An Analytical Review of the Past and Current Effectiveness of Cosmetic Safety Regulations and Future Direction," *Food and Drug Law Journal* 63 (2008): 257, 273.

115. Gogoi, "An Ugly Truth."

116. For an overview, see Sopher, "Weight Loss Advertising," 933; see also Termini and Tressler, "American Beauty," 265–74 (discussing gaps in safety regulations and misleading claims).

117. Gogoi, "An Ugly Truth" (quoting Scott Bass, the partner heading the international food and drug practice at the law firm Sidley, Austin, Brown, and Wood).

118. Gogoi, "An Ugly Truth" (quoting Allen Harper).

CHAPTER 7

1. Annette Kellerman, *Physical Beauty: How to Keep It* (New York: George H. Doran, 1918), 14.

2. See Princeton Survey Research, *Progress and Perils: How Gender Issues Unite and Divide Women* (Princeton, NJ: Princeton Survey Research, 2001), 66; Shaun Dreisbach, "How Women Feel Now," *Glamour*, April 2009, 259.

3. Carl Bialik, "The Slimming Figures of Childhood Obesity," *Wall Street Journal*, July 22, 2009, A11. For eating disorders, see chapter 2.

4. Kelley D. Brownell, *Food Fight* (New York: McGraw Hill, 2004), 46.

5. Linda Bacon, *Health at Every Size: The Surprising Truth about Your Weight* (Dallas: BenBella Books, 2008), 225.

6. "Oliver's Own Goal," *Sunday Times* (London), March 29, 2009, np; "Jamie's Food Fuels Pupils' Brain Power," *Sunday Times* (London), February 1, 2009, np; Michele Belot and Jonathan James, *Healthy School Meals and Educational Outcomes* (Essex: Institute for Social and Economic Research, 2009), available at http://www.iser.essex.ac.uk.

7. Alex Witchel, "Putting America's Diet on a Diet," *New York Times Magazine*, October 11, 2009, 50.

8. Websites with cautionary examples can be helpful. Margaret M. Gullette, "Plastic Surgery (Thankfully) Is Under the Knife," *Women's eNews*, December 4, 2008, http://www.womensenews.org.

9. Michael Pollan, *In Defense of Food: An Eater's Manifesto* (New York: Penguin, 2008), 1. See also David A. Kessler, *The End of Overeating: Taking Control of the Insatiable American Appetite* (New York: Rodale, 2009), 12–18, 139–44.

10. Kessler, *The End of Overeating*, 12–18, 139–44. For addiction generally, see Rudd Center for Food Policy and Obesity, "Food and Addiction" (2007), available at http://www.yaleruddcenter.org/resources/upload/docs/what/reports/RuddCenterAddictionMeeting.pdf.

11. Participants in a Health at Every Size program did not lose weight but did experience improvements in cholesterol, blood pressure, and self-esteem, as well as lower rates of depression; Bacon, *Health at Every Size*, 161–63. See Linda Bacon, Judith Stern, Marta Van Loan, and Nancy L. Kelm, "Size Acceptance and Intuitive Eating Improve Health for Obese, Female Chronic Dieters," *Journal of the American Dietetic Association* 105 (2005): 929; Deb Burgard, "What is 'Health at Every Size'?" in Esther P. Rothblum and Sondra Solovay, eds., *The Fat Studies Reader* (New York: New York University Press, 2009).

12. Elizabeth Haiken, *Venus Envy: A History of Cosmetic Surgery* (Baltimore, MD: Johns Hopkins University Press, 2004), 174.

13. The case was *Cassista v. Community Foods, Inc.* 856 P.2d 1143 (Cal. Sup. Ct. 1993).

14. Sandra Solovay, *Tipping the Scales of Justice: Fighting Weight-Based Discrimination* (Amherst, NY: Prometheus Books, 2000), 236.

15. For examples, see Margo Maine, *Body Wars: Making Peace with Women's Bodies* (Carlsbad, CA: Gurze Books, 2000).

16. Sanjay Gupta, "Taking On the Thin Ideal," *Time*, June 5, 2008, 50.

17. "Facebook Group Challenges Traditional Notions of Beauty," February 7, 2008, available at http://www.cbc.ca/canada/prince-edward-island/story/2008/02/07/beauty-industry.html.

18. Martin Lindstrom, *Buyology: Truth and Lies About Why We Buy* (New York: Broadway Business, 2008), 191−92.

19. Committee on Women's Rights and Gender Equality of the European Parliament, Report on How Marketing and Advertising Affect Equality Between the Sexes, 40−41st Session (2008), Paragraph 21.

20. Robin Givhan, "Milan's Beef about Skeletal Models," *Washington Post*, December 8, 2006, C01; "Milan Bans Too Thin Models," *New York Times*, December 20, 2006, A6.

21. Michael Gove, "Fatten Up Models and You'll End Starvation Slavery," *London Times*, September 18, 2007, 7; Brenda Gazzar, "Spain Sizes Up Fashion World Measuring Stick," Women's eNews, February 21, 2008, http://www.womensenews.org.

22. Michael Rich, "Are American Girl Dolls a Better Choice for My Niece Than Barbies or Bratz?," Boston Children's Hospital Health and Science blog, http:childrenshospitalblog.org/are-american-girl-dolls-a-bettter-choice-for-my-niece-than-the-more-sexualized-barbies-or-bratz?.

23. Abigail C. Saguy and Rene Almeling, "Fat in the Fire? Science, the News Media, and the Obesity Epidemic," *Sociological Forum*, 23 (2008): 53, 57−67, 72.

24. Paul Campos, Abigail Saguy, Paul Ernsberger, Eric Oliver, and Glenn Gaesser, "The Epidemiology of Overweight and Obesity: Public Health Crisis or Moral Panic," *International Journal of Epidemiology* 35 (2006): 55; Steven N. Blair and Michael J. LaMonte, "Commentary: Current Perspectives on Obesity and Health: Black and White, or Shades of Grey?" *International Journal of Epidemiology* 35 (2006): 69; Michael Gard and Jon Wright, *The Obesity Epidemic: Science, Morality, and Ideology* (London: Routledge, 2005), 127−28.

25. Saguy and Almeling, "Fat in the Fire?" quoting Surgeon General Richard Carmona, 53; Campos, Saguy, Ernsberger, Oliver, and Gaesser, "The Epidemiology of Overweight and Obesity," 55; Abigail Saguy and Kevin W. Riley, "Weighing Both Sides: Morality, Mortality, and Framing

Contests over Obesity," *Journal of Health Politics, Policy and Law* 30 (2006): 869–923. For moral panic generally, see Stanley Cohen, *Folk Devils and Moral Panics* (New York: Routledge, 1972); Erich Goode and Nachman Ben-Yehuda, *Moral Panics: The Social Construction of Deviance* (Malden, MA: Blackwell, 1994). For extension of the concept to obesity, see Campos, Saguy, Ernsberger, Oliver, and Gaesser, "The Epidemiology of Overweight and Obesity," 58; Gard and Wright, *The Obesity Epidemic*, 174.

26. Richard Freeman and Joel Rogers, "Worker Representation and Participation Survey: First Report of Findings" (December 5, 1995), http:// www.dol.gov, September 16, 2008, Appendix A.

27. United States Department of Health and Human Services, "Prevention Makes Common Cents," available at http://aspe.hhs.gov/ health/prevention/prevention.pdf; Anne Ciesla Bancroft, "Corporate Wellness: Is It Healthy for Employers?" *Practical Lawyer* 55 (June 2009): 39, 40; Kathryn Hinton, "Employer by Name, Insurer by Trade: Society's Obesity Epidemic and Its Effects on Employers' Healthcare Costs," *Connecticut Insurance Law Journal* 12 (2005–2006): 137, 153.

28. For the limitations of current research, see Eric J. Finkelstein and Laurie Zuckerman, *The Fattening of America: How the Economy Makes Us Fat, If It Matters, and What to Do about It* (Hoboken, NJ: John Wiley and Sons, 2008), 189–90; United States Department of Health and Human Services, "Prevention Makes Common Cents"; Kenneth R. Pelletier, "A Review and Analysis of the Clinical and Cost-Effectiveness Studies of Comprehensive Health Promotion and Disease Management Programs at the Worksite: Update IV 200–2004," *Journal of Occupational and Environmental Medicine* 47 (2005): 1051.

29. Kessler, *The End of Overeating*, 71.

30. Ibid., 131.

31. Ibid.

32. Pollan, *In Defense of Food*, 39–41, 154. For other examples, see Marion Nestle, Food Politics (Berkeley: University of California Press), 124.

33. Datamonitor, *Profiting from Consumers' Desire for Health Indulgence* (India: Bharat Book Bureau, 2005) available at http://www.bharatbook .com/detail.asp?id=8333; Kessler, *The End of Overeating*, 130.

34. See, e.g., Bryan A. Liang and Kurt M. Hartman, "It's Only Skin Deep: FDA Regulation of Skin Care Cosmetics Claims," *Cornell Journal of Law and Public Policy* 8 (1999): 249, 276 (arguing for greater support for claims by cosmetic manufacturers); Roseann Termini and Leah Tressler, "American Beauty: An Analytical View of the Past and Current Effectiveness of Cosmetic Safety," *Food and Drug Law Journal* 63 (2008): 257, 271 (surveying gaps in the current regulatory framework and proposing ways to educate consumers about cosmetic products); Natasha Singer, "Should You Trust Your Makeup?" *New York Times*, February 15, 2007, G1 (describing state and local policy initiatives to promote safety in cosmetic products).

35. World Health Organization, *Global Strategy on Diet, Physical Activity, and Health* (Geneva: World Health Organization, 2004), paragraph 43.

36. Diane Brockett, "School Cafeterias Selling Brand Name Junk Food: Who Deserves a Break Today?" *School Board News*, October 1998, 56, 5. Katherine W. Bauer, Y. Wendy Yang, and S. Bryn Austin, "How Can We Stay Healthy When You're Throwing All of This in Front of Us? Findings from Focus Groups and Interviews in Middle Schools on "Environmental Influences on Nutrition and Physical Activity," *Health Education and Behavior* 31 (2004): 34. 41; Andrew Martin, "The School Cafeteria, on a Diet," *New York Times* online, September 5, 2007, np, http://www.nytimes.com.

37. Bauer, Yang, and Austin, "How Can We Stay Healthy?" 41.

38. Ibid., 38, 43.

39. Hinton, "Employer By Name, Insurer by Trade," 165 n. 219; Kelly Brownell and Katherine B. Horgen, *Food Fight: The Inside Story of The Food Industry, America's Obesity Crisis, and What We Can Do about It* (New York: McGraw Hill, 2004), 103–4, 121, 196, 213–14; Zoltan J. Acs, Ann Cotten, and Kenneth R. Stanton, "The Infrastructure of Obesity," in Zoltan J. Acs and Alan Lyles, eds., *Obesity, Business and Public Policy* (Northampton, MA: Edward Elgar, 2007), 135, 147; John Cawley, "The Economics of Childhood Obesity Policy," in Acs and Lyles, *Obesity, Business and Public Policy*, 27–44.

40. Brownell and Horgen, *Food Fight*, 91, 103–4, 154–55. For restrictions on advertising, see Finkelstein and Zuckerman, *The Fattening of America*, 177; Margaret Sova McCabe, "The Battle of the Bulge: Evaluating Law as a Weapon against Obesity," *Food Law and Policy* 3 (2007): 135, 152–57; Nestle, *Food Politics*, 179–80.

41. For surveys, see Finkelstein and Zuckerman, *The Fattening of America* (noting that three-quarters of surveyed Americans support restricting unhealthy foods, and over four-fifths support more physical education and promotion of healthy foods). For experts on marketing, see ibid., 177; J. Michael McGinnis, Jennifer Appleton Gootman, and Vivica I. Kraak, eds., *Food Marketing to Children and Youth: Threat or Opportunity* (Washington, DC: National Academies Press, 2006); Federal Trade Commission and Department of Health and Human Services, *Perspectives on Marketing, Self-Regulation and Childhood Obesity* (Washington, DC: Federal Trade Commission, 2006); Nestle, *Food Politics*, 179–80.

42. For restrictions, see Haitham M. Ahmed, "Obesity, Fast Food Manfacture and Regulation: Revisiting Opportunities for Reform," *Food and Drug Journal* 64 (2009):565, 566. For bans on junk food marketing on children's television in the United Kingdom and the inadequacy of U.S. physical education programs, see Finkelstein and Zuckerman, *The Fattening of America*, 173, 177. For the availability of junk food and beverages, see Cynthia Kopkowski, "The Dish on Schools," *Neatoday*, February 2008, 32.

43. See Finkelstein and Zuckerman, *The Fattening of America*, 171–72 (advocating report cards but acknowledging self-esteem concerns); McCabe, "The Battle of the Bulge," 168–72 (advocating such strategies without providing evidence of their long-term impact or possible stigmatizing effects).

44. See Centers for Disease Control and Prevention, *Differences in Prevalence of Obesity among Black, White and Hispanic Adults, United States, 2006–2008* (Washington, DC: Centers for Disease Control and Prevention, 2009) (describing Los Angeles coalition targeted at improving fitness and diet among African Americans); Brownell and Horgen, *Food Fight*, 103–4, 121, 196, 213–14; Zoltan J. Acs et al., "A Policy Framework for Confronting Obesity," in Zoltan and Lyles, *Obesity, Business and Public Policy*, 245 (reviewing policy options); Nestle, *Food Politics*, 367–69.

45. Mimi Hall, "Massachusetts Town Takes Lead in Trimming Fat," *USA Today*, April 21, 2009, 5A.

46. World Health Organization, *Global Strategy on Diet, Physical Activity, and Health*, paragraph 41 (4).

47. Pollan, *In Defense of Food*, 116–17; Daniel Imhoff, *Food Fight: The Citizen's Guide to a Food and Farm Bill* (Berkeley: University of California

Press, 2007), 33–36, 90–92; Michael Pollan, "You Are What You Grow," *New York Times Magazine*, April 22, 2007, 15.

48. Sander L. Gilman, *Fat: A Cultural History of Obesity Policy* (Cambridge: Cambridge University Press, 2008), 105.

49. Jennifer Pomeranz and Kelly D. Brownell, "Legal and Public Health Considerations Affecting the Success, Reach, and Impact of Menu Labeling Laws," *American Journal of Public Health* 98 (2008): 1578; Tony Kuo, Christopher J. Jaroosz, Paul Simon, and Jonathan E. Fielding, "Menu Labeling as a Potential Strategy for Combating the Obesity Epidemic: A Health Impact Assessment," *American Journal of Public Health* 99 (2009): 1; Scot Burton, Elizabeth Creyer, Jeremy Kees, and Kyle Huggins, "Attacking the Obesity Epidemic: The Potential Health Benefits of Providing Nutrition Information in Restaurants," *American Journal of Public Health* 96 (2006): 1669; Ahmed, "Obesity, Fast Food Manufacture and Regulation," 569.

50. For the percentage of restaurant purchases, see Mary T. Bassett et al, "Purchasing Behavior and Calorie Information at Fast-Food Chains in New York City, 2007," *American Journal of Public Health* 98 (2008): 1457, 1458. For consumer misperceptions, see Finkelstein and Zuckerman, *The Fattening of America*, 138–39, Pomeranz and Brownell, "Legal and Public Health Considerations," 1578; Burton, Creyer, Kees, and Huggins, "Attacking the Obesity Epidemic," 1669.

51. Calories dropped by 52 for patrons of Subway restaurants that posted the information near the point of purchase. Mary T. Bassett et al, "Purchasing Behavior and Calorie Information at Fast-Food Chains in New York City, 2007," *American Journal of Public Health* 98 (2008): 1457, 1458. Although such decreases are small, if sustained over repeated purchases, the cumulative effect can be significant. Kuo, Jaroosz, Simon, and Fielding, "Menu Labeling as a Potential Strategy for Combating the Obesity Epidemic," 1.

52. Brian Ebel, Rogan Kersh, Victoria L. Brescoll, and L. Beth Dixon, "Calorie Labeling and Food Choices: A First Look At the Effects On Low-Income People In New York City," *Health Affairs*, October 6, 2009, w1110, w1114. For other studies finding no effects, see ibid, w1111.

53. For studies on tobacco warnings, see Lindstrom, *Buyology*, 14; Martin Lindstrom, "Inhaling Fear," *New York Times*, December 12, 2008, A31. For studies on nutritional labeling, see Finkelstein and Zuckerman, *The Fattening of America*, 114; Tomas J. Philipson and Richard Posner, "Is

the Obesity Epidemic a Public Health Problem? A Review of Zoltan J. Acs and Alan Lyles's *Obesity, Business, and Public Policy,*" *Journal of Economic Literature* 46 (2008): 974, 979. For the need for evaluation generally, see World Health Organization, *Global Strategy on Diet, Physical Activity, and Health*, paragraph 46(a).

54. See Julie Ann Elston et al., "Tax Solutions to the External Costs of Obesity," in Acs and Lyles, *Obesity, Business and Public Policy*, 171; Jeff Strnad, "Conceptualizing the 'Fat Tax': The Role of Food Taxes in Developed Economies," *Southern California Law Review* 78 (2005): 1221, 1224–26; Sandy Kobrin, "Plastic Surgeons Say 'Vanity Tax' Discriminates," Women's eNews, Aug. 8, 2005, http://www.womensenews.org.

55. Eric Oliver, *Fat Politics: The Real Story Behind America's Obesity Epidemic* (New York: Oxford University Press, 2005), 174.

56. For evidence suggesting declines in consumption based on modest price increases, see evidence reviewed in Kelly D. Brownell and Thomas R. Freiden, "Ounce of Prevention: The Public Policy Case for Taxes on Sugared Beverages," *New England Journal of Medicine* 360 (2009): 1805, 1806. For skepticism about the impact of taxes, see Elizabeth Frazao and Jane Allshouse, "Strategies for Intervention: Commentary and Debate," *Journal of Nutrition*, 133 (2003): 844S; Helen L. Walls, Anna Peeters, Bebe Loff, Bradley R. Crammond, "Editorial: Why Education and Choice Won't Solve the Obesity Problem," *American Journal of Public Health* 99 (2009): 590, 591; research summarized in Ahmed, "Obesity, Fast Food Manufacture and Regulation," 573.

57. H.B. 2918, introduced March 3, 2009, to amend the Code of West Virginia, Article 25, Section 47–25–1.

58. L. A. Johnson, "West Virginia State Lawmaker Proposes Ban on Barbie Just before She Turns Fifty," *Pittsburgh Post Gazette*, March 5, 2009, available at http://www.post-gazette.com/pg/09064/953363-455.stm.

59. For the Mississippi bill see HB. 282, Mississippi State Legislature, 2008, proposed by Representative W. T. Mayhall, available at http://billstatus.ls.state.ms.us/documents/2008/pdf/HB/0200–0299/HB0282IN.pdf. The bill died in committee. For the Texas cupcake amendment, aka "Lauren's Law," see Texas Educational Code §28.002, discussed in Martin, "School Cafeteria," C1, C5. For the Massachusetts proposal, see Philip McKenna, "Can This Spread Be Stopped? Lawmaker Wants to Put a Lid on Fluff," *Boston Globe*, June 19, 2006, B1. For the counterproposal, see

Lemont Calloway, "The War on Fluffernutter Escalates in Legislature," *Boston Globe*, June 21, 2006, B1. National news ridicule caused the sponsor of the ban to drop his proposal; "Barrios Ends Effort to Limit Fluff," *Boston Globe*, June 27, 2006, B2.

60. Diane Barthel, *Putting on Appearances: Gender and Advertising* (Philadelphia: Temple University Press, 1988), 137 (quoting Baudrillard).

Index

...

Abercrombie and Fitch, 106
academia, appearance in, xi–xii, 3, 27
adolescents
  eating disorders in, 26, 60, 150
  effect of media on, 60
  importance of appearance to,
    26, 60
  See also children
advertising. See marketing
Africa
  FGM, 36
  Skin bleach, 38
African Americans
  in beauty pageants, 56, 57, 75
  cosmetic surgery in, 43
  cultural grooming styles of, 15, 72,
    99–100
  obesity rates, 43, 102
  and white–based grooming codes,
    9, 15, 71–72, 96, 100, 122
  and workplace discrimination,
    211n.55
age discrimination
  appearance bias compounding,
    12, 96

  in workplace, 28, 63, 103
aging
  double standards for men and
    women, 11, 28, 31, 61–63, 76
  fears of, 80
  See also age discrimination
American Academy of Cosmetic
  Surgery, 38
American Association of Retired
  Persons, 132
American Bar Association,
  ix–x, 3
American Board of Plastic Surgery,
  38
American Girl dolls, 151
American Medical Association, 38
American Psychological Association,
  52
Americans with Disabilities Act
  (ADA), 112, 122–23
anorexia nervosa
  dangers of, 39, 40
  description of, 39
  in fashion industry, 151
  See also eating disorders

antidiscrimination laws
  appearance discrimination claims
    under, 118
  customer preference as defense in,
    13, 20, 106–7, 155
  protection for voluntary traits
    under, 109
  scope of, 92
  See also appearance–related law;
    civil rights law; disability law
appearance
  in academia, xi–xii, 3, 27
  affect on psychological well-being,
    5, 7, 39–40
  and class identity, 8, 96, 117
  costs of, 2, 5–7, 32–35, 147,
    160–61
  and cultural identity, 8, 12, 72,
    99–100
  cultural preoccupation with, 2, 3,
    5, 19, 68, 80–81, 146, 160–61
  effect on income, 5, 6, 27, 28
  feminist perspectives on. *See*
    feminists
  gender differences in importance,
    30–32
  ideals for, 86–89
  market forces on, 8, 19, 49–53,
    65–67
  media impact on. *See* media
  and quality of life, 29–30
  in relationships, 5, 26–27, 30–31,
    48, 188n.5
  and self-esteem, 5, 6, 28–29, 30,
    39–40, 76, 87, 96, 97
  as self-expression, 2, 10, 66, 75, 77,
    80, 87, 99–101, 147
  sociobiological frameworks of, 2, 5,
    7, 45–48, 109–10, 188n.5
  as source of pleasure, 11, 87
  technology's impact on, 5, 8, 24,
    30, 53–54, 68

in workplace. *See* employment
  See also appearance discrimination;
    appearance-related law;
    attractiveness
appearance discrimination
  activism against, 20–21, 149–50
  business role in combating,
    152–53, 154–55
  by children, 6, 26, 41
  continuum of, 3, 25–26, 92, 111
  costs of, 2–3, 146
  double standards for men and
    women, xi, xii–xiii, 5, 7, 9, 10,
    11, 12, 28, 31, 87, 147
  equal opportunity denied through,
    11, 93–95, 101
  individual costs of, 11, 94, 101
  individual role in combating, 89,
    148–50
  media role in combating, 151–52
  minimization of, 2, 13, 112
  reinforcement of group
    disadvantages through, 12,
    95–99, 101, 103
  as restriction of self-expression, 12,
    99–101
  sexual harassment parallel, 114–15
  social costs of, 94, 101
  stigmatization in, 3, 11–12, 95
  strategies for change, 5, 19–22,
    142–43, 146–61
  toward overweight/obese people.
    See weight discrimination
  in workplace. *See* employment
  See also appearance-related law
appearance-related law
  anti-discrimination statutes, 118,
    120–22
  arguments against, 13–14, 101–14,
    118
  arguments for, 13, 14, 93–101,
    112–16, 147

Australia model, 17, 134–36, 140
as burden on business, 13–14, 16,
118, 126
and consumer protections, 19, 89,
141–42, 147, 154
as dilution of other civil rights
claims, 118
constitutional law, 118–20
disability law, 15–16, 20, 118,
122–25, 153, 154
European, 17, 137–39, 205n.1
history, 15, 48, 117
local jurisdictions, 14, 16, 21,
94–95, 125–32, 150, 157, 158
limitations of, 5, 17–18, 139–40
Michigan statutes, 16–17, 113, 125,
126, 132–34
Regulation of propriety, 117–18
social contributions of, 14, 18–19,
140, 147
strategies for change in, 20–22,
142–43, 147, 154–55, 159–60
appearance-related pursuits
consumer costs of, 2, 32–35
criticisms of, 71–77
feminist conflicts over, 73–86
gender differences in, 30–32,
33, 97
health risks of, 7, 35–41
Appiah, Anthony, 94
A Room of One's Own (Woolf), 70–71
Asia, cosmetics use in, 38
Asian Americans, 43, 211n.55
athletes, media portrayals of, 9,
64–65
Atlantic City casinos
sexualized grooming codes of,
21–22, 116
See also Borgata Hotel/Casino sex
discrimination suit
Atlantic City, N.J., beauty pageants
in, 56

Atlantic Richfield Co. v. D.C.
Commission on Human Rights, 129
attractiveness
as business selling point, 13, 20,
106
character traits attributed to, 6,
26–27, 171n.31
in children, 6, 26, 27, 46
in court settings, 27
cultural preoccupation with, 2, 3,
5, 19, 68, 80–81, 146, 160–61
defining, 24
income bonus from, 6, 27, 28
measuring, 24–25
media role in defining, 54–65
in relationships, 5, 26–27, 30–31,
48, 188n.5
and self-esteem, 5, 6, 28–29, 30,
39–40, 76, 87, 96, 97
in sociobiological terms, 2, 5, 7, 24,
45–47, 109–10, 188n.5
See also appearance; appearance
discrimination
Australia, 17, 134–36, 140

Balkin, Jack, 96
Barbie, 51–52, 159
Barry, Dave, 69–70
Bartky, Sandra, 75
"Beautiful People" (social network),
53–54
beauty. See appearance;
attractiveness
beauty bias. See appearance
discrimination
beauty industry
critics of, 74–77
founding of, 49
marketing in, 10, 19, 49
See also appearance-related
pursuits

Beauty Junkies (Kuczynski), 32
Beauty Myth (Wolf), 10, 74–75
beauty pageants
  children in, 57–58
  minorities in, 56, 57
  origins of, 56
  racial and ethnic bias in, 57
  unattainable ideals of, 8
  wholesome images cultivated by,
    56–57
  See also specific beauty pageants
binge eating disorder, 39
  See also eating disorders
The Birthmark (Hawthorne), 75–76
Bloomer, Amelia, 9, 72
body dysmorphic disorder, 38
body mass index (BMI), 24–25, 167n.9
Body Project, 150
Bordo, Susan, 85
Borgata Hotel/Casino sex
    discrimination suit, 21, 22, 98,
    106, 115, 116
Boston Herald, 61
Botox, 38, 50, 62, 89
Boyle, Susan, 63, 83
"bra-burning" protest, 9–10, 73
Bratz dolls, 51, 52
breast implants, 21, 78, 80, 89
Breslauer, Jan, 79, 82
Brice, Fanny, 50
Britain's Got Talent, 83
Brokaw, Tom, 61
Brownmiller, Susan, vii, 11, 31, 79, 84
Brown v. Board of Education, 112
bulimia, 39
  See also eating disorders
Bush, Barbara, 76
Business Week, 106

Caribbean, cosmetics use in, 38
The Case Against Perfection (Sandel), 96

celebrities
  cosmetic procedures by, 76, 88
  obsession with appearance, 63
  as unattainable ideal, 9, 59
Centers for Disease Control (CDC)
  definitions of overweight/obesity,
    24–25
  obesity rates, 43
Chakvetadze, Anna, 64
Chancer, Lynn, 83–84
Chapkis, Wendy, 77, 84
Chastain, Brandi, 64
children
  advantages for attractive, 6, 26, 27,
    46
  appearance discrimination by, 6,
    26, 41
  beauty pageants for, 57, 58
  encouraging healthy lifestyles in,
    148–49, 155, 156–57
  media impact on, 60
  obesity rates in, 148
  television exploitation of, 58
  See also adolescents
Chinese footbinding, 35
Civil Rights Act of 1964, 120
"Civil Rights for the Aesthetically
    Challenged, " 111
civil rights law
  appearance-discrimination
    claims under, 110, 122,
    132–34, 143
  as catalyst for social change,
    106–7, 114
  sexual harassment claims under,
    114–15
class identity, role of appearance in,
    8, 96, 117
class inequality, role of appearance
    in, 5, 7, 12, 96, 117
Clement of Alexandria, 37
Clinton, Hillary, 10, 60, 78

clothing
    dangerous female, 36
    dress reform campaigns, 9, 71, 72,
        117
    sumptuary laws, 15, 48, 117
    See also footwear
Coming Into the End Zone
    (Grumbach), 68
"Coming of Age" (Heilbrun), 80
Connery, Sean, 61
constitutional law, appearance
    discrimination claims under, 118,
        119–20, 143, 154 55
consumer protection
    and cosmetics industry, 37–38,
        143, 154
    individual responsibility in, 89,
        149, 154
    role of law in, 19, 89, 141–42, 147,
        154
    and weight loss industry, 33–34,
        141 42, 154
Consumer Reports, 34
Continental Airlines, 107, 214n.80
Cook, Bonnie, 123–24
"cosmeceuticals," 34, 142
cosmetic procedures
    and body dysmorphic disorder, 38
    breast implants, 21, 78, 80, 89
    by celebrities, 76, 88
    consumer spending on, 7, 8, 35
    critics of, 70, 75, 79–80, 88–89
    foot surgeries, 4
    liposuction, 7, 50, 51, 79
    marketing of, 8, 50–51, 52, 77
    men, 32, 52
    minorities, 43–44
    motives for, 8, 75, 76, 77–78, 79, 81
    rise in, xiv, 3, 7, 8, 88–89
    risks of, 7, 10, 38–39, 79–80, 88,
        89, 97
    television portrayals of, 8–9, 58–59

women, xiv, 4, 32, 97
    See also plastic surgeons
cosmetics
    ancient use of, 48
    costs of, 6, 32, 34–35
    effectiveness of, 32
    exports of, 37–38
    gender-based purchases of, 32
    government regulation of, 37–38,
        143
    historical objections to, 9, 37,
        71–72, 117
    ingredients in, 34, 37–38, 67, 142
    marketing of, 6, 8, 10, 19, 34,
        54–55, 67, 72, 141, 142
    production costs, 6, 34
    use by men, 32, 207n.25
    use in workplace, 81
    and well-being, 78–79
cosmetics industry
    animal testing in, 38
    consumer protection from, 37–38,
        143, 153, 154
    criticism of, 82
    regulation of, 37–38
    women employed in, 76
Costco, 122
Council on Size and Weight
    Discrimination, 149
Couric, Katie, 62–63
Craft, Christine, 107
Cronkite, Walter, 61
cultural identity, appearance as
    expression of, 8, 12, 72,
        99–100
Cuomo, Mario, 110

Daily Show, 62
Dancing on My Grave (Kirkland &
    Lawrence), 140
Darwin, Charles, 2

Davenport, Lindsay, 64
Davis, Kathy, 77–78, 81
depression. *See* psychological health
diets/dieting
    American preoccupation with, 60
    failure rate of, 6, 32
    health risks of, 7, 40–41
    marketing of, 10, 67
    media focus on, 60
    spending on, 6, 32
    yo-yo, 7, 40–41, 63, 149
    See also weight reduction
disability bias
    appearance discrimination
        compounding, 96
    legal remedies for, 14
    in workplace, 211n.55
disability law
    appearance discrimination claims
        under, 110, 118, 122–25, 143
    definitions of disability under,
        122–23
    weight discrimination claims
        under, 15–16, 20, 92, 104,
        123–25, 155
    See also appearance-related law
discrimination based on appearance.
    See appearance discrimination
District of Columbia appearance
    statutes, 16, 113, 125, 126,
    128–29, 140
dress reform, 9, 71, 72, 73, 117

eating disorders
    in adolescents, 26, 60, 150
    combating, 150, 151
    in fashion industry, 151
    media role in, 9, 54, 60
    rise in, 3
    risks of, 10, 39, 40
    types of, 39

unrealistic standards exacerbating,
    7, 9, 115
websites supporting, 54
education. *See* schools
Edwards, John, 62, 97
Eldridge, Jeff, 159
Elle (magazine), 78
employment
    appearance discrimination in, 12,
        13, 23, 27–28, 93, 94–95,
        102–4
    attractiveness as selling point in,
        13, 20, 106
    encouraging fitness in, 152–53
    ideals for appearance in, 87, 89,
        152–53
    role of appearance in, 5, 6, 27–28,
        72, 79, 105
    sex-based double standards in, 11,
        12, 31, 89, 96–98, 147
    use of cosmetics in, 81
    weight discrimination in, 13,
        15–16, 28, 43, 93, 94–95,
        103–5
    See also grooming codes
Ensler, Eve, 59, 77, 80
Environmental Working Group, 37
Ephron, Nora, xiii, 33, 80
Equal Employment Opportunity
    Commission, 107, 114, 123
Estee Lauder, 55
Esther, Queen, 56
Etcoff, Nancy, 86
ethnic inequality, 7, 12, 96, 103
ethnic minorities. *See* minorities
Europe
    appearance-related law in, 17,
        137–39, 205n.1
    eating disorders policy responses,
        150, 151
    history of cosmetic procedures in,
        53

sumptuary laws, 15, 48, 117
European Union, 38, 137
evolution. *See* sociobiological
    frameworks
Ewen, Stewart, 65
exercise. *See* fitness
Extreme Makeover (television show),
    58

Facebook, 54, 150
fashion industry
    eating disorders in, 151
    models for, 60, 151
    women employed in, 76
    See also clothing
fast-food industry
    nutrition labeling by, 153, 157–58
    in schools, 63, 156, 157
fat
    as preferred term of activists, 25
    See also overweight/obese people
fat acceptance movement, 25, 74,
    102, 149
Fat is a Feminist Issue (Orbach), 89
Fat Land, 42
The Fat of the Land (Fumento), 42
FDA (Food and Drug
    Administration). *See* Food and
    Drug Administration
Federal Trade Commission (FTC),
    33, 141
"Feed Me Better" campaign,
    148–49
feet
    cosmetic procedures for, 4
    See also footwear
female genital mutilation (FGM),
    35–36
feminists
    critique of beauty ideals, 9–10, 11,
    66, 70, 73–77, 79–86, 88–89

dress reform by, 9, 71, 72, 73, 117
first wave views on dress,
    cosmetics, 71, 72
negative perceptions of, 10, 64,
    73–74, 76
second wave views on beauty
    products, 73–74
suffragists, 72
third wave views on fashion,
    femininity, 74
Fifth Amendment, 119
Fiji, 60
fitness
    encouraging in children, 148–49,
    155, 156–57
    gender differences in, 33
    and longevity, 41
    in overweight/obese people,
    18–19, 115, 149
    as predictor of health, 115
    spending on, 32
    workplace initiatives for, 152–53
Fitzgerald, Zelda, 72
Fonda, Jane, 76
Food and Drug Administration
    hearings on breast implants, 80
    regulation of cosmetics, 34, 37, 142
food industry. *See* fast food industry
footbinding, 35
footwear
    high heels, 3–5, 35, 79, 97, 160
    for men, 5, 31
    sexualization of, 35
Ford, Richard, 14, 102, 104, 110
Fourteenth Amendment, 119
France, 17, 138, 139
freedom of speech. *See* constitutional
    law
Freud, Sigmund, 86
Friday, Nancy, 86
Friedan, Betty, 61
Frye, Donna, 62

FTC (Federal Trade Commission), 33
Fumento, Michael, 42

Garvey, Marcus, 72
Gaskell, Elizabeth, viii
Gaud, Renee, 21, 116
gays and lesbians
  combating sexualized grooming
    codes, 98–99, 116
  impact of laws in promoting
    acceptance of, 112–13,
    216n.109
  interest in appearance, 32, 52
Gear (magazine), 64
gender inequality
  in employment, 12, 31, 96–97
  legal remedies for, 14
  rates of, 102–3
  role of appearance in, 5, 7, 12, 44,
    48, 75, 76
  See also grooming codes
Germany, 17, 138, 139
GI Joe, 52–53
The Good Body (Ensler), 59, 77
Goodman, Ellen, 61, 83
Good Morning America, 21, 98
Gore, Al, 62
Greer, Germaine, 76
grooming codes
  court cases on, 99–101, 120–21
  customer preference as defense
    for, 13, 20, 107–8, 155
  double standards in, 12, 89, 96–99,
    147
  and religious expression, 15
  strategies for change, 20, 87, 147,
    154–55
  See also Borgata Hotel/Casino sex
    discrimination suit; Harrah's
    Casino decision
Grumbach, Doris, 68

hair
  consumer spending on, 32
  treatments for, 53, 79
  Harper's Bazaar, 55
Harrah's Casino decision, 12, 14, 15,
  20, 109, 116, 121, 229n.109
Harris, Katherine, 61
Hart, H.L.A., 120
Hart, Trisha, 21, 116
Harvard Business Review, 114
Hawthorne, Nathaniel, 75–76
healthy lifestyles
  for children, 148–49, 155, 156–57
  promoting, 19, 20, 147, 149, 155–59
  See also fitness
"hedonic treadmill," 30
height
  character traits associated with, 27
  discrimination because of, 21, 28,
    93, 125, 126, 127–28
Heilbrun, Carolyn, 31, 80
high heels
  advantages of, 79
  dangers of, 3–4, 35, 97, 160
Hispanics
  in beauty pageants, 56, 57
  obesity rates, 43
  workplace discrimination against,
    211n.55
Hollander, Nicole, 45
Holton, Angela, 83
Hooters, 13, 108
Howard County, Md., 16, 130
How to Be Beautiful, 36

I Feel Bad About My Neck (Ephron),
  xiii
income
  effect of appearance on, 5, 6,
    27, 28
  effect of weight on, 28, 30, 171n.35

importance in relation to
appearance , 30–31, 46, 47
India, 53
Indonesia, 36
information technology. *See* technology
"in-group favoritism," 112
International Size Acceptance
Organization, 149
Internet, reinforcement of appearance
through, 53–54, 150

Jarrell, Randall, viii–ix
Jazzercise, 18, 105, 115, 127, 229n.109
Jespersen, Darlene, 12, 14, 109, 116,
121, 217n.119
Jews
in beauty pageants, 57
cosmetic surgery in, 43
and workplace discrimination, 99,
211n.55
Johnson, Samuel, 70

Keefer, Fredrika, 127–28
Keefer, Krissy, 127, 128
Kerr, Jean, *23*
Kerry, John, 62
Kessler, David, 153
Knowlton, Libby, 134
Kournikova, Anna, 64
Kuczynski, Alex, 32

Larry King Live, 60–61
laws concerning appearance. *See*
appearance-related law
Lehman, Karen, 84
Leno, Jay, 63
lesbians. *See* gays and lesbians
lifestyles. *See* healthy lifestyles
Limbaugh, Rush, 61, 73

liposuction, 7, 50, 51, 79
L'Oreal, 66, 106
Louisiana, appearance statutes in,
117–18

Madison, Wis., 16, 113, 130–32, 140
magazines
cosmetics advertising in, 8, 54–55
role in defining attractiveness, 8,
54–55
unattainable ideals reflected in, 59
weight loss as topic in, 60
See also media
makeovers, media portrayals of, 8,
58
makeup. *See* cosmetics
Malaysia, 36
Marie Claire (magazine), 79
marketing
of cosmetic procedures, 8, 50–51,
52, 77
of cosmetics, 6, 8, 10, 19, 34,
54–55, 67, 72, 141, 142
to girls, 51–52
on Internet, 54
of junk food in schools, 156, 157
to men, 51, 52–53
misleading claims in, 19, 34,
66–67, 89
spending on, 34
tactics in, 65–67, 77
of weight reduction products, 10,
19, 49–50, 67
marriage
gay, 216n.109
gender roles in, 48
role of appearance in, 27, 30–31, 72
McDonald's, 16
Mead, Margaret, 53
media
effect on adolescents/children, 60

media (*continued*)
female athletes in, 9, 64–65
images of older women in, 61–62
images of overweight/obese people,
8–9, 58–59, 63–64, 151–52
images of prominent women in,
60–63
impact on self-esteem, 60
portrayal of feminists, 10
role in eating disorders, 9, 54, 60
role in promoting appearance, 5,
8–9, 53, 54–65, 68
and standards of attractiveness, 24
strategies for reform, 89, 151–52
See also beauty pageants;
magazines; television
Michigan appearance statutes, 16–17,
113, 125, 126, 132–34, 140
Mideast, 36
Miers, Harriet, 62
Militant (journal), 82
minorities
and Anglo-based grooming norms,
96
antidiscrimination laws protecting,
13
in beauty pageants, 56, 57, 75
cosmetic surgery by, 43–44
obesity rates in, 43, 102
and workplace discrimination, 28
See also African Americans; Asian
Americans; Hispanics
Miss America pageant
bra–burning protest, 9–10, 73
minority winners of, 57, 75
origins of, 56
unattainable ideal, 59
wholesome image cultivated by,
56–57
"Miss Bimbo" (website), 54
Miss Bronze America pageant, 56
Miss Universe pageant, 57

Miss USA pageant, 56, 57
Miss World pageant, 56
modeling industry, women employed
in, 76
models, as unattainable ideal, 9, 59, 60
morbid obesity
defined, 123
See also overweight/obese people
Morgan, Kathryn, 75
Mowrey, Daniel B., 34, 142
Muslims
appearance-related court cases,
119, 122, 138, 228n.102
and workplace appearance-related
discrimination, 99, 211n.55

NAAFA (National Association to
Advance Fat Acceptance), 25
National Association to Advance
Fat Acceptance (NAAFA), 25, 149
Neustatter, Angela, 82
The New Republic, 110
New York Daily News, 88
New Yorker cartoons, *1*, 40, *91*, *145*
New York Times
on Condoleezza Rice, 62
on Katie Couric, 62
on women's footwear, 4–5
New York Times Sunday Magazine, 64

Obama, Michelle, 10
obesity. *See* overweight/obese people
objectification of women
athletes, 9, 64–65
in beauty pageants, 56–57, 75
cosmetic practices leading to,
70, 75
prominent women, 9, 10
in workplace, 57–58
O'Brien, Conan, 63

older women. *See* age discrimination; aging
Oliver, Jamie, 148–49
Onion, 85–86
Orbach, Susie, 50, 89
overweight/obese people
activism on behalf of, 21, 25, 74, 102, 149
definitions for, 24–25, 167n.9
fitness in, 18–19, 115, 149
gender differences in, 30–31, 44
health of, 41, 152, 173n.49
income penalties for, 28, 30, 171n.35
media portrayals of, 8–9, 58–59, 63–64, 151–52
in minority populations, 43, 102
poverty experienced by, 42–43, 102, 171n.35
as preferred terms of social scientists, 25
psychological problems in, 29, 39–40
and relationships, 27, 30
in sociobiological terms, 47–48
stigma attached to, 6, 11, 27, 29, 41–44, 63, 93, 94, 95, 105, 124, 125, 152, 170n.27
surgical interventions for, 40
U.S. rates of, 25, 151–52
See also weight discrimination
Ovid, 37

Palin, Sarah, xiii, 9, 10, 62, 97
Penthouse (magazine), 75
People (magazine), 61
Pet World Warehouse Outlet, 131–32
Physical Beauty: How to Keep It, 146
Pictures from an Institution (Jarrell), viii–ix
Pius XII, Pope, 70

plastic surgeons, 38–39, 189n.25
plastic surgery. *See* cosmetic procedures
Playboy (magazine), 59, 64, 79
Plessy v. Ferguson, 112
Pogrebin, Letty, 63
political values, appearance as expression of, 8, 12
politics, appearance in, 28
Pollan, Michael, 149, 153
Pollitt, Katha, 81, 85, 86
Portnick, Jennifer, 18, 105, 127
Posner, Richard, 111
The Power of Beauty (Friday), 86
Prohibition, 113
psychological health
effect of appearance on, 5, 7, 39–40
impact of media images on, 9
in overweight/obese people, 29, 39–40

racial inequality
appearance bias compounding, 7, 12, 96, 103
overcoming, 14, 112
in workplace, 103
racial minorities. *See* minorities
The Rambler (Johnson), 70
reality television. *See* television
Rehabilitation Act, 122, 124
relationships, role of appearance in, 5, 26–27, 30–31, 48, 188n.5
religion
appearance as expression of, 8, 12
and workplace discrimination, 103
religious freedom, appearance claims filed under, 118, 119
Reno, Nev., 12, 14
reproduction
in evolutionary terms, 8, 46–48
role of appearance in, 7, 45–46

Republican National Committee, 97
Rice, Condoleezza, 62
Richards, Janet Radcliffe, 73
Riot Grrrls, 74
Risman, Barbara, 87
Rogers v. American Airlines, 100
Rubenstein, Helena, 49
Rudner, Rita, 52
Russell, Sharon, 105

Sam's Club, 132
Sandel, Michael, 96
Sand Hotel, 21–22
San Francisco appearance statutes,
    16, 18, 21, 113, 125, 127–28, 140,
    150
San Francisco Ballet School, 127–28,
    229n.109
San Francisco Human Rights
    Commission, 18, 21, 127, 150
Santa Cruz appearance statutes, 16,
    94–95, 113, 125, 126–27, 140,
    150, 222n.44
The Sceptical Feminist (Richards), 73
schools
    appearance discrimination in, 27,
        89, 93, 156
    role in children's health, 148–49,
        156–57
Schroeder, Gerhard, 31
self-esteem
    effect of appearance on, 5, 6,
        28–29, 30, 39–40, 76, 87, 96, 97
    effect of reality television shows
        on, 59
self-expression
    appearance as, 2, 10, 66, 75, 77, 80,
        87, 99–101, 147
    cosmetics as, 72
    ethnic grooming styles as, 15, 72,
        99–100

Selmi, Michael, 111
sex discrimination law
    appearance claims filed under, 121,
        143
    See also Borgata Hotel/Casino sex
        discrimination suit
"sex-plus" grooming requirements,
    120–21
    See also grooming codes
sexual harassment, 114–15, 229n.108
sexual objectification. *See*
    objectification of women
sexual orientation
    discrimination based on, 96
    See also gays and lesbians
"Shape Up" program, 157
Shepherd, Cybill, 55
shoes. *See* footwear
shopping
    gender differences in, 33
    positive effects of, 78–79
Sikhs, 15, 122
Skadden, Arps, Slate, Meagher &
    Flom, 57–58
*Skin Deep: The Truth about Beauty
    Aids*, 55
smoking, 40
sociobiological frameworks
    attractiveness in, 2, 5, 7, 24, 45–47,
        109–10, 188n.5
    male provider role in, 46, 47, 188n.5
    weight in, 7–8, 47–48
Sommers, Christina Hoff, 73–74
Sontag, Susan, 31, 99
Sotomayor, Sonia, 94
Sports Illustrated, 64
Stanford, ix, 14
Stanton, Elizabeth Cady, 9, 72
statutory provisions
    banning appearance
        discrimination under, 143
    See also appearance-related law

INDEX

Steinem, Gloria, xiii, 73
Stewart, Jon, 62
Streisand, Barbara, 50
StriVectin wrinkle cream, 34, 142
Sullivan, Andrew, 110
.sumptuary laws, 15, 48, 117
Sunday Times, 110
Sunstein, Cass, 96
Supreme Court. *See* United States
  Supreme Court
surgeons. *See* plastic surgeons
Sylvia (cartoon), 45

Tardif v. Quinn, 119
Taylor, Elizabeth, 61
technology
  role in promoting appearance, 5, 8,
    24, 30, 53–54, 68
  as villain in weight gain, 63
television
  appearance-related reality shows,
    8–9, 58–59
  double standards in, 107–8
  effect on adolescents, 60
  See also media
thinness
  health risks of, 41
  in reproductive biology, 8, 47
Title VII, 120
Toddlers and Tiaras (television show), 58
Tufts, 157

Ugly-Girl Papers, 55
United States Congress
  and civil rights law, 107
  female members of, 79
  health care reform, 157–58
United States Supreme Court
  sex discrimination cases, 120, 121
  on sexual harassment, 114

Urbana, Ill., appearance statutes, 16,
  125, 126, 127, 223n.48

Van Buren, Martin, 52
Van Susteren, Greta, 88
Vashti, Queen, 56
Veblan, Thorstein, 8
Victoria, Australia, 17, 135, 140
Vindication of the Rights of Women
  (Wollstonecraft), 70
Virginia, appearance statutes in,
  117–18

Wall Street Journal, 3, 51
Walmart, 132
Walzer, Michael, 94
Washington Post, 44, 61
websites, appearance–related, 53–54,
  150
weight discrimination
  court cases, 104, 123–25
  educating public about, 152
  as most common appearance
    discrimination, 102
  rationalizations for, 103–6
  rise in, 41–42
  strategies for change, 155
  under disability law, 15–16, 20, 92,
    104, 123–25, 155
  in workplace, 13, 15–16, 28, 43, 93,
    94–95, 103–5
  See also appearance
    discrimination; overweight/
    obese people
weight reduction
  benefits of, 41
  difficulty of, 104–5, 109
  drugs for, 41
  health risks of, 39, 40–41
  in men v. women, 60

[251]

weight reduction (*continued*)
  success rate of, 50, 105
  television shows about, 8–9,
    58–59
  See also diets/dieting
weight reduction industry
  marketing in, 10, 19, 49–50, 67
  misleading claims in, 19, 33–34,
    141–42, 154
  women employed in, 76
Wharton, Edith, 99
"When She Asks How She Looks,
  Any Answer Could Get Ugly"
  (Barry), 69–70
Wilde, Oscar, 44
Williams, Patricia, 84
Winfrey, Oprah, xiii–xiv, 63, 69

Wisconsin, 16, 18
Wolf, Naomi, 10, 74–75
Wollstonecraft, Mary, 70
"Women Against Pornography," 75
women's rights movement. *See*
  feminists
Woods, Tiger, 65
Woolf, Virginia, 70–71
workplace. *See* employment
World Health Organization, 36, 155,
  157

Youngblood, Nikki, 98, 116
You've Got Talent (television show), 63
yo-yo diets, 7, 40–41, 63, 149
  See also diets/dieting